LOCAL HEROES

To Chuck,
Best Regards & Keep Fit.
Richard M. Lapp

The Memorial Cup, donated by the Ontario Hockey Association in 1918 to signify junior hockey supremacy.

LOCAL HEROES

A History of the Western Hockey League

Richard M. Lapp
&
Silas White

with a foreword by Vince Leah

HARBOUR PUBLISHING
Vancouver & Madeira Park, BC

HARBOUR PUBLISHING
P.O. Box 219
Madeira Park, BC Canada V0N 2H0

This book is the result of good teamwork: Richard provided the hard work and determination that set it up and Silas the good hands that finished the play; Greg Drinnan, Tony Parker, Randy Jensen and Vince Leah get assists for their yeoman work in the corners digging out stories. Thanks also to Norm Dueck, the WHL, Dan Francis and Herb Lapp for their heads-up contributions.

Cover design by Jim Brennan.
Cover photos, clockwise from bottom left: Lanny McDonald (Morley L. Fach), Cam Neely (Art Thompson, courtesy WHL), Theoren Fleury (courtesy WHL), Joe Sakic (courtesy WHL), Mark Recchi (Allan Fedorak, courtesy Mrs. Ruth Recchi).
Photos pages 10, 29, 32, 34, 38, 50, 57, 72, 89, 91, 124, 127, 129, 130, 135, 139, 142, 160, 164, 172, 173, 178, 179, 187, 192, 193, 195, 196, 198, 199, 216, 220, 221, 225, 227, 228, 230 are from the collection of Richard M. Lapp.
Photos pages 13, 41, 47, 53, 62, 114, 119, 123, 133, 144, 165, 174, 186, 201 courtesy Western Hockey League/*Canadian Hockey Magazine*. Photo page 21 by Tony Smith courtesy WHL/*Canadian Hockey Magazine*. Photo page 23 by A.T. Bieguin, Lapp collection. Photo page 69 courtesy Mrs. Yvonne Clarke. Photos frontispiece, pages 77, 79, 81, 84, by Fedorak Photo, Lapp collection. Photo page 82 courtesy Mrs. Ruth Recchi. Photo page 92 courtesy the Sutter family. Photos pages 103, 105, 108, 111 by Morley L. Fach, Lapp collection. Photo page 120 by Brad Watson courtesy the Calgary Flames. Photo page 226 by Bob Holliday, Lapp collection.
Printed and bound in Canada.

Canadian Cataloguing in Publication Data

Lapp, Richard M.
    Local heroes

    Includes index.
    ISBN 1-55017-080-5

    1. Western Hockey League—History.   2. Hockey—Canada, Western—History.   I. White, Silas.   II. Title.
GV847.8.W48L36 1993   796.962'62'06071   C93-091912-2

Contents

Foreword

A century or more has rolled by since hockey came to the West. Its history is studded with great names and great teams. At the junior level in particular its growth has been exceptional. Teams from Winnipeg, Regina, Saskatoon and Calgary wrote their own pages in the history of competition for the Memorial Cup, the trophy donated at the end of World War One by the Ontario Hockey Association to remember the young men who lost their lives fighting for Canada.

The advent of the Western Canada Junior Hockey League, formed in June, 1966 at a meeting at the Riding Mountain National Park summer resort village of Clear Lake, ushered in a period of unbelievable expansion for hockey in the West. At its inception, the new circuit called itself the Canadian Major Junior Hockey League and declined to affiliate with the Canadian Amateur Hockey Association. Of course, this left it branded as "outlaw," but no matter. It quickly attracted other communities to take part. From Brandon and Winnipeg in the east to the great Pacific Northwest the interest grew. And the league became international in scope with the additions of teams from Seattle, Portland, Tacoma and Spokane. In some centres the expansion of the NHL provided too much competition at the box office and franchises disappeared. But in many smaller communities the Western Junior Hockey League has become the "big leagues."

When one realizes that the Western league has won seven Memorial Cup championships in the last ten years one can see where the balance of junior hockey power lies.

The authors, whose love for hockey is an all-consuming passion, have become tireless researchers in revealing the story of the Western Hockey League, of the great teams whose names grace the Memorial

During the WCHL's 1969—70 season, Wayne Chernecki of the Winnipeg Jets fires the puck at Saskatoon Blades goalie Kevin Migneault while Blades defenceman Jermoe Engele battles Archie MacDonald in front of the net.

Cup, and of the players who achieved their own kind of immortality in the world's fastest game. They are to be commended for their zeal and devotion in recording the league's exciting history. It is indeed a welcome addition to North American sports literature.

VINCE LEAH
Winnipeg, Manitoba

Introduction

The Western Hockey League was formed in June, 1966 at a meeting of junior hockey executives in the resort village of Clear Lake, 110 kilometres north of Brandon, Manitoba. Known originally as the Canadian Major Junior Hockey League, it was a blend of franchises from Saskatchewan and Alberta. When play began that fall there were seven teams in the circuit: Estevan Bruins, Regina Pats, Moose Jaw Canucks, Saskatoon Blades, Weyburn Red Wings, Edmonton Oil Kings and Calgary Buffaloes.

No sooner had the league been organized than it was suspended by the governing body of junior hockey, the Canadian Amateur Hockey Association. The establishment branded the newcomers an outlaw league and prohibited the Moose Jaw Canucks, winners of the first post-season playoffs, from appearing in the Memorial Cup tournament.

Somewhat chastened, the new league changed its name to the Western Canada Hockey League and agreed to abide by the policies of the CAHA. It also expanded for its second season, adding teams from Swift Current, Flin Flon, Winnipeg and Brandon.

In the summer of 1968 the WCHL once again fell out with the CAHA. This time the issue was the use of over-age players. The CAHA had lowered the age limit for junior players to 19 while the western league wanted the cut-off to be 21. WCHL owners argued that older players increased revenue for the teams and allowed for a more consistent lineup from one year to the next. The league also permitted players who entered an accredited four-year university program to continue playing Junior A until they were 22. The result was that once again the WCHL was out in the cold, operating as an independent league with no right to participate in the Memorial Cup.

The WCHL decided to form its own umbrella organization. Along with the Western Ontario Junior Hockey League it formed the Canadian Hockey Association to administer its affairs. Initially NHL president Clarence Campbell said he would not recognize the CHA but he relented and the NHL began recruiting from the ranks of the new association.

Three teams dropped out of the WCHL in 1968, preferring to play in leagues accredited with the CAHA, but the western league soldiered on with eight teams, organized into two divisions. Then, in 1970, the WCHL patched up its differences with the CAHA and embarked on an era of steady expansion. Regina rejoined the fold that year, along with a new franchise from Medicine Hat. The next season, 1971–72, the league became truly western when three cities from British Columbia joined—Vancouver, New Westminster and Victoria.

In 1978 the league changed its name once again, to the Western Hockey League, to reflect the fact that it was no longer exclusively Canadian. Teams from Portland, Seattle and Billings, Montana were now part of the circuit and before too long there were expansion teams or relocated franchises in three more Washington centres—Spokane, Tacoma and Kennewick.

There is no reason to think that this kind of growth will end soon. The Red Deer Rebels joined the league in 1992, and several cities in Oregon and Washington are waiting for franchises. Even Boise, Idaho, and Sacramento, California, have been mentioned as possible future locations for WHL teams.

Junior hockey is thriving as never before. The Canadian Hockey League, the parent organization for junior hockey in Canada, representing the WHL, the Ontario Hockey League and the Quebec Major Junior Hockey League, consists of 44 teams across Canada and the US. Sixteen of these teams are in the WHL and, if the past decade is any indication, the western league is overshadowing its eastern counterparts. Attendance figures are climbing, especially in the American Northwest, and the calibre of hockey being played is at an all-time high. Since 1983, when the Portland Winter Hawks became the first team based south of the border to win the Memorial Cup, seven WHL teams have won the junior championship.

It has been a quarter century of steady growth for the Western Hockey League, an appropriate time to look back at the 39 teams which have comprised the league and some of the star players who honed their skills in its ranks.

Ed Chynoweth: "Mr. President"

Since its inception the Western Hockey League has had two kinds of presidents—Ed Chynoweth and everybody else. Chynoweth has led the WHL since the early seventies. Most franchise executives have never

Ed Chynoweth.

known the league without him. It hasn't been a problem-free couple of decades—Chynoweth has too strong a personality not to stir up some opposition—but it's hard to argue with the evidence of his success. Under his leadership, the Western Hockey League has grown and prospered until, today, it is healthier than it has ever been.

Born in Dodsland, Saskatchewan, Chynoweth grew up in nearby Coleville, then moved to Saskatoon. During 20 years in the City of Bridges, he was one of the great contributors to the sports scene. A fastball player of note, he captained the Saskatoon College Lads, a team that appeared in four Canadian championships. "They called me fancy field, no hit," Chynoweth once said. It was his love of fastball that led him to become one of the kingpins behind the construction of the Gordon Howe Bowl, a facility used for baseball and football. Chynoweth was the charter president of the Pow City (Saskatoon) Kinsmen Club, and he served as president of the Saskatoon Minor Hockey Association.

Chynoweth's involvement in the WHL began in 1970 when Jack McLeod was hired on as coach and general manager of the Saskatoon Blades, and brought Chynoweth along as assistant GM. He stayed with the Blades for only one season before quitting to give the hotel business a try. But a year later it was back to junior hockey and into the league office as aide to the president. Before long he was in the chair himself, and, with the exception of one season as general manager of the Calgary Wranglers, he has remained there ever since.

If Chynoweth has demonstrated anything during his tenure in junior hockey, it has to be foresight. He has been several years ahead of his time with suggestions for league expansion, for a drug and alcohol abuse program, for a crack-down on violence in hockey, for improving the league's educational assistance program.

In the middle and late 1970s, Chynoweth told team operators they were going to have to start promoting their product, that they could no longer open the arena doors and expect fans to flock to their games. Chynoweth warned them about the advancing popularity of VCRs and satellite dishes and the numerous ways in which people were being asked to spend their entertainment dollars.

"He's the most qualified hockey guy, with respect to being a league president or a league commissioner, that you're going to find," one team owner has said. "He's been around long enough that he knows the business. When he phones a general manager of an NHL team, they take his call."

Perhaps the first real test faced by Chynoweth came in the 1975–76 season, the bloodiest of all seasons, a season of discontent if ever there was one. There was brawl after brawl after brawl. At one point, after a particularly nasty incident between the Victoria Cougars and the Saskatoon Blades, Saskatoon city council voted to lock the doors to the arena so the two teams could not play a scheduled rematch.

And on top of everything else, the World Hockey Association was actively raiding junior teams.

Fed up with all the frustrations, Chynoweth offered his resignation. "It isn't a play for money," he said at the time. "It is simply that there is too much hassle. It is starting to bother me that all my friends in Saskatoon are going to the airport to take flights south for winter holidays, I go to the airport and fly to Flin Flon."

But things settled down, and Chynoweth remained in the president's chair. As it turned out, worse was yet to come. For bad luck and tragedy, absolutely nothing could top the 1986–87 season.

On December 30, the Swift Current Broncos were on their way to Regina for a game with the Pats when their bus rolled into a ditch. Four players died in the accident. Then, on March 1, in a game in Regina, Pats centre Brad Hornung suffered a broken neck that left him paralysed from the neck down.

"It was the most trying season in the time I have been involved," Chynoweth told a reporter. "They say sometimes adversity brings strength and certainly we've had our share of adversity. The loss of the four lives in the bus accident is something that is hard to put into words. An accident of that magnitude was just heart-wrenching. To have the Brad Hornung situation—to have two of those things happen in one year—certainly it is something that tests you."

Along with the presidency of the WHL, Chynoweth presides over the Canadian Hockey League, the umbrella organization under which the western league, the Ontario Hockey League and the Quebec Major Junior Hockey League operate. As the CHL president, he takes up the challenges of organising the Memorial Cup and the inter-league European draft and all-star game, acting as a liaison between Canadian junior hockey and the NHL, and administrating rules and regulations for the three leagues.

Many NHL teams have recognised Chynoweth's hard work, and his name often pops up when there is a general manager position vacant.

If junior hockey is healthier than ever today, a lot of the credit belongs to Ed Chynoweth.

BILLINGS

The Billings Bighorns

The city of Billings, Montana, lies between the Yellowstone River and the towering Rimrocks, close to Yellowstone National Park and the site of the Battle of Little Bighorn. The history of hockey in Billings goes back to 1975, when the professional South West Hockey League organized a circuit of teams in the American Midwest. With the benefit of hindsight, it seems the enterprise was doomed from the start. Who was interested in hockey in Amarillo, Texas, or Reno, Nevada or Albuquerque, New Mexico, all franchises in the SWHL? But it seemed like a good idea at the time, and Billings iced a team which played in the brand-new 8600-seat Yellowstone Metra arena.

The SWHL folded in February 1977, less than two years after it began, but fans in Billings didn't have to wait long for a replacement. The previous year, the Edmonton Oil Kings of the WHL had moved to Portland, where junior hockey took the city by storm. The instant success of the Winter Hawks franchise indicated to WHL executives that the league had a future in the US. In Calgary the venerable Centennials franchise was looking for a new home. Since the World Hockey Association had come to town, and rumours of NHL expansion began circulating, junior hockey was no longer the draw it once was in Cowtown. Dick Koentges, owner of the Centennials, hired a new general manager, Bob Strumm, a former hockey writer with the Saskatoon *Star-Phoenix*, and together the two men won approval to move the team to Billings in time for the 1977–78 season.

Strumm did not take over a very powerful hockey club. In their last season of operation, the Centennials finished third-worst in the league,

GRADUATES TO THE NHL

Billings Bighorns

1979: **Lindsay Carson**—Philadelphia, Hartford. **Don Nachbaur**—Pittsburgh, Hartford, Edmonton, Philadelphia. **Harvey Pocza**—Washington.

1980: **Andy Moog**—Edmonton, Boston, Dallas. **Murray Brumwell**—Minnesota, New Jersey. **Jim McTaggart**—Washington. **Mike Eagles**—Quebec (drafted from the Kitchener Rangers of the Ontario Hockey League in 1981), Chicago, Winnipeg.

1981: **Jim McGeough**—Washington, Pittsburgh.

1982: **Gord Kluzak**—Boston. **Rocky Trottier**—New Jersey. **Mark Lamb**—Calgary, Detoit, Edmonton, Ottawa. **Bob Rouse**—Minnesota, Washington, Toronto. **Brian Ford**—Quebec, Pittsburgh. **Mike Zanier**—Edmonton.

Nanaimo Islanders

1983: **Richard Zemlak**—Quebec, Minnesota, Pittsburgh, Calgary.

surrendering 397 goals in 72 games. Strumm hoped to turn things around in Billings, and to do so he hired Dave King as head coach. A university graduate with degrees in education and physical education, the 30-year-old King had coached in the university and junior ranks before coming to Billings. He would go on to earn fame as coach of the Canadian National and Olympic teams and the NHL's Calgary Flames.

The 1977–78 season turned into something special for Billings. The team finished the regular season one game above .500, good enough for second place in the Central Division. Dell Chapman sparked the Bighorns attack with 107 points, followed by Doug Robb, Pat Conacher and Blake Sullivan. Tim Thomlinson was a standout in the nets, recording a 4.36 goals-against average and winning a place on the league all-star team. Another player many people remember from that team is Brent Gogol, a right-winger acquired early in the season from Victoria. The fans called him Go-Go, and it wasn't for his dancing ability—he earned a total of 511 minutes in penalties during that year, a league record. In the playoffs, the Bighorns, led by Pat Conacher's 15 goals and Kevin Willison's 23 assists, made it through to the final series, where they were swept by the New Westminster Bruins on their way to a second consecutive Memorial Cup. When it was all over, King shared Coach-of-the-Year honours with Victoria's Jack Shupe.

During the initial season, Koentges sold the franchise to Sheldon Ferguson, owner of the Red Deer Rustlers of the Alberta Junior Hockey League. Ferguson only kept the team for four months before he sold it to Joe Sample, a Billings broadcasting executive. When their second season began, the Bighorns picked up where they had left off in the previous year's playoffs. One of the team's brightest prospects was Gord Stafford, a centre from Banff, who was on his way to becoming the team's all-time scoring leader. Cal Roadhouse chipped in with 50 goals, while Harvey Pocza added 42. And a young player named Andy Moog was starting to make a name for himself in the nets. As well, Billings had matured into one of the best defensive teams in the league. Then, unexpectedly, the Bighorns crashed in the playoffs, failing to get past the first round. The season of promise was over.

A front-office shakeup followed. King quit as coach and returned to the University of Saskatchewan. Bob Strumm followed suit, taking over as general manager of the Regina Pats. They were replaced in time for the 1979–80 season by Les Calder, over from the Seattle Breakers. The bright spots that year included Gord Stafford's 52 goals, Andy Moog's goaltending and the debut of defenceman Gord Kluzak. The Bighorns finished respectably in the middle of the pack but bowed out in the first round of the playoffs. This was the beginning of the end for the franchise. The next two seasons the Bighorns finished below .500 and were twice eliminated from the playoffs early, despite the brilliant scoring touch of Jim McGeough and the play of pesky centre Mark Lamb. In 1981–82 McGeough racked up 93 goals, still a franchise record and the fourth-highest single season total ever scored by a WHL player. However, Billings' problem that season was defence, giving up 432 goals and going through eight netminders while trying to find someone to stem the tide. There was confusion behind the bench as well—the club changed coaches twice.

In the spring of 1982 Sample sold the Bighorns to Bill Zeitlin, a minority shareholder in the Chicago White Sox, and Real Turcotte, a Detroit businessman, for $300,000. One of the main problems for the franchise was its location so far away from other cities in the WHL. The time on the road was wearing and made it hard for the players to keep up their education—not to mention what it did to the team budget. Another factor was the lack of a local practice facility, forcing the Bighorns to travel 300 kilometres to Great Falls for workouts. The new owners recognized these limitations and immediately moved the team to Nanaimo on Vancouver Island.

But the franchise did not leave the United States for very long. During its first year in Nanaimo it was purchased by Vancouver business-man Ron Dixon, who moved it to New Westminster in 1983. When that didn't work out, Dixon packed up and took the team back south of the border to Kennewick, Washington, where it entered a successful new phase as the Tri-City Americans.

Dave King

Although better known for his work with Canada's Olympic hockey program, Dave King had a successful sojourn in the WHL in the 1970s, first as assistant coach with the Saskatoon Blades and then as head coach of the Billings Bighorns. But his development as one of hockey's new-look scientific coaches began as a student at the University of Saskatchewan (Saskatoon), where the North Battleford native was an exceptional athlete, lettering in football, basketball and track and field. Along the way to a degree in physical education, he captained the varsity hockey team. When he became a lecturer at the university in 1972 he also took on the job of coaching the hockey team. After moving across town to work for the WHL Blades, King moved on to a head coach position with the Billings franchise, newly relocated from Calgary. King led the Bighorns to the championship of the Central Division in his first season at the helm, but dropped the league final to New Westminster in four straight. There was no shame in that; the powerful Bruins lost only two games in the entire playoffs that year, and went on to win their second consecutive Memorial Cup. King, meanwhile, shared Coach-of-the-Year honours with Victoria's Jack Shupe.

In his second season in Billings, 1978–79, King's team finished first in the division, third place overall. But the Bighorns faltered badly in the playoffs. In the first round-robin series against Lethbridge and a Calgary team they had bested by 25 points in the regular-season, King's squad was eliminated from further play. King found the constant travel in the far-flung junior circuit exhausting, and in 1979 he decided to return to university hockey in Saskatchewan.

As coach of the Huskies from 1979 to 1983, King took the team to the Canadian Inter-university Athletic Union finals three times. In 1981 and 1982 the Huskies lost to the University of Moncton, the second time in overtime. It was third time lucky, however, and in 1983 the Huskies defeated Concordia to win the CIAU championship. During the same period he coached the national junior team to a gold medal at the World Championships in 1982.

King signed on as coach of the Olympic team in 1983. At the 1984 Winter Olympics in Sarajevo, the Canadian team advanced to the medal round, and at the 1988 showdown in Calgary it recorded an excellent 5–2–1 record but still couldn't pick up a medal. In the 1992 games at Albertville, King finally realized his dream of making it to the coveted gold-medal game. Bolstered by holdout NHL veteran Sean Burke, high-scoring Bruins prospect Joe Juneau and Eric Lindros, widely considered the best player in the world outside the NHL, Canada's Olympians still lost 3–1 to a Soviet squad making its farewell tour under the euphemism "Unified Team." King had to settle for silver, but it was the first medal of any kind Canada had taken home since 1968.

After years of speculation over which team would succeed in wooing King into the NHL, he finally signed on as head coach of the Calgary Flames in 1992–93. King, who was also given some responsibility for player personnel decisions, led the team to second place in the division with 97 points, 23 more than the 1991–92 squad had posted with virtually the same roster. Like his star forward in Albertville, Dave King had long been considered one of the best hockey talents not working in the NHL. After the 1992 season, he appeared to be well on his way to changing that line to one of the best *in* the NHL.

Andy Moog

A native of Penticton, BC, Andy Moog played his Junior A hockey with the Kamloops Braves and Penticton Vees before moving on to the WHL's Billings Bighorns for the 1978–79 season. In two years with Billings he posted a respectable 3.89 goals-against average and was named to the league's second all-star team after his senior season. (The first-team all-star was future teammate Grant Fuhr.) He emerged from the junior

Andy Moog of the Billings Bighorns reaches down to glove a rolling puck.

ranks with a reputation as a solid, dependable goaltender with a quick glove hand. He wasn't flashy, the scouts said, but he would get the job done.

The Edmonton Oilers made Moog their sixth pick in the 1980 entry draft and sent him to play for Wichita in the now-defunct Central Hockey League. In 1982 he came up to the NHL for good, but it looked as if he would spend his career as a backup, since the Oilers already had Grant Fuhr, then at the top of his game. For five seasons, 1982–87, Moog and Fuhr split the goaltending duties in Edmonton, but when it came to the playoffs, Fuhr got most of the action. Edmonton went to the Stanley Cup finals four times during this stretch, winning it all three times, and as long as Fuhr was healthy he was obviously the Oilers number one netminder.

Even though he made the NHL all-star team twice, and had three Stanley Cup rings, the situation in Edmonton began to gnaw at Moog. He wanted to prove that he could be a first-string goalie in the NHL. He demanded a trade, and when the 1987 training camp rolled around he stayed at home, waiting for someone to call with an offer. Then, in October, Moog announced that he was joining the Canadian National team under coach Dave King. In an unusual arrangement, the IGA grocery store chain agreed to pick up his salary.

Not long after the Olympics, in March 1988, Moog was traded to Boston for goaltender Bill Ranford and left-winger Geoff Courtnall. In Boston, he would finally be a number one goaltender. Moog put together a stretch of great seasons, starting in 1989–90, when the Bruins finished with the best record in the league. Moog and Boston's other netminder, Reggie Lemelin, ended up sharing the William M. Jennings Trophy, which goes to the team allowing the fewest goals. Moog's goals-against average was 2.89, fourth best in the league. Only three goalies posted more victories than Moog, and only one had more shutouts. In the playoffs he was spectacular, starting the Bruins' last 16 games as they went all the way to the final before losing to Edmonton in five games.

Statistically, Moog had an even better season in 1990–91, playing in 51 games, getting 4 shutouts and recording a 2.87 goals-against average. He took the Bruins to the Wales Conference Finals in the playoffs, but failed to stop the high-powered offence of the Pittsburgh Penguins. The next season Moog played a career-high 62 games but was foiled again by the Penguins in the playoffs. Despite obtaining 37 wins and recording a 3.16 average in 1992–93, Moog was inconsistent and the Bruins management was disappointed in his performance. On June 25, 1993, he was traded to the Dallas Stars for netminder Jon Casey.

As Moog matured as a goaltender he came to rely less on his cat-like reflexes and more on the angle game. Small in stature, he is an intense, aggressive competitor who has proved he belongs in the front ranks of NHL goaltenders.

Gord Kluzak

A native of Climax, Saskatchewan, Gord Kluzak played midget hockey for the famous Notre Dame College Hounds in 1979–80, the year the Hounds won the Canadian championship. He graduated to the Billings Bighorns of the WHL in 1980. During his two seasons in Montana the Bighorns were a mediocre team but Kluzak developed into a standout defenceman, a heavy hitter known also for his deft passing. In 1981–82 he was named to the league second all-star team and was picked first overall in the NHL entry draft by Boston. At 6'4", 220 pounds, Kluzak looked like a sure bet for professional hockey stardom. In 1982 he played a prominent role in Team Canada's gold-medal-winning performance, and won the award as the country's finest junior male athlete.

Unfortunately, after only four full seasons in Boston, Kluzak's career was blighted by injuries, mainly to his knee. He played through a string of ten operations, sitting out two entire seasons and skating in pain for most of the others. His sterling play in the 1988 playoffs showed Kluzak could still be a dominant defenceman when given the chance. His courage and tenacity were honoured in 1990 when hockey writers chose him winner of the Bill Masterton Memorial Trophy for the player best exemplifying the qualities of perseverance, sportsmanship and dedication to hockey.

During Kluzak's last three seasons with Boston he played fewer than ten games a year and he finally retired in 1991. He stayed in Boston to study law at Harvard University and run a chain of restaurants.

Gord Kluzak is perhaps the best player to wear a Billings uniform.

BRANDON

The Brandon Wheat Kings

The story of the Brandon Wheat Kings can be telescoped into a single three-year period, 1976–79, when the Wheaties proved themselves to be one of the great major junior hockey teams in WHL history.

Not that Brandon hasn't had some talented players since they joined the league in its second season. There was Ron Chipperfield, a prolific scorer whose 261 goals puts him second on the league's all-time scoring list. There was Ray Ferraro, whose 108 goals during the 1983–84 season set a single-season record that has never been bested. And the goalie on that team, Ron Hextall, went on to win the Vezina Trophy, playing for the Philadelphia Flyers in 1986–87.

But there has never been another team in the WHL to compare to the Wheat Kings of the late 1970s. Managed by Jack Brockest, coached by Dunc McCallum and powered by the goal-scoring of Bill Derlago, Ray Allison, Brian Propp and Laurie Boschman, Brandon compiled a three-year record of 158–27–31 for an astonishing .803 winning percentage.

And of all that glorious run, it is the 1978–79 season which Brandon hockey fans remember as the absolute zenith of their franchise.

This was back before the NHL began poaching the best players from the junior ranks, back when management could count on having a player for three years. It was just such a three-year plan, engineered by Brockest, McCallum and chief scout Ron Dietrich, that produced the 1978–79 Wheat Kings.

The team was anchored by three-year veterans Tim Lockridge and Brad McCrimmon on defence, and wingers Propp and Allison. Seven other players—goaltender Rick Knickle, defencemen Wes Coulson and

GRADUATES TO THE NHL

Brandon Wheat Kings

1969: **Jack Borotsik**—St. Louis.

1970: **Ernie "Butch" Deadmarsh**—Buffalo, Atlanta, Kansas City. **Bob Fitchner**—Pittsburgh, Quebec. **Chuck Lefley**—Montreal, St. Louis.

1971: **Curt Ridley**—NY Rangers, Vancouver, Toronto.

1972: **Dave McLelland**—Vancouver.

1974: **Ron Chipperfield**—California, Edmonton, Quebec. **John Paddock**—Washington, Philadelphia, Quebec.

1975: **Rick Blight**—Vancouver, Los Angeles.

1977: **Glen Hanlon**—Vancouver, St.Louis, NY Rangers, Detroit. **Wayne Ramsey**—Buffalo. **Dan Bonar**—Los Angeles. **Dave Semenko**—Edmonton, Hartford, Toronto.

1978: **Bill Derlago**—Vancouver, Toronto, Boston, Winnipeg, Quebec.

1979: **Laurie Boschman**—Toronto, Edmonton, Winnipeg, New Jersey, Ottawa. **Brian Propp**—Philadelphia, Boston, Minnesota. **Brad McCrimmon**—Boston, Philadelphia, Calgary, Detroit, Hartford. **Ray Allison**—Hartford, Philadelphia. **Don Gillen**—Philadelphia, Hartford. **Walt Poddubny**—Edmonton, Toronto, NY Rangers, Quebec, New Jersey

1980: **Steve Patrick**—Buffalo, NY Rangers, Quebec. **Don Dietrich**—Chicago, New Jersey. **Dave Chartier**—Winnipeg. **Tony Camazzola**—Washington.

1981: **Dean Kennedy**—Los Angeles, NY Rangers, Buffalo, Winnipeg. **Carl Mokosak**—Calgary, Los Angeles, Philadelphia, Pittsburgh, Boston.

1982: **Tom McMurchy**—Chicago, Edmonton. **Ron Hextall**—Philadelphia, Quebec, NY Islanders.

1983: **Cam Plante**—Toronto.

1984: **Derek Laxdal**—Toronto, NY Islanders. **Jim Agnew**—Vancouver, Hartford. **Ray Ferraro**—Hartford, NY Islanders.

1985: **Dave Thomlinson**—Toronto, St. Louis, Boston. **Eldon "Pokey" Pokey"Reddick**—Winnipeg, Edmonton.

1987: **George Maneluk**—NY Islanders. **Terry Yake**—Hartford, Anaheim.

1990: **Trevor Kidd**—Calgary. **Cam Brown**—Vancouver. **Jeff Odgers**—San Jose.

Mike Perovich and forwards Laurie Boschman, Don Gillen, Brad Kempthorne and Dave Stewart—were in their second complete season and
most had appeared, at least briefly, in 1976–77. Then there were the
rookies and the acquisitions from other teams. Forwards Steve Patrick
and Dave McDonald showed up early in the season, choosing the Wheat
Kings over US colleges. Defencemen Don Dietrich and Kelly Elcombe fit
in well, as did forwards Brant Kiessig, Darren Gusdal and Kelly McCrimmon (Brad's younger brother), a trio of tremendous penalty killers.
When injuries hit the defence, Greg Mann came in and played exceptionally well. And centre Dave Chartier, a fiery pepper-pot, arrived from St.
Lazare. Oftentimes, when the club was going stale, he was the straw that
stirred the drink.

This collection of talented juniors spent the winter of 1978–79
rewriting the WHL record book. Their accomplishments included: most
points in a season, 125; most wins, 58; fewest losses, 5; longest unbeaten
streak (overlapping seasons), 49; longest unbeaten streak (one season),
29; longest winning streak on the road, 10; longest unbeaten streak on
the road, 17; most goals, 491; most shots on goal in a single game, 85.

The Wheaties began the season with a 29-game winning streak.
They did not lose a game until December 13. When they clinched the
East Division pennant on February 7, there was still two months left in
the regular season and the team had only lost two games.

Despite being so overpowering, Brandon did suffer a pair of
setbacks during the season which, in retrospect, hurt their chances in
post-season play. Walt Poddubny, who would go on to play in the NHL
with the Toronto Maple Leafs, New York Rangers and Quebec Nordiques, started his major junior career with the Wheat Kings. He struck
for 11 goals and 22 points in 20 games before leaving the club and ending
up in the Ontario Hockey League. More devastating was the broken arm
suffered by defensive stalwart Mike Perovich during a game against
Regina in March. Both players might have made a difference when
Brandon reached the Memorial Cup.

This was not a conventional run-and-gun junior club. Nor was it a
team full of intimidators. It was a tough, hard-working, close-knit team.
McCallum, who had played his junior hockey with the Wheat Kings
before going on to a pro career as a defenceman, was prouder of his
club's defensive abilities than its knack for scoring goals. It was no secret
that if a forward didn't do his job defensively, he didn't play.

When the regular season ended, the Wheat Kings, with 125 points,
had a 59-point edge on the second-place Saskatoon Blades in the East
Division. A single line—Propp, Allison and Boschman—finished one-
two-three in the scoring race. In the playoffs, Brandon dominated in the
early going. The team set a record by running up an 11-game unbeaten
string. They twice tied a playoff record by scoring 13 goals in one game,

and they set a record for the fastest two goals in a playoff game, when Brad McCrimmon and Boschman scored 6 seconds apart in a victory over the Lethbridge Broncos.

In the final, however, they came up against a very good Portland team, featuring the likes of Perry Turnbull, Blake Wesley, Bart Hunter, Jim Dobson, John Multan, Keith Brown and Dave Babych. The series opened in Brandon, with the Winter Hawks getting 2 goals from each of Multan and Dobson, and picking up a 4–2 victory. The Wheat Kings won the next two games, also in Brandon, 3–1 and 6–5. The teams then moved to Portland, and the Winter Hawks tied the series with a 5–2 victory. That was it for the Winter Hawks, though, as Brandon won the fifth game 4–3 when Gillen scored on an overtime breakaway, then took the sixth game 6–3. It was the first, and so far the only, WHL championship for the franchise.

At the Memorial Cup tournament, Brandon opened play against the Trois-Rivieres Draveurs and things got ugly early. It started with a pre-game brawl, when Mario Tardif of the Draveurs jabbed his stick at Kempthorne during the warmup. Then, when the teams lined up for the opening faceoff, Draveurs left-winger Jean-Pierre Petit went right after Kempthorne. That about set the tone for the entire game, which the Draveurs won 4–3.

The Wheat Kings went on to lose to the tournament's other entry, the Peterborough Petes, 7–6 in overtime and, with a 0–2 record, found themselves almost written off. But they bounced back to thump the Draveurs 6–1, then edged the Petes 3–2 to qualify for the Cup final. The final game against the Petes was a classic in every sense of the word. The teams exchanged first-period goals, and that was it until overtime. The play that resulted in the winning goal started with the Petes clearing the puck from their own zone. Brad McCrimmon got to the puck first and played it, assuming icing would be called. It wasn't. The Petes' Terry Bovair stole the puck and passed it to defenceman Larry Murphy high in the slot. His shot was stopped, but Bob Attwell got the rebound and slid it into the net for the victory and the Cup.

The NHL entry draft in August confirmed just how good that season's Wheat Kings really were. Four Brandon players—Boschman, Propp, McCrimmon and Allison—were picked in the first round, and ten went in all of the six rounds.

The 1978–79 Wheat Kings won a lot of individual awards as well. Five players—Knickle, McCrimmon, Boschman, Propp and Allison—were named to the WHL's first all-star team. Dunc McCallum won Coach-of-the-Year honours, taking home the trophy that was named for him following his untimely death in the spring of 1983. Brian Propp won the scoring title and league Player-of-the-Year award, Rick Knickle was named top goaltender, and four Wheat Kings—McCrimmon, Boschman, Allison, and goalie Bart Hunter, whom Brandon had acquired from Portland—were selected to the Memorial Cup all-star team.

Through it all, there was one mystifying thing. Despite the fact they enjoyed the most successful on-ice season in WHL history, the Wheat Kings did not do very well at the gate. The Keystone Centre, with 5022 seats, was rarely sold out and in a good year, the club averaged only around 2500 fans per game. The Wheat Kings were the talk of the major junior hockey world, but the fans simply didn't turn out.

On the ice, Wheat Kings hockey has since tumbled downhill. In the 1980s, the team recorded a losing record in every season but one. That exception was 1983–84, when record-breaker Ray Ferraro, high-scoring defenceman Cam Plante, and goaltender Ron Hextall led the team to 90 points in the regular season. Ferraro scored 108 goals, a WHL record, and 192 points. Plante set the records for assists by a defenceman, 118, and points by a defenceman, 140.

Low attendance was a problem that stayed with the franchise throughout the 1980s, when victories were much more scarce, and the 1978–79 Wheat Kings were only a glorious memory.

The 1992–93 edition of the Wheat Kings turned the team's losing woes around, picking up 43 wins and 90 points. Led by Chicago draft pick Bobby House, centre Marty Murray, defenceman Aris Brimanis, former Lethbridge Bronco star Darcy Werenka and Goalie of the Year Trevor Robins, Brandon finally recorded its first winning season in nine years.

Ron Chipperfield

Ron Chipperfield's brilliant career as a junior hockey player began in 1969 when, as a 15-year-old from Minnedosa, Manitoba, he joined the Dauphin Kings of the Manitoba Junior Hockey League. During his one season with the Kings, Chipperfield accumulated 79 points, including 39 goals, to finish second in the league's scoring race by a single point.

In the 1970–71 season, Ron made the leap to major junior hockey with the Brandon Wheat Kings, then coached by Gerry Brisson. It was the beginning of a four-year stint with the Wheaties, a length of time totally unheard of in junior ranks nowadays. Chipperfield earned the nickname "Magnificent Seven" by scoring 40 goals in his first season in the WCHL, but that was just a taste of what was to come. During his next two seasons, 1971–72 and 1972–73, he scored 59 and 72 goals respectively, finishing in the top ten both years and twice winning the Frank Boucher Trophy as the league's most sportsmanlike player.

Chipperfield's final junior season was 1973–74. He capped off his career by winning the WCHL scoring crown with 90 goals and 162 points. He was the league's MVP and started at centre for the first all-star team.

During his four years at Brandon he scored a total of 261 goals, at that time the most in league history. (The record has since been surpassed by Glen Goodall who scored 262 goals with the Seattle Thunderbirds.)

Chipperfield was selected by the California Golden Seals in the NHL entry draft, but the World Hockey Association's Vancouver Blazers also picked him and he played his first pro season in Vancouver, where he had a mediocre campaign with only 39 points. In 1975–76 the franchise became the "Cowboys" and shifted to Calgary where Chipperfield scored 42 goals, his highest total in professional ranks. After another season with the Cowboys, the Edmonton Oilers, then still a WHA team, purchased his rights in a dispersal of several league teams, also including the San Diego Mariners and Phoenix Roadrunners.

Chipperfield's first season with Edmonton, 1977–78, was his last successful one. He scored 33 goals and totalled 85 points. He finally made it to the NHL in 1979, when Edmonton became one of four cities awarded expansion franchises. Chipperfield was traded to the Quebec Nordiques before his first season in the National Hockey League was over, and in 1980 knee problems ended his NHL career, though he had a brief fling in 1980–81 with the Rochester Americans of the American Hockey League.

Chipperfield later made a prominent name for himself in Italy, winning several Italian hockey championships as coach and general manager of a team in Milan.

Ron Chipperfield (r.) with coach Rudy Pilous, during Chipperfield's final season with the Wheat Kings.

Glen Hanlon

Brandon, Manitoba has produced many goaltenders who have gone on to become big-league stars from the junior ranks in the farming city. The list is impressive and contains the names of Bill Ranford, Ken Wregget, Ron Hextall and Walter "Turk" Broda. Still others from nearby towns and cities have played junior hockey in the Wheat City and many names once again are familiar, such as Eldon "Pokey" Reddick, Trevor Kidd, "Sugar" Jim Henry, Ray Frederick, Rick Knickle and Dave McLelland. One other name however comes to mind when speaking of great goaltenders in the era of junior hockey. That name is Glen Hanlon, a star performer during the Dunc McCallum era of the mid to late 1970s.

Hanlon was born in Brandon on February 20, 1957. He stepped into junior hockey in the 1973–74 season with the Brandon Travellers of the Manitoba Junior Hockey League, when he played an average season with a 3.63 goals-against average. He then arrived in the Western Canada Hockey League in the 1974–75 season and created an impressive picture for three seasons as the Wheat Kings' top netminder. He was twice chosen to the first team Western Hockey League all-star squad in 1975–76 and 1976–77. During the 1976–77 season he led the league in goaltending with an average of 3.09, and obtained 4 shutouts to win the Del Wilson Trophy as the league's top goaltender. In that season's playoffs the Wheat Kings lost out to the New Westminster Bruins in five games.

Hanlon was then selected from the Wheat Kings by the Vancouver Canucks in the third round of the 1977 amateur draft. He was immediately placed with the Tulsa Oilers of the Central Hockey League where he continued his fine netminding. While playing in Tulsa in 1977–78, Hanlon topped the league with 3 shutouts, was named to the all-star team and was selected Rookie of the Year.

He appeared in a four-game stint with the Canucks in 1977–78 and became a regular in the 1978–79 season with Vancouver. Hanlon played in 57 games in 1979–80, one in which he allowed Wayne Gretzky's first-ever NHL goal, immortalizing his name in the minds of trivia buffs forever. He remained with the team until a March 1982 trade with the St. Louis Blues involving four players. The trade featured Hanlon going to the Blues for Tony Currie, Jim Nill, Rick Heinz and a fourth-round 1982 entry draft pick, who turned out to be Shawn Kilroy. The trade seemed to favor the Blues, but played an important role in Vancouver reaching the Stanley Cup Final later that spring.

Hanlon later made stops with the New York Rangers and Detroit Red Wings, where his career ended in the 1990–91 season. Hanlon's highlight in Detroit was leading the Red Wings to the Clarence Campbell championship against the Edmonton Oilers. Despite the fact Detroit lost in five games, Hanlon had a fine season with 4 shutouts and a 3.23 goals-against average for the Red Wings.

Hanlon closed out his professional career in the 1990–91 season as a member of the San Diego Gulls of the International Hockey League. He remained in hockey as the goaltending coach of the Vancouver Canucks.

Dunc McCallum

In any discussion about the best coach in the history of the Western Hockey League, you don't get much argument when Dunc McCallum's name is mentioned.

McCallum coached the Brandon team from 1975 until his untimely death of cancer two days shy of his 43rd birthday on March 27, 1983. During that time he compiled the best winning percentage of any WHL coach, with more than three years behind the bench. In six seasons with Brandon he posted a won-lost record of 251–123–41 for a .651 winning percentage. By comparison, the legendary Ernie "Punch" McLean was .582 and Pat Ginnell was .573.

During an unbelievable three-year streak, 1976–79, McCallum's teams won 80% of their games, a feat unlikely ever to be matched. During that stretch McCallum won Coach-of-the-Year honours twice (1976–77 and 1978–79), and it is fitting that the trophy for the league's top coach is now named for him.

A native of Flin Flon, Manitoba, McCallum played junior hockey in Brandon in the late 1950s. He was a minor-league pro for a while, then made it to the NHL with Pittsburgh following the 1967 expansion. After four years with the Penguins, two more in the World Hockey Association with Houston and Chicago, and another year out of the pros, McCallum joined the Wheat Kings.

As a coach, McCallum turned out more than a few talented NHL players. Ex-Philadelphia Flyers scoring machine Brian Propp, 14-year NHL veteran Brad McCrimmon, former Canucks first-round draft pick Bill Derlago, Ottawa Senators captain Laurie Boschman, Winnipeg Jets captain Dean Kennedy, former Oilers enforcer Dave Semenko, and Canucks goaltending coach Glen Hanlon all matured in Brandon under McCallum's watchful eye.

Dave Semenko

Dave Semenko was one of the many players to come out of Winnipeg and to graduate to the NHL by way of the Western Hockey League. Dave, who grew up in Winnipeg's East St. Paul suburb, was placed on the negotiating list of the Brandon Wheat Kings.

31

Dunc McCallum, a Pittsburgh Penguin in 1970–71.

Semenko, born on July 12, 1957, learned his hockey from Dunc McCallum, one of the great coaches in junior hockey. When left-winger Dave arrived in Brandon during the 1974–75 season, he was first sent down to the Tier II Brandon Travellers.

After a disappointing season in 1974–75, the Wheat Kings brought in several new players, including Semenko and Bill Derlago, and a new coach, Dunc McCallum, a recently retired professional hockey player who went on to pile up a very impressive record with the team.

Under McCallum, Semenko and his fellow Wheat Kings players were taught how to prepare for the pro game. Over the next two seasons in Brandon, 1975–76 and 1976–77, Dave established his rough reputation as he compiled 459 penalty minutes and accepted every challenge to fight. This was a far cry from the 55 penalty minutes that he had received in his season with the Travellers. During his first full season in Brandon, Semenko will always be remembered for a wild fight he had with left-winger Wes George of the Saskatoon Blades at Brandon's Keystone Centre. The two had scrapped on the ice and were banished to their dressing rooms, when they decided to go at it again on the concrete floor by the stage area in the northwest corner of the Keystone Centre. Ironically, they later became teammates in 1978–79 with the WHA Edmonton Oilers.

After his second complete WHL season, Dave Semenko was chosen in the 1977 amateur drafts by the Minnesota North Stars of the NHL and Houston Aeros of the World Hockey Association. The Aeros had no money left to sign Semenko, and they transferred his rights to Glen Sather's Edmonton Oilers.

In a time when tough players were in demand, Semenko held out for a good salary and a one-way contract (meaning he wouldn't have to play in the minor leagues and be paid less) in the fall. He began the 1977–78 season as an over-age left-winger with the Brandon Wheat Kings. He played 7 games in the WCHL that season and was the star of the team, scoring 10 goals and 5 assists. He recollects those games as being the most unusual that he ever played. In November, he came to terms with the Oilers and played the final two seasons of the World Hockey Association in Edmonton. On May 20, 1979 he scored the final goal in the history of the WHA in the league's final playoff game.

After a deal was worked out between the North Stars and the Oilers for Semenko to remain in Edmonton as they moved to the NHL, he went on to play seven more seasons in the blue and orange. During that time, he became famous for being Wayne Gretzky's personal bodyguard. When opposing players knew that they would have to deal with Semenko if they even touched Gretzky, the Great One had a lot more room to perform his dazzling play. When Gretzky won a new car for being the MVP of the 1989 all-star game, he gave it to Semenko. Semenko experienced the satisfaction of winning two Stanley Cups with the Oilers in 1984 and 1985, but by December 1986 Semenko was gone, traded to the Hartford Whalers.

After a contract conflict with the Whalers, Semenko was sent to the Toronto Maple Leafs in 1987. Semenko grew tired of the role of beating people up that was forced on him by Leafs coach John Brophy, so he announced his retirement in March 1988.

After leaving the ice surface, Dave got into real estate and became a color commentator on Edmonton Oilers radio broadcasts. He also served the Oilers as a sales representative. Semenko's final NHL statistics were 65 goals, 153 points and 1175 penalty minutes.

Bill Derlago

Born on August 25, 1958, in Birtle, Manitoba, "Billy" Derlago began his junior career as a 16-year-old playing with the Brandon Travellers of the Manitoba Junior Hockey League. In 1975 he graduated to the Wheat Kings, where for two years he centred a line with Brian Propp at left wing and Ray Allison on the right side. It was one of the greatest scoring lines in junior hockey history.

During his second season in the WHL, 1976–77, Derlago led the

Dave Semenko—ex-Wheatie made his mark looking out for No. 99.

Bill Derlago—Brandon scoring phenom stands third in all-time scoring.

league in both regular season and playoff scoring. During the regular season he scored 96 goals and added 82 assists for 178 points in 72 games. Not surprisingly, he was named centre on the WCHL first all-star team. Despite playing in only 52 games in 1977–78, Derlago managed to lead the league in goals scored with 89, and finish fifth in the scoring race. If he had played in all 72 WHL games that season and kept up his scoring at the pace he was at, Bill Derlago's point totals would have been 123 goals and 210 points (projected). Those totals would currently give him the single season goal scoring record, the career goal scoring record, and the title of being the first WHL player ever to amass 100 goals and 200 points. Derlago now stands third on the list of all-time WHL goal scorers, behind Seattle's Glen Goodall and fellow Wheat King Ron Chipperfield.

The Vancouver Canucks chose Derlago in the first round of the 1978 draft, fourth overall. After a season and a half in Vancouver, he was part of an important trade with the Toronto Maple Leafs which saw Jerry Butler and Dave "Tiger" Williams come to Vancouver in return for Derlago and Rick Vaive. Despite severe knee ligament problems, Derlago went on to enjoy his most successful seasons in the NHL with the Maple Leafs, scoring more than 30 goals on four occasions. During the 1985–86 season he was traded twice, to Boston and then to Winnipeg, and in 1986–87 his NHL career drew to a close.

After playing hockey with a Swiss first-division team for three seasons, Bill Derlago is currently operating a general insurance business in Toronto.

Brian Propp

The Ron Chipperfield era had hardly finished when another prolific goal scorer arrived in Brandon to rewrite the record books.

A native of the tiny farming community of Neudorf, Saskatchewan, Brian Propp was a standout as a 16-year-old with the Melville Millionaires of the Saskatchewan Junior Hockey League, scoring 90 goals and 192 points in just 69 games. But Propp was unselfish and unassuming, and when he went to Brandon in the fall of 1976 all he would admit to local reporters was that he had a "decent shot" at making the team.

He did a lot more than make the team; he remade the team, helping to turn it into one of the most successful teams in WHL history.

During his first season in the league, Propp scored 55 goals, finished third in scoring behind teammates Bill Derlago and Ray Allison, and won Rookie-of-the-Year honours for his play. By the end of the following season, 1977–78, he had vaulted to the top of the league scoring race. And in his final season, he set new WHL records for goals, 94 and points, 194, in 71 games.

Propp was much more than just a goal scorer. In one season he had

112 assists while at the same time piling up 200 minutes of penalty time. He was an all-around hockey player—a sniper, a playmaker and a grinder all rolled into one.

On the famous 1978–79 Wheat Kings, Propp, at left wing, combined with linemates Allison and Laurie Boschman to form the (arguably) most feared offensive unit in the history of major junior hockey. The trio finished one-two-three in the WHL scoring race, leading Brandon to an overall 58–5–9 record, a league championship and the final game of the Memorial Cup.

Propp was picked 14th in the 1979 NHL entry draft by Philadelphia, where he led the Flyers offensively almost from the day he arrived. A 4-time 40-goal scorer, he enjoyed his best scoring season in 1985–86 when he accumulated 40 goals, 57 assists and 97 points in 72 games. Propp was traded to Boston in 1990 and, after a brief fling with the Bruins, the Minnesota North Stars signed him as a free agent in July of the same year.

Brian Propp's greatest achievements were being member of the triumphant Team Canada squad in 1987, and playing in four Stanley Cup finals (but never winning) with Philadelphia (1984–85, 1986–87), Boston (1989–90) and Minnesota (1990–91). Propp remained the property of the Stars, but injuries and his age made him expendable. During the 1992–93 season, he was assigned by the team to play in Lugano, Switzerland for several months.

Brad McCrimmon

Brad McCrimmon, a standout defenceman on the Philadelphia Flyers team which reached the Stanley Cup finals twice in the mid-1980s, was a product of the Saskatchewan minor hockey system. Born in Dodsland, Saskatchewan, on March 29, 1959, and raised down the road in Plenty, he played his early hockey in Rosetown. Following an impressive 1973–74 season at the midget level, the 15-year-old McCrimmon graduated to the Prince Albert Raiders of the Saskatchewan Junior Hockey League, where he remained for two years, eventually joining the league's first team all-star roster and winning honours as the top defenceman.

McCrimmon joined the Brandon Wheat Kings in 1976 and was in Brandon for the three most successful years that the franchise ever experienced, capped off by the heart-breaking overtime loss to Peterborough in the 1979 Memorial Cup Final. McCrimmon was the Wheaties' top defenceman each year he played in Brandon. He made the WHL second all-star team in his first season and won first-team honours the next two years. In 1977–78 he was named the league's top defenceman. His WHL career statistics are 61 goals and 218 assists for 279 points in 203 games, plus 480 penalty minutes.

McCrimmon was one of four NHL first-round draft selections from the Wheat Kings in August, 1979. He was selected 15th overall by Boston, where he played three solid seasons before being dealt to the Philadelphia Flyers for all-star netminder Pete Peeters in 1982. In Philadelphia, McCrimmon, an old-fashioned stay-at-home defensive player, also began to shine on offence, upping his point production dramatically and playing a key role on a Flyers team that came very close to winning the Stanley Cup.

After five years with Philadelphia, McCrimmon clashed with Flyers' general manager Bobby Clarke and was promptly traded to Calgary in the summer of 1987. Without McCrimmon, the Flyers dropped from second in league standings in 1987 to eighth in 1988 and have declined as a team ever since his trade. Meanwhile, he was having his best season in the NHL in his first with the Flames. McCrimmon was named to the league's second all-star team and won the Emery Edge Award for the defenceman with the best plus-minus record. After one more season in Calgary, McCrimmon had accomplished what his Flyers had always fell short of.

On May 25th, 1989, Brad McCrimmon hoisted the Stanley Cup over his head in the Montreal Forum after his Flames beat the Canadiens in six games. McCrimmon's point production dramatically dropped that year, but he played as well as ever defensively, and led the Flames' defence to the President's Trophy and the franchise's first-ever Stanley Cup. After another season in Calgary, he was traded to Detroit for a second-round draft pick. He completed three more seasons in Motown, where he played alongside Mark Howe, his former defence partner in Philadelphia, during the 1992–93 season. On June 1, 1993, McCrimmon was once again traded, this time from the Red Wings to the Hartford Whalers, in exchange for a sixth-round draft pick.

Ron Hextall

One of the most impressive goaltenders to explode onto the hockey scene from Manitoba in recent memory is Ron Hextall. A graduate of the Brandon franchise, Hextall is best known for his fabulous 1986–87 season, when he led the Philadelphia Flyers to within one game of the Stanley Cup and won both the Vezina Trophy as the league's leading netminder and the Conn Smythe Trophy for Most Valuable Player in the playoffs.

Hextall's heroics are deservedly well known. What is less well known is that he is part of a hockey dynasty. No fewer than four Hextalls from three generations have played in the NHL: Ron himself, his grandfather Bryan Aldwyn Hextall, who made it into the Hockey Hall of Fame, his father Bryan Lee Hextall, and his uncle Dennis Hextall. Unquestionably, the Hextalls are one of the first families of hockey.

Ron Hextall, a Brandon grad, won the NHL's Conn Smythe and Vezina tropies in 1987.

Ron Hextall was born in Winnipeg on May 3, 1964, and learned his hockey in the Brandon minor league system. As a 16-year-old netminder he joined the Melville Millionaires of the Saskatchewan Amateur Junior A League. Experience was what he was after, and with Melville he got lots of it. In one game the Prince Albert Raiders peppered him with 105 shots for a 21–2 shellacking.

The next season, 1981–82, Hextall reported to the Brandon Wheat Kings training camp and surprised everyone by making the team as backup to Todd Lumbard. In three seasons with Brandon he proved he was a capable netminder, but at times he let his fiery temper get the best of him. One memorable night at Regina's Agridome in March 1984, Hextall precipitated a melee which resulted in $3000 worth of fines and the suspension of four players for 24 games. Brandon general manager Les Jackson got himself an eight-game suspension by jumping on the Regina coach during the fireworks. For Hextall, it was a sign of things to come.

After being drafted by the Philadelphia Flyers, he played for two seasons in the minor leagues. With the Hershey Bears of the American Hockey League in 1985–86, he posted a 3.41 goals-against average, registered 5 shutouts, made the first all-star team and was named Rookie of the Year. The Flyers called him up in 1986–87 and it turned out to be a dream season. Hextall finished the regular season with a fine 3.00 goals-against average, good enough to win the Vezina Trophy, but it was his brilliant play in the playoffs that remains in the minds of hockey fans. He won 15 games and posted a 2.77 goals-against average as the Flyers went all the way to the Stanley Cup Finals. They lost in seven games to Edmonton, but Hextall won the Conn Smythe Trophy as playoff MVP. Among post-season honours he was named to the all-rookie team and the first all-star squad. His 37 victories set a new club record for rookie goaltenders and was the fourth highest total for a rookie in league history.

Hextall played for Team Canada at the 1987 Canada Cup tournament and was a starting netminder in the 1988 NHL all-star game. Meanwhile, his quick temper had not deserted him and he was gaining a reputation around the league for piling up penalty minutes. During the 1986–87 Cup final against Edmonton, he earned an eight-game suspension for slashing Kent Nilsson, then went one better with a 12-game suspension for an attack on Chris Chelios during the Flyers' playoff loss to Montreal in 1989.

Strangely enough, Hextall is also famous as a goal scorer. On December 8, 1987, he became only the second netminder in NHL history to directly score a goal when, in the dying seconds of a game against Boston, he lifted the puck the length of the ice and into an empty net. Not content with one goal, Hextall repeated the feat during a playoff game at Washington on April 11, 1989. It was the first goal ever scored by a goaltender in Stanley Cup play. Once again it was an empty-netter with 62 seconds remaining in the game.

After six years with Philadelphia, Hextall moved to the Quebec Nordiques for the 1992–93 season as part of a package of six Flyers traded for the budding superstar Eric Lindros. He took the Nordiques, the youngest team in the NHL, to a fourth overall finish in the regular season, but failed to get the team past the first round of the playoffs. In a surprise move before the 1993 expansion draft, Quebec traded Hextall and a first-round draft pick to the New York Islanders for goaltender Mark Fitzpatrick and their first-round pick.

Ray Ferraro

In the history of the Western Hockey League, Brandon centre Ray Ferraro occupies a place all by himself. He is the only player ever to score more than 100 goals in a single season. In fact, only two players in all of major junior play have scored more goals in a season than Ferraro. Mario Lemieux totalled 133 with the 1983–84 Laval Voisins, and Guy Lafleur scored 130 with the 1970–71 Quebec Remparts.

Born and raised in Trail, BC, Ferraro was pretty well the lone bright spot for the Brandon franchise during the entire decade of the 1980s. After the 1979 overtime loss to Peterborough in the Memorial Cup Final, the Wheat Kings fell on hard times, finishing no higher than fifth in their division for four successive seasons. But then young Ray Ferraro arrived on the scene.

Ferraro began his junior hockey career with the Penticton Knights in 1981–82, winning the BC junior league scoring title with 65 goals and 135 points in 48 games. He graduated to the Portland Winter Hawks, where he broke his wrist after 50 games but still managed to contribute 56 goals and rejoin the team to win the Memorial Cup.

Despite such a promising rookie season, Portland traded Ferraro to Brandon, along with four other players, for rookie centre Blaine Chrest. It may have been the biggest talent steal in WHL history. Chrest's career faltered, while four of the new Wheat Kings were good enough at least to get a cup of coffee in the NHL.

The story of the trade turned out to be Ferraro. When he showed up in Brandon for the 1983–84 season, head coach Jack Sangster let him know he was going to be the key player. "The only thing I was leery about was his toughness," Sangster recalled. "I didn't know how he'd handle the rough going. But he proved to me that it doesn't matter to him how the other team plays."

Defenceman Dana Murzyn, who played in the same division as Brandon with the Calgary Wranglers that year, remembered Ferraro well. "He used to score goals by the bucketful in junior," Murzyn told a reporter. "He'd skate down on you and say, 'Here I come.' Then, he'd skate by you and say, 'Here I go.' As a junior, he was cocky, but when you score that many goals you have a right to be. We used to kid him that he was scoring goals even when he wasn't on the ice."

For the most part, Ferraro centred a line with Dave Curry on right wing and Stacy Pratt on left wing. "All through the year, he [Coach Sangster] played me consistently and he played me a lot," recalled Ferraro, "and, at that point in my career, that's exactly what I needed. He gave me the chance to play and prove myself."

Ferraro won the scoring title with 192 points, 11 more than Prince Albert Raiders centre Dan Hodgson. Besides setting a single-season record with 108 goals, Ferraro also established a record of 43 power-play goals.

The Wheat Kings benefited at the gate, too. In 1982–83, they averaged 1340 fans per game. With Ferraro in high gear the following season, that figure rose to 2300.

Despite his dream year, Ferraro did not go directly to the NHL. The Hartford Whalers drafted him but, concerned that he was too

As a member of the Brandon Wheat Kings, Ray Ferraro set the WHL single-season goal-scoring record.

small—he was 5'10" and 160 pounds—and too slow, they sent him to Binghamton of the American Hockey League. By the 1985–86 season he was up with the parent club for good, however, scoring 30 goals (a team-high 14 on the power play) and 77 points in 76 games.

The 1988–89 season was Ferraro's best in the NHL—he scored 41 goals—but late the next season the well dried up. He tallied just one goal in Hartford's last 27 games and when he began the 1990–91 season slowly the Whalers wasted no time trading him to the New York Islanders for defenceman Doug Crossman. In New York, Ferraro finished off the year at the same pace, but the next season would be his best in the NHL, playing in every game, scoring 40 goals, and picking up 80 points.

Unfortunately, Ferraro wasn't so lucky in 1992–93. After a slow start, he fractured his right fibula and missed 38 games. When he came back late in the season he continued to play poorly, but when playoff time came for the Islanders, he was ready to play the best hockey of his professional career.

Ferraro rebounded from his dismal regular season to take the team to the Patrick Division Championship and the Wales Conference Finals by leading the Islanders in goals, 13 (second in the league after Wayne Gretzky), and points, 20. By finishing sixth in overall playoff scoring, racking up 4 goals in a losing cause against the Capitals (including 3 while individually trying to mount a comeback in the third period), and either scoring or assisting 7 of the Islanders' 9 game-winning goals in the playoffs, Ray Ferraro proved that he could still play like that young superstar who tore apart the WHL ten years earlier.

CALGARY

The Calgary Buffaloes, Centennials & Wranglers

When the Canadian Major Junior Hockey League, the forerunner of the WHL, began operations in the fall of 1966 one of the early disappointments was the performance of the fledgling Calgary Buffaloes franchise. On the ice, and at the box office, the Calgary team was a disaster. It managed only four victories during its first season, which is still a WHL record for ineptitude. Thinking that a name change might help, the franchise began the second season as the Calgary Centennials, but it didn't make much difference. Under coach Cec Papke, the team won 15 games and finished in tenth place, 12 points ahead of the woeful Weyburn Red Wings. At this point, no one would have predicted that the Centennials would become one of the most successful WHL franchises of the 1970s. Or that the team would consistently challenge the powerful Edmonton Oil Kings for bragging rights in Alberta junior hockey circles. But that is exactly what happened, thanks largely to the efforts of one man.

In 1967–68 Scotty Munro was part-owner of the Estevan Bruins. The Bruins went all the way to the Memorial Cup that season, dropping the final game to the Niagara Falls Flyers, but, following the tournament, Munro sold his shares in the team and took over the struggling Calgary franchise. The change was almost miraculous. The first season under his leadership, 1968–69, the Centennials suddenly became respectable, finishing above .500 for the first time and advancing to their division final before losing to Edmonton. Among the exciting players on the roster were Tom Serviss and Bob Liddington, who finished third and fourth in

GRADUATES TO THE NHL

Calgary Buffaloes

1967: **Al McLeod**—Detroit. **Lyle Moffat**—Toronto, Winnipeg.

Calgary Centennials

1969: **Bob Liddington**—Toronto. **Darryl Maggs**—Chicago, California.

1970: **Ed Dyck**—Vancouver. **Randy Rota**—Oakland, Montreal, Los Angeles, Kansas City, Colorado. **Len Frig**—Chicago, California, Cleveland, St. Louis. **Brian Carlin**—Los Angeles.

1972: **Bob Nystrom**—NY Islanders. **Jim Watson**—Philadelphia. **Ron Homenuke**—Vancouver. **Doug Horbul**—NY Rangers, Kansas City.

1973: **John Davidson**—St.Louis, NY Rangers.

1974: **Grant Mulvey**—Chicago, New Jersey. **Danny Gare**—Buffalo, Detroit, Edmonton. **Jerry Holland**—NY Rangers. **Mike Rogers**—Vancouver, Hartford, NY Rangers, Edmonton.

1975: **Don Ashby**—Toronto, Colorado, Edmonton.

1976: **Rick Hodgson**—Atlanta, Hartford.

1977: **Roy Sommer**—Toronto, Edmonton. **Gary Rissling**—Washington, Pittsburgh.

Calgary Wranglers

1979: **Warren Skorodenski**—Chicago, Edmonton.

1980: **Kelly Kisio**—Detroit, NY Rangers, San Jose. **Glenn Merkosky**—Hartford, New Jersey, Detroit. **Brian Tutt**—Philadelphia, Washington.

1981: **Darrel Anholt**—Chicago. **Mike Vernon**—Calgary. **Colin Chisholm**—Buffalo, Minnesota. **Danny Bourbonnais**—Hartford. **Raymond Cote**—Edmonton.

1982: **Mike Heidt**—Los Angeles. **Leigh Verstraete**—Toronto.

1984: **Doug Houda**—Detroit, Hartford. **Ken Quinney**—Quebec. **Ross McKay**—Hartford.

1985: **Dana Murzyn**—Hartford, Calgary, Vancouver.

1987: **Mark Tinordi**—NY Rangers, Minnesota, Dallas.

the league scoring race. It was the beginning of a bitter rivalry with Bill Hunter's Oil Kings. For four straight seasons the teams finished one-two in their division. Each time, Edmonton defeated Calgary in the playoffs to move on to the league championship, winning it twice. Games between the two teams were brutal and more than once erupted in bench-clearing fights.

During this time the Centennials were a solid team from the goal mouth out. John Davidson, who played in Calgary from 1969 to 1973, posted the best single-season goals-against average in league history during 1971–72 (2.37) and had 8 shutouts. Meanwhile, forwards like Bob Nystrom, Wayne Bianchin, Derek Black and Doug Horbul filled up the opponents' nets. Calgary featured two of the finest lines in junior hockey at this time—Mike Rogers, Danny Gare and Jerry Holland on one line and Don Ashby, Denny McLean and Grant Mulvey on the other. And along the blue line, Jim Watson and Jim McMasters provided a solid defence.

Under Munro the franchise prospered at the box office as well. After drawing less than 50% of capacity during its first two seasons, the team became a hit with fans who flocked to the Calgary Corral in record numbers. While the Centennials romped to three division crowns in seven years, it was not uncommon to have more than 6000 fans at a home game.

The good times peaked for Calgary in 1973–74. Led by Rogers, Gare and Holland, all of whom finished among the scoring top ten, the Centennials ended the regular season atop their division and only dropped two games in the first two rounds of the playoffs. The team desperately wanted to go to the Memorial Cup that year since the tournament was being played in Calgary but it turned out they did not have the horses. In the final, they ran into Dennis Sobchuk and his Regina Pats and came away on the short end of a four-game sweep.

For whatever reason, the franchise was never the same again. The following season, 1974–75, the Centennials tumbled to last place in their division, posting only 11 victories all year. A string of coaches appeared behind the bench, including Eric Sutcliff, Dave Amadio and Jim Munro, Scotty's son. None could stem the tide. Then, on September 19, 1975, an era came to an end when Scotty Munro died of cancer at the age of only 57.

The team continued to flounder. In 1975–76 it went through four coaches and still finished in the divisional basement, where it remained through the next season. A low point came on February 23, 1977, in Lethbridge when Calgary's Grant Morin, that season's league leader in penalty minutes, spat in the face of the Bronco's Mike Sauter. Sauter retaliated, other players jumped in, and pretty soon a brawl was underway. When it was all over Sauter was suspended for 12 games, Morin for 4 and several other players from both teams for various lengths of time.

In 1977, the owners of the franchise, suffering from competition from the Calgary-based World Hockey Association team, decided to move to Billings, Montana, where the team reappeared for the 1977–78 season as the Billings Bighorns. But this did not mark the end of junior hockey in Cowtown. The Winnipeg Monarchs, another struggling WHL franchise, immediately moved its operation to Calgary and launched the Calgary Wranglers, with Doug Barkley as general manager and Gerry Brisson continuing as coach.

The Wranglers did not win many games their first season—18 to be exact—but they caught the attention of Calgary fans with some "unusual" escapades. In one instance, after a fight broke out as the game ended, coach Brisson stormed into the officials' room and had to be restrained from attacking the referee. On another occasion, during a game at the Lethbridge Sportsplex, the referee awarded a penalty shot to Lethbridge centre Steve Tambellini. The game was tied and the Wranglers were shorthanded. As Tambellini started down ice, Calgary winger Dave Morrison left the bench and skated in front of him. Then, as Tambellini approached the net, goalie Warren Skorodenski lifted the net off its moorings and skated away. Tambellini got the goal, Lethbridge got the win, and Calgary got a $2500 fine.

The Wranglers' most successful season was 1980–81, with Doug Sauter behind the bench and Mike Vernon in the nets. After finishing second in its division, the team advanced easily through the playoffs to the finals where it faced the Victoria Cougars. Calgary actually had a three games to one lead in the series, and seemed certain to win a berth in the Memorial Cup, but then it lost three straight games and the championship to the Cougars.

In 1983, Marcel Comeau took over as coach from Doug Sauter, who left for a job with the Springfield Indians of the American Hockey League. With the departure of the defensive-minded Sauter, the Wranglers began a swan dive from which they never fully recovered. By 1985–86 they were at the bottom of their division and fan interest had dissipated badly. Once again professional hockey, this time the NHL Flames, was making the junior game a hard sell. At the end of the 1986–87 season the owners of the franchise sold to a community-based group in Lethbridge, and the long association between the City of Calgary and the Western Hockey League came to a close.

Scotty Munro

A list of the towns in which Scotty Munro coached hockey reads like a road map of Western Canada. Yorkton, Moose Jaw, Gravelbourg, Lethbridge, Bellevue, Edmonton, Blairmore, Humboldt, Melfort, Estevan, Calgary—Munro saw them all during his peripatetic coaching career. And in almost every case he managed to produce a winner. From 1943 to 1946, for example, he coached a Moose Jaw team to four consecutive Saskatchewan juvenile championships. (The team was owned by hardware merchant Ross Thatcher, later premier of the province.) In Lethbridge his Native Sons went to the 1948 Abbott Cup championship finals, losing the seventh game to Port Arthur in Toronto's Maple Leaf Gardens in front of 11,000 fans. In Humboldt his Indians won the 1955 Saskatchewan Junior Hockey League championship. And in Estevan, where Munro arrived in 1956 to lay the groundwork for the Estevan Bruins, his teams won the SJHL title three times, the Abbott Cup once, and made one trip to the Memorial Cup, in 1968, when the Bruins won the WHL championship.

This was the record of success that Munro brought to Calgary in the summer of 1968, when he arrived to take over the floundering Centennials franchise. Prior to his arrival, the team had managed just 19 victories over two seasons. Then, as if by magic, Munro accomplished a complete turnabout. In his first year with the club, the Centennials finished second in their division and went to the second round of the playoffs. In the years which followed, the franchise won three division crowns in seven seasons. Munro's teams always played good defensive hockey, with a fair amount of roughhouse tactics thrown in for good measure. He was known as "The Fighting Scotsman," but it was usually his players who did the fighting.

R.N. "Scotty" Munro.

He would not tolerate any member of his team who would not drop his gloves and start swinging, and the long rivalry between the Centennials and the Edmonton Oil Kings saw some memorable blow ups. The fans, of course, loved it and flocked to the Calgary Corral in record numbers.

When the World Hockey Association was launched in 1972, Munro became general manager of the Calgary Broncos franchise. Before play began, the Broncs withdrew from the league and Munro carried on with the Centennials, but later he got involved with the Calgary Cowboys of the WHA. When he died of cancer in 1975 he was vice-president of finances for the Cowboys. Today his long affiliation with the WHL is honoured with the Scotty Munro Memorial Trophy, given to the league's regular-season champions.

John Davidson

John Davidson, who was born on February 27, 1953 in Ottawa, has given an outstanding goaltending performance for every league he has joined.

He spent two seasons stopping pucks for the Lethbridge Sugar Kings in the Alberta Junior Hockey League. In the 1970–71 AJHL season, he was named MVP and won the top-goaltender award. Scotty Munro, the Centennials bench boss, took notice of Davidson's impressive talents and brought him to Calgary to spend a sensational two-year career in the Western Canada Hockey League.

His two years spent in Cowtown were sparkling in every sense of the word. In 1971–72 he posted 8 shutouts and a 2.37 goals-against average to top the league in both categories. The goals-against average is still a Western Hockey League record. Davidson followed this up with a 3.30 average in the 1972–73 season and, by this time, pro scouts had John at the top of their scouting reports.

Davidson was drafted fifth overall by the St. Louis Blues in the 1973 amateur draft. He became an early pioneer, as the first goalie ever to jump directly from junior hockey into the National Hockey League.

Davidson was not, however, an instant hit with the various coaches and general managers of the St. Louis Blues. He was even dispatched briefly in the 1974–75 season to the Denver Spurs in the Central Hockey League.

Due partly to a knee injury and his bad balance attributed to his lanky size of 6'3" and 205 pounds, Davidson's St. Louis years were seen

John Davidson----holds WHL goals-against average record.

by the management as unsuccessful. But perhaps the goalie's worst fate was being drafted by the Blues so high, with the impossible expectations placed upon his shoulders right from the outset. Davidson was simply handed the Blues starting netminding position straight out of juniors and was proclaimed as the saviour in the nets. "There is a lot of pressure on a kid coming out of juniors and playing in the NHL right away," admitted Davidson. "For a goalie, it is more intense, he's on display every time a shot is taken and everybody can see when he makes a mistake."

It came as a big surprise to many people when, after just two years in the Blues organization, Davidson found himself on Broadway in the uniform of the New York Rangers. He was traded along with Bill Collins to New York for Ted Irvine, Bert Wilson and Jerry Butler in June 1975. In his first few seasons in New York, his goals-against average and netminding took a turn for the worse.

"I don't think I got comfortable with the Rangers for a while," admitted Davidson. He claimed "the team didn't do too well and frankly, neither did I."

By 1978–79, when Fred Shero arrived on the Ranger scene as coach, Davidson had emerged as the club's number one goalie. A broken leg and knee surgery had hampered his earlier career in New York until that season. In 1978–79, a sciatic condition had kept him sidelined for five and a half weeks. He recovered in time for the final two weeks of the schedule and Shero used those games to get Davidson in shape for the post-season action. The gamble worked and Davidson took the Rangers to the finals almost single-handedly.

Davidson was the hero of the Rangers' unlikely dash into the 1978–79 Stanley Cup Final and would have been a cinch for playoffs MVP if New York hadn't been defeated by Montreal. In 18 play-off games and 1106 minutes of pressure cooker action, Davidson allowed only 42 goals for a 2.28 goals-against average.

"He's always had the talent," said opposing Montreal goalie Ken Dryden. "Now it looks like he's put the talent he knew he had, and everyone knew he had, together with the consistency he needs."

Mainly due to back problems, Davidson concluded his NHL career as a New York Ranger after completion of the 1982–83 season. Davidson, who wore the number 00 as a Ranger, had a fine netminding average of 3.52 in his decade in the NHL spotlight.

Since leaving the ice, Davidson has certainly not abandoned the game. In fact, many hockey fans came to know him better for his work as hockey announcer on the New York Rangers' Madison Square Garden Network, ABC-TV and ESPN than they ever did for his work between the pipes.

Bob Nystrom

As commonplace as European hockey stars are in the NHL today, 20 years ago a Swedish player in a Canadian uniform was a rarity. Bob Nystrom, a hard-working right-winger with the legendary New York Islanders dynasty of the early 1980s, is not usually thought of as a hockey import, but he was born in Sweden in 1952 and did not arrive in Canada until he was five years old. As a youngster coming up through the ranks in Hinton, Alberta, he wasn't a player who was ever looking for a fight. It was when he made the jump to the junior level with the Kamloops Rockets of the BCJHL that he met the late Joe Tennant who taught him to take a more physical approach to his game. Still, it was Nystrom's blistering shot that impressed Scotty Munro, who invited the youngster to join the Calgary Centennials for the 1970–71 season. Like Tennant, Munro favoured the physical game. Nystrom was a modest goal scorer

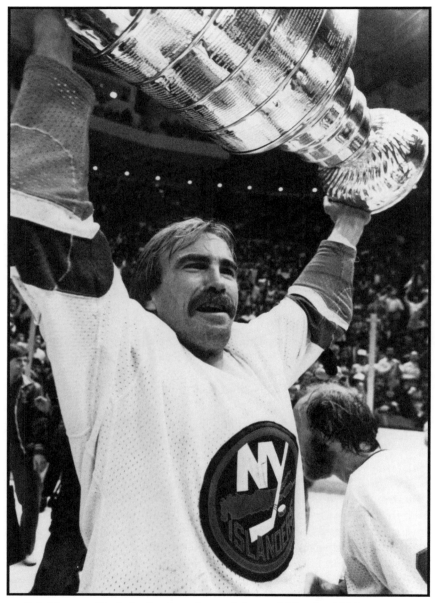

Bob Nystrom fired the shot heard round the world for the 1980 Islanders.

in his junior career but Munro worked on turning him into a player with a reputation for toughness. This was the era when Calgary battled the Edmonton Oil Kings for supremacy of the West Division, and longtime WHL fans still talk about the night that Nystrom took on Oil Kings defenceman Phil Russell, the most penalized player in the league, in a classic toe-to-toe slugfest. No matter who won the bloody fight—it seems to have been considered a draw—it served to establish Nystrom's reputation for major league muscle.

In 1972 the New York Islanders, preparing for their initial season in the NHL, made Nystrom their third draft pick, behind Billy Harris and Lorne Henning. He remained with the Islanders as they built the team that won four consecutive Stanley Cups, 1980–83. Playing in the shadow of more celebrated teammates such as Bryan Trottier, Mike Bossy and Denis Potvin, Nystrom was chosen most popular player by the fans six times. He was known as an exceptional pressure player, the guy you went to when you just had to have a goal. Take the 1980 playoffs, for instance, when his famous goal at 7:11 of overtime in the sixth game of the final series against Philadelphia brought the Islanders their first Stanley Cup. A photograph of "the shot heard round the world" was on the front page of the New York Times the next day, showing a blond-haired Bob Nystrom snapping the puck past Pete Peeters.

The Islanders' reign at the top of the hockey world ended in 1984 when they lost in the playoffs to the next dynasty, the Edmonton Oilers. After a dozen years in the NHL, Nystrom was slowing down, along with the entire team. During the 1985–86 he suffered an eye injury in practice which eventually finished his playing career. Nystrom, always a workhorse, earned two new jobs—the Islanders' Director of Community Relations and a radio announcer for the team.

Mike Rogers

Mike Rogers, a standout centre, was certainly one of the best and widely underrated players to emerge from the Western Hockey League. He did not perform the heroics of a Gretzky or a Dionne, but in the category of overall competence at his job, there were few better.

"He could do it all," says the great Gordie Howe, "He was quick as a cat and very strong for his size. And he could play all night."

"Not many guys could skate better than Rogers," says former teammate Dave Keon.

Rogers was born on October 24, 1954 in Calgary, Alberta. He grew up in Calgary and played three seasons of junior hockey there. Before playing in his hometown, Rogers played Tier II Junior A Hockey in the 1970–71 season with the Lethbridge Sugar Kings of the Alberta Junior Hockey League.

Playing on a line with Jerry Holland and Danny Gare, he was considered a terror to opposing netminders throughout his major junior career. He twice scored more than 50 goals and 100 points as a member of the Calgary Centennials. Rogers shares a WHL playoff record with several players for the most goals in one period—three. He banged in 67 goals in his final year of 1973–74, and added another 13 goals and 29 points in the playoffs, but the big league teams weren't overly impressed. The Philadelphia Flyers, also known as the Broad Street Bullies, had just battled their way to the Stanley Cup and scouts were on the prowl for big, brawny intimidators, not 5'9", 170-pound smoothies.

In the May 1974 amateur draft, Vancouver Canucks selected Rogers, 77th overall, in the fifth round. The rival Edmonton Oilers of the World Hockey Association also picked him in the fifth round, 61st overall. He elected to sign with the Oilers in the World Hockey Association.

"It wasn't a matter of money," said Rogers. "The Canucks informed me they would send me to the minors, and Edmonton told me that I was a big pick and that they intended to play me. I didn't want to go to the minors so I signed with Edmonton." He went on to win the WHA's Most Sportsmanlike Player Award in 1974–75, as he recorded only two minutes in penalty time.

After a season and a half with the Oilers, he was traded to the New England Whalers in January 1976 for centre/left-winger Wayne "Swoop" Carleton. Rogers figures his development as a player was highly accelerated when he centred Gordie Howe, one of the greatest players ever to play the game, and another fine player, Gordie's son Mark.

Spurned by Vancouver on the advice of coach Harry Neale, who thought his ex-WHA star wasn't NHL material, Rogers moved with the Whalers when they joined the National Hockey League for the 1979–80 season. Rogers became one of the few players in NHL history along with Wayne Gretzky, Mario Lemieux and Peter Stastny to score more than 100 points in each of his first three seasons in the NHL. Rogers played on a line with Blaine Stoughton and Pat Boutette, which was formed on a trial-and-error basis and, in due course, evolved into one of the more efficient units in the National Hockey League.

In October 1981, Rogers was traded from Hartford with Simo Saarinen to the New York Rangers for Chris Kotsopoulos, Doug Sulliman and Gerry McDonald. He was 27 at the time. "Although I didn't realize it then," Rogers says. "I had a lot to learn about hockey."

Rogers went on to enjoy four solid seasons in New York before being traded once again to, of all teams, the Edmonton Oilers. But after spending much of the season in the minor leagues with the Nova Scotia Oilers of the American Hockey League, Rogers headed over to Switzerland to play hockey in the 1986–87 season.

His final statistics in the NHL were 202 goals, 317 assists totalling 519 points, proof enough that even during one of hockey's tougher periods a little guy with skill and smarts could make his mark in the NHL.

Danny Gare

Born in Nelson, BC, in 1954, Danny Gare came from a family of skaters. His father, Ernie Sr., was a physical education instructor at the University of Notre Dame in Nelson. His older brother Ernie Jr. played senior hockey with the Spokane Flyers in the Western International League and later coached the Vernon Lakers in the BC junior league. His younger brother Morrison was drafted by the New York Islanders, and three sisters were all figure skaters.

Danny played his minor hockey in Nelson, where he was scouted by the Calgary Centennials and in 1971, at age 17, he made the jump to the WHL. He put in three seasons in Calgary and each year became a tougher, more polished hockey player. He scored ten goals his first year, 45 his second and 68 his final year, when he finished seventh in the league scoring race and was named to the all-star team. Despite his small stature, he developed into a very rugged customer in the fighting department as well. It was not his style to ever give an inch to an opposing player. During his final two seasons of junior hockey he combined on a line with Jerry Holland and Mike Rogers, two other future NHLers.

The Buffalo Sabres selected Gare in the second round of the 1974 amateur draft, 29th overall, and promptly signed him to a contract. He went on to have a fabulous rookie season in 1974–75. In his very first regular season game he scored a goal at the 18-second mark on his first shot in the NHL. Playing on a line with Craig Ramsey and Don Luce, he scored 30 more goals that season and finished runner-up to Atlanta's Eric Vail in the voting for Rookie of the Year. In the playoffs, the Sabres made it all the way to the Stanley Cup final before losing to Philadelphia in six games.

Gare remained with Buffalo for seven and a half seasons. During that time he notched 50 or more goals twice and scored more than 30

Danny Gare----pride of Nelson, BC captained two NHL teams.

goals five times. His 56 goal season was a Buffalo team record for many years. Not only a prolific marksman, he was also a team leader and served as the Sabres' captain for four seasons. In 1981, however, a nagging back injury was hurting his play and Buffalo traded him to Detroit in a seven-player deal. Once again a team captain, Gare topped the 25-goal plateau twice for the Red Wings, but his back problems persisted and in 1986 Detroit released him. He signed on as a free agent with the Edmonton Oilers for one more NHL season, but only dressed for 18 games and in 1987 he retired.

Gare went back to Buffalo to own a restaurant and work in broadcasting, but was hired on as the first radio and television voice of the Tampa Bay Lightning in 1992. After a year behind the microphone in Tampa Bay, the Lightning made Gare an assistant coach for the 1993–94 season.

Doug Sauter

Doug Sauter has been called the unofficial mayor of Fairlight, Saskatchewan, a farming community southeast of Regina. If not that, he is, at the very least, Fairlight's goodwill ambassador to the world of hockey. The man with the second most famous moustache in the West (Lanny McDonald takes top honours, of course) got his start in junior hockey as a goaltender with the Estevan Bruins in 1970–71. The next season he made the move to New Westminster with the franchise. Sauter was no hall-of-famer in goal. His entire WHL playing career consisted of 31 games over three seasons. He does claim to have invented the curved goalstick, making it easier for goaltenders to fish the puck out of the net after a score. He'd be the first to tell you that his own career gave him lots of experience.

After his playing days ended, Sauter spent five seasons, 1973–78, in New Westminster as an assistant coach to the legendary Ernie McLean. During this time the Bruins won four WHL championships and two Memorial Cups. If you are going to learn the coaching trade, you might as well study with the master. Sauter didn't spend all his time with the parent club, though. In 1975–76 he was sent to Butte, Montana, to take charge of the Butte Copper Kings of the now-defunct South West Hockey League. He was general manager and player/coach of the team and, in a game against Billings, he scored the only two goals of his life. Naturally he picked himself first star.

Following the 1977–78 season, Sauter left the Bruins to become head coach of the Calgary Wranglers. In Calgary, he established a reputation for producing strong defensive teams with solid goaltending. During a stretch of four consecutive seasons—with Calgary and Medicine Hat—his clubs had the WHL's best defensive record, not once surrendering more than 266 goals. He coached such goaltenders as Warren Skorodenski, Mike Vernon, Gary Johnson, Troy Gamble and Mark Fitzpatrick, all of them having superb WHL careers.

Sauter spent five seasons with the Wranglers, and by the time he moved on he was a celebrity in Calgary. Everybody knew him—the moustache, the cowboy hat, the boots—and he knew everybody. He even spent a week in July helping out in the chutes at the Stampede. Sauter had a good deal of on-ice success in Calgary, too, running off four straight seasons of 40-plus victories. In 1980–81 the Wranglers won the East Division title before losing to Victoria in the championship series, four games to three.

In the fall of 1983 Sauter took a crack at the pro game with the Springfield Indians, the American Hockey League farm team of the Chicago Blackhawks. He lasted just one season as coach, finishing with a 39–35–6 record, then returned to the WHL with the Medicine Hat Tigers. The Tigers, with Sauter at the controls, put together a pair of magnificent seasons, going 53–17–2 in 1984–85 and following that up with a 54–17–1 campaign in 1985–86 when they won the East Division title.

Enter the Regina Pats. The Pats organization was in a bit of turmoil at the time. The league had had to step in and buy the club, then resell it to a group of Regina businessmen. The new owners decided Sauter was their man and offered him two jobs—general manager and coach. Sauter signed on and immediately hired Dennis Sobchuk, perhaps the most popular player in Regina hockey history, as his assistant. The first season was a nightmare. The Pats finished under .500 and bowed out of the playoffs without winning a game. Worse than that, there was the bus accident which claimed the lives of four members of the Swift Current Broncos while they were on their way to Regina, then the tragic injury to Brad Hornung which left the young centre paralyzed.

Sauter remained in Regina for two seasons, then moved on briefly to the Brandon Wheat Kings. During the 1989–90 season in Brandon he developed a body-crippling syndrome and had to step down from the coaching ranks to recuperate. He recovered sufficiently by the 1992–93 season to coach professionally with the Winston-Salem Thunderbirds of the East Coast Hockey League and in 1992–93 with the Wheeling Thunderbirds (ECHL).

His 417 career WHL victories puts him fifth on the all-time list. Only Ken Hodge, Ernie McLean, Pat Ginnell and Jack Shupe won more games.

Kelly Kisio

Kelly Kisio, a native of Peace River, Alberta, began his junior hockey career in pretty fast company. When he joined the Red Deer Rustlers of the Tier II Alberta Junior Hockey League for the 1977–78 season, he found himself skating with the likes of Duane and Brent Sutter, Rod Buskas, the future NHL defenceman, and Dave Babych, a 14-year NHL veteran with Winnipeg, Hartford and Vancouver. Kisio scored 74 goals with Red Deer, amassing 142 points in just 58 games and catching the attention of the Calgary Wranglers management who put the young centre on their protected roster.

During his two seasons in the WHL with the Wranglers, Kisio continued to score goals at an impressive rate. During 1978–79, his rookie year, he notched 60 goals to finish sixth in the scoring race and win Rookie-of-the-Year honours. The subsequent year he moved up to fourth place in scoring with 65 goals and a total of 138 points.

Surprisingly for a player with those numbers, Kisio was not drafted by an NHL team when his junior career ended. Undiscouraged, he spent a couple of seasons in the minors with teams in the American, International and Central leagues. In 1981–82 he scored 62 goals for the Dallas Black Hawks, good enough to lead the entire Central Hockey League. After a season in Switzerland with the Davos Hockey Club, in which he scored 49 goals in 40 games, Kisio finally attracted an offer from an NHL club and he finished the 1982–83 season in a Detroit Red Wings uniform. A consistent 20-plus goal scorer, he remained in Detroit for three more years, played for the Rangers for five, and at age 34, was the team scoring leader and Most Valuable Player for the San Jose Sharks in his tenth NHL season. In the summer of 1993 he became a free agent and signed a multi-year contract with the Calgary Flames.

Mike Vernon

Mike Vernon was born on February 24, 1963 in Calgary, Alberta. He played his minor hockey in the Calgary Southwest Association and was placed on the roster of the Billings Bighorns. When the Bighorns decided on Andy Moog as their number one goaltender, the Calgary Wranglers acquired Vernon and, as they say, the rest is history.

After being farmed down to the Calgary Canucks of the Alberta Junior Hockey League in 1979–80 and posting a fine goals-against average of 2.91, he made the roster of the Wranglers for the next season. The highlight of his rookie WHL season was no doubt reaching the championship final against the Victoria Cougars and jumping to a three-games-to-one lead before losing in seven games to Grant Fuhr and the Cougars.

During the next two seasons, Vernon went on to enjoy tremendous success with his hometown Calgary Wranglers as he made the first all-star team both in 1981–82 and 1982–83, and was also the Most Valuable Player in the league for those same two seasons. As well, in 1981–82 and

1982–83 he captured the Del Wilson Trophy as the league's top goaltender. He was also chosen as the 1981–82 Molson/Cooper Player of the Year.

After the 1981–82 season, the Calgary Flames selected Vernon 56th overall in the third round of the amateur draft and, except for a short stay with the Oklahoma City Stars during the 1981–82 playoffs in the Central Hockey League, remained with the Wranglers the entire 1981–82 season. At the end of the following campaign, the Portland Winter Hawks gained approval to use Vernon in the 1982–83 Memorial Cup Tournament in Portland and he led the Winter Hawks to an upset victory over the heavily favoured Lethbridge Broncos in the four-team tournament. That same season, Vernon appeared in two games with the Calgary Flames and, although he didn't win either game, gained valuable experience for future seasons.

In the 1983–84 season, the Flames shipped Vernon down to the Central Hockey League's Colorado Rockies where he was chosen to the second all-star team and made marked improvement in his goaltending skills.

Mike Vernon's World Junior Championships card.

Except for the 1984–85 and 1985–86 seasons when he spent time in hockey's minor leagues with the Moncton Golden Flames and Salt Lake City Golden Eagles, Vernon remained with the Calgary Flames.

His major highlights with the Flames were appearing in two Stanley Cup championship series. The Flames lost to the Montreal Canadiens in five games in 1986 and subsequently defeated Montreal in 1989 in an exciting six-game series.

Among Vernon's personal career highlights are playing in four straight all-star games from 1988 to 1991 as well as leading the NHL with 37 wins in 1988–89. He was also named to *The Sporting News* second all-star team in 1988–89. He suited up for Team Canada at the 1991 World Hockey Championships as Dave King's squad clinched a silver medal. In his days as a junior with the Calgary Wranglers, Vernon also participated in a World Junior Hockey Championship series.

EDMONTON

The Edmonton Oil Kings

In the early years of the Western Hockey League, one of the power-house teams was the Edmonton Oil Kings. Between 1966, when the league was formed, and 1973, the Oil Kings topped the regular season standings twice, led their division three times, went to the final round of the playoffs four years in a row, and travelled east twice to the Memorial Cup tournament as WHL champions. With all the success of the NHL Oilers through the 1980s, it should not be forgotten that Edmonton had a hockey dynasty long before the professionals came to town.

The WHL Oil Kings franchise had its roots in a Junior A team which began play in 1950. Growing quickly in reputation, this team became a perennial contender as Western Canada's representative in the Memo-rial Cup. During the early 1960s the roster included future NHL greats Norm Ullman and Johnny Bucyk, not to mention three future coaches—Glen Sather, Pat Quinn and Bert Marshall. The talent-laden franchise actually won the national championship twice, in 1963 and again in 1966. The 1966 team defeated Bobby Orr's Oshawa Generals for the Cup, and was so strong that it played at the senior level in Alberta.

When the WHL, known as the Canadian Major Junior Hockey League in those days, began play in 1966, Edmonton was one of the seven original franchises. Bill "Red" Hunter was part-owner of the team and the coach was NHL hall-of-famer Bill Gadsby. The Oil Kings led the league that inaugural season, behind the scoring of Garnet "Ace" Bailey, Galen Head and Ron Walters, but were ambushed in the playoffs by the surprising Moose Jaw Canucks.

In the 1968–69 season Edmonton finished atop its division and

GRADUATES TO THE NHL

Alberta Senior League Franchise

1966: **Ace"Garnet "Ace" Bailey**—Boston, Detroit, St. Louis, Washington.

WCHL Franchise

1967: **Galen Head**—Detroit. **Don "Smokey" McLeod**—Detroit, Philadelphia.

1968: **Kerry Ketter**—Detroit, Atlanta. **Harold "Hap" Myers**—Detroit, Buffalo.

1969: **Frank Spring**—Boston, St. Louis, California, Cleveland. **Gregg Boddy**—Los Angeles, Vancouver. **Frank Hughes**—Toronto, California. **Bobby Whitlock**—Minnesota.

1970: **Larry Bignell**—Pittsburgh. **Randy Wyrozub**—Buffalo. **Ted McAneeley**—California.

1971: **Ron Jones**—Boston, Pittsburgh, Washington. **Dave Kryskow**—Chicago, Washington, Detroit, Atlanta.

1972: **Phil Russell**—Chicago, Atlanta, Calgary, New Jersey, Buffalo. **Don Kozak**—Los Angeles, Vancouver. **Tom Bladon**—Philadelphia, Pittsburgh, Edmonton, Winnipeg, Detroit. **Brian Ogilvie**—Chicago, St. Louis.

1973: **Darcy Rota**—Chicago, Vancouver. **Bob Murdoch**—California, Cleveland, St. Louis.

1974: **Harold Snepsts**—Vancouver, Minnesota, Detroit, St. Louis.

1975: **Doug Soetaert**—NY Rangers, Winnipeg, Montreal.

1976: **Paul Messier**—Colorado.

1979: **Craig "Cowboy" Levie**—Montreal, Winnipeg, Minnesota, St. Louis, Vancouver. **Ray Neufeld**—Hartford, Winnipeg, Boston.

made the first of four consecutive trips to the league championship. During this stint the franchise changed head coaches as often as the players changed their uniforms as "Buster" Brayshaw, Gerry Melnyk and Harvey Roy played musical chairs behind the bench until 1971 when Brian Shaw settled into the job. Standout players during this period included Don Kozak, who notched 60 goals in 1970–71, Danny Spring, the team scoring leader that season with 122 points, Dave Kryskow and Darcy Rota. In 1971, after twice being eliminated by Flin Flon in the final series, Edmonton finally succeeded in knocking off the Bombers, winning the WHL championship and earning a berth in the Memorial Cup tournament. That year, however, the tournament belonged to Guy Lafleur and his Quebec Remparts and the Oil Kings came home empty-handed.

After the 1971–72 season Edmonton was back in the league finals, facing the Regina Pats for the championship. The first game of the final series went to Regina, but then the Oil Kings closed the door, allowing just two more goals as they dumped the Pats in four straight games. The team consisted of Darcy Rota, John Rogers, Terry McDonald, Don Kozak, Henry Van Drunen, Marcel Comeau and Brian Ogilvie up front, Phil Russell, Tom Bladon and Dave Inkpen on defence, and Larry Hendrick and Doug Soetaert in goal. Management picked up netminder John Davidson for Memorial Cup play, hoping he would make the difference between winning and losing. The tournament was a round-robin affair, featuring Edmonton, the Peterborough Petes and the Cornwall Royals. In their first game the Oil Kings were battling Peterborough to a 4–4 tie after two periods when Petes coach Roger Neilson asked that the referee measure Darcy Rota's stick. The ploy worked; Rota was penalized for playing with an illegal stick. The Petes scored on the power play and went on to win the game 6–4. Bill Hunter was furious. "It's the cheapest method I know to win a hockey game," he bellowed. Two nights later Cornwall shut out the Oil Kings behind the goaltending of Richard Brodeur and Edmonton's hunt for the Memorial Cup was over for another year.

The Oil Kings were back atop their division in 1972–73, led by the line of Darcy Rota, John Rogers and Fred Comrie. Rota finished fourth in the scoring race with a league-leading 73 goals. Rogers added 63 goals and Comrie, 30. However, the team was knocked off by the surprising Medicine Hat Tigers in the second round of the playoffs, the first time in five seasons that Edmonton was not in the finals.

It was a sign of things to come. Ken Hodge joined the team in 1973 as head coach, but the Oil Kings slumped badly for the next three seasons. The franchise struggled off the ice as well. The World Hockey Association had come to Edmonton, there was talk of the NHL arriving soon, and the audience for junior hockey was falling off. In 1976 Brian Shaw, then general manager, gambled on moving the team south of the border to Portland where it was reborn as the Winter Hawks. Portland turned out to be the first of five successful WHL franchises now located in the US Pacific Northwest.

However, Edmonton still had not seen the end of the Oil Kings. In 1978 the Flin Flon franchise was on the move. It was supposed to transfer to Winnipeg but at the last minute the deal fell through and Bill Hunter and Vic Mah, a wealthy restaurateur, brought the team to Edmonton. Donald Scott was general manager, while Norm Ferguson and Wayne Tennant shared coaching duties. The new Oil Kings had a pretty dismal year, winning only 17 games and suffering a first-round loss in the playoffs. When the year ended, the franchise was on the move again, this time to Great Falls, Montana, where it lasted only 28 games before folding.

With NHL ticket prices rising beyond the means of many fans, and junior hockey still being a big draw in Western Canada, there has been talk in the early 1990s of one day bringing WHL hockey back to the Alberta capital.

Bill Hunter

The biggest hockey booster in western Canada has to be Bill Hunter. At every level Hunter has dared to think big and to believe in doing the seemingly impossible. Born in North Battleford in 1920, "Wild Bill" Hunter began his love affair with hockey back in the senior leagues of post-war Saskatchewan, first as owner/coach/manager of the Regina Capitals, then as coach of the Saskatoon Quakers. In the early 1950s Hunter made his first foray into the ranks of junior hockey with the Medicine Hat Tigers as coach/manager/trainer/bus driver and all around dogsbody. Then, after several seasons out of junior hockey, some of them spent as a controversial executive with the Edmonton Eskimos football team, he returned to the rink to coach the Edmonton Oil Kings of the Alberta Senior League. He would stay with the team from his first year, when it won the Memorial Cup, to the early seventies when it was an established dynasty in the new WHL.

In 1965, as manager of the Edmonton Oil Kings, he was convinced that a cross-Canada junior circuit was possible and began importing teams from Ontario to play exhibition games in Alberta. When that dream failed to materialize, he was one of the moving spirits behind the creation of the Canadian Major Junior Hockey League, the forerunner of the WHL, and was the league's first chairman in 1966.

Meanwhile, his Oil Kings reached the league finals four years in a row. In 1971, when the major junior leagues in Quebec and Ontario threatened not to take part in the Memorial Cup with Edmonton because of a dispute over travel expenses and over-age players, Hunter called on the prime minister to invoke the War Measures Act to ensure that the tournament took place. (In the end the disagreements were settled and Guy Lafleur's Quebec Remparts captured the Cup.) Hunter, ever the visionary, took another sabbatical from junior hockey in 1972 to play a major role in the creation of the World Hockey Association, the upstart competitor of the NHL.

Hunter founded the Edmonton Oilers WHA franchise, served as coach and general manager and even won the league's Executive-of-the-Year trophy once. In 1976 he sold the Oilers to a group headed by Nelson Skalbania, Mitch Kilmore, Bep Guidolin and Peter Pocklington and he returned to the WHL for one last fling in 1978–79, trying unsuccessfully to breathe new life into the old Oil Kings franchise.

Hunter's next crusade was to bring an NHL expansion franchise to

Bill Hunter established an Edmonton dynasty.

Saskatoon. Fans would come from all over Saskatchewan to fill SaskPlace arena, he argued. In 1983 he came very close to buying the St. Louis franchise and turning it into the Saskatchewan Blues. The St. Louis owners agreed, but the NHL governors turned down the deal. Undeterred, Hunter remains the foremost booster of pro hockey for Saskatoon. "That's the heritage of western Canada," he has said, "when others say it can't be done, we know it can be done."

Hunter is known for his persuasive oratory, and his skills as an after-dinner speaker are much in demand across Canada and the United States. His activities out of hockey have been operating two companies—Batoni-Hunter Enterprises in Saskatoon and Bill Hunter's Enterprises in Edmonton—as well as selling automobiles in Saskatoon and dabbling in the publishing business with *Saskatchewan Report*.

In the early nineties, Hunter moved to San Diego to help operate the San Diego Gulls IHL franchise as vice-president of operations and marketing. Still dreaming of starting up a successful hockey league, Bill Hunter teamed up with other visionaries like Dennis Murphy to begin Roller Hockey International. He and former Oil King Fred Comrie, the brother of BC Lions owner Bill Comrie, own the San Diego Barracudas, who began play with the rest of the league in the summer of 1993.

Darcy Rota

Darcy Rota, a high-scoring left-winger during Edmonton's glory days in the early 1970s, was raised in Prince George, BC, where he began playing hockey at the age of seven. In 1970, he attended a tryout with the Oil Kings, immediately impressing coach Harvey Roy with his talents. In his rookie season he scored 43 goals for an Edmonton team that won the league championship and went all the way to the Memorial Cup tournament in Quebec City. But that was just the beginning for Rota. He returned in 1971–72 to score 51 times in the regular season, then led all Edmonton scorers in the playoffs. Once again the Oil Kings represented Western Canada at the Memorial Cup, and once again they failed to win it. Then, in his third and final season, Rota finished fourth in the scoring race with a league-leading 73 goals and made the first all-star team.

The Chicago Blackhawks made Rota their number one pick in the 1973 draft, 13th overall, hoping he would help to make up for the loss of Bobby Hull who had jumped to the Winnipeg Jets of the World Hockey Association. Rota played almost six seasons in Chicago before he was dealt to the Atlanta Flames in 1979. Then, a year later, he was traded again, this time to the Vancouver Canucks. He played his best hockey for Vancouver, making an important contribution to the Canucks team that made it to the Stanley Cup finals in 1982. His finest NHL season was 1982–83, when he scored 42 goals and 81 points, club records for Vancouver left-wingers. He ended that season on fire, with 15 goals and 15 assists in 14 games in March.

Injuries began to take their toll and Rota retired following the 1983–84 campaign. During 11 seasons in the NHL he scored a very respectable 256 goals and added 239 assists. After working as the Director of Public and Media Relations for the Canucks, Rota joined the NHL front office as a special assistant to the president.

Harold Snepsts

When Harold Snepsts cracked the lineup of the WHL Edmonton Oil Kings back in the 1972–73 season, he was not a very pretty sight. Even Snepsts himself admits that a lengthy and distinguished career in the NHL was the farthest thing from his mind. "I was a very clumsy player when I joined the Oil Kings," recalls the Edmonton native. "I remember guys like Darcy Rota walking around me in practice every day. I was also a goon. I was the guy who protected the skill guys. I mean, after I turned 13 I barely made every team I played on."

But what Snepsts lacked in skill, he more than made up for with determination. He worked at his game, and then he worked at it some more. "He was a very clumsy, awkward player with limited skills," says Rota, the Oil Kings' leading scorer in 1972–73. "He was tough, he had size and he loved to practise but I still thought he was a long-term project. When I look back on my NHL and junior career and all the players I played with and against, I would have to say Harold fell into the category of the guy you thought was never going to make it."

Snepsts was recommended to the Oil Kings by his juvenile coach, Bill Comrie, and practised with the team briefly in 1971. The next season he was invited back to training camp and managed to stick. In his rookie year he had 2 goals, 24 assists and 155 penalty minutes. The next season he scored 8 times, picked up 41 assists and spent 239 minutes in the penalty box. "The league was rough and we had some pretty tough teams in those days," Snepsts admits. "My most memorable Western League fight was with Clark Gillies (Regina Pats). We fought, we stopped, and then we fought again. We both ended up with black eyes."

The 1974 NHL entry draft featured a banner crop of WHL players and Snepsts watched 13 of them go in the first two rounds before the Vancouver Canucks chose him in the third round. "That was a power-house draft," he says. "All I wanted was to get drafted anywhere and get a tryout." He began the 1974–75 season in the minors but was called up to the Canucks part way through, and remained with Vancouver for the next nine years, even representing the team in the all-star game twice. Probably the most popular player of the Canucks' first two decades, Snepsts was traded to Minnesota in 1984, then signed as a free agent with Detroit a year later. He played three injury-plagued seasons for the Red Wings and in 1988, when they made it plain they had no intention of re-signing him, it appeared that his playing career was over. But then the Canucks came calling. Pat Quinn, Vancouver's general manager, was looking for a "character" player to add to his lineup. Snepsts remained with the Canucks for one season and most of a second before being traded to St. Louis, where he finally ended a long career in 1991.

The Blues generously gave Snepsts a chance at coaching, with their International Hockey League farm team in Peoria, and he made good on it, taking the team to third place in the league (105 points). St. Louis brought him up to the NHL as an assistant coach in 1992–93, but after having differences with head coach Bob Berry, he was fired at the end of the season. "I was stunned and just a little bitter," related Snepsts, who was rejuvenated later in the off-season when the Mighty Ducks of Anaheim selected him to be the head coach of their farm team in San Diego.

FLIN FLON

The Flin Flon Bombers

Located in the Shield country of northern Manitoba, Flin Flon emerged in the late 1920s as the centre of a huge zinc-copper mining operation owned by Hudson Bay Mining and Smelting Company. During the 1930s it was hard hit by the Depression and a bitter labour dispute, but gradually Flin Flon developed the wide range of services and activities typical of most towns. And high on the list of must-haves for any community in Western Canada was a junior hockey team.

The Flin Flon Bombers joined the Saskatchewan Junior Hockey League in 1948, coached by Bryan Hextall Sr., newly retired from the New York Rangers where he had played for 11 seasons and four times made the NHL all-star team. With the support of the mining company, the Bombers progressed steadily and in 1957 won the Memorial Cup as the best junior hockey team in the country. Pat Ginnell, who later made his name synonymous with Flin Flon hockey, played on that championship team.

In 1966 the Bombers jumped to the Manitoba Junior Hockey League for one very successful season. Ginnell returned to coach the team to the league championship, losing to Port Arthur in the final of the Abbott Cup.

By this time the WHL, then known as the Western Canada Hockey League, was in operation and Ginnell's Bombers joined up in time for the 1967–68 season. For a bunch of newcomers, they put on quite a show. Bobby Clarke and Reggie Leach combined on a line with Cal Swenson to power Flin Flon to the top of the league standings. Clarke was the league's scoring champion with 117 assists and 168 points in 59 games.

GRADUATES TO THE NHL

Flin Flon Bombers

1968: **Chris Worthy**—Detroit, Oakland, California. **Gerry Hart**—Detroit, NY Islanders, Quebec, St. Louis. **Lew Morrison**—Philadelphia, Atlanta, Washington, Pittsburgh. **Steve Andrascik**—Detroit, NY Rangers.

1969: **Bobby Clarke**—Philadelphia. **Larry Romanchych**—Chicago, Vancouver. **Brian Marchinko**—Toronto, NY Islanders. **Murray Anderson**—Montreal, Washington.

1970: **Reggie Leach**—Boston, California, Philadelphia, Detroit. **John A. Stewart**—Pittsburgh, Atlanta, California, Quebec.

1971: **"Chuck" (Ernest) Arnason**—Montreal, Atlanta, Pittsburgh, Kansas City, Colorado, Cleveland, Minnesota, Washington. **Gene Carr**—St. Louis, NY Rangers, Los Angeles, Pittsburgh, Atlanta. **Ken Baird**—California.

1972: **Garry Howatt**—NY Islanders, Hartford, New Jersey. **Jack McIlhargey**—Philadelphia, Vancouver, Hartford.

1973: **Blaine Stoughton**—Pittsburgh, Toronto, Hartford, NY Rangers. **Ron Andruff**—Montreal, Colorado. **Dennis Polonich**—Detroit.

1974: **Cam Connor**—Montreal, Edmonton, NY Rangers. **Doug Hicks**—Minnesota, Chicago, Edmonton, Washington. **Ray Maluta**—Boston.

1977: **Kim Davis**—Pittsburgh, Toronto.

1978: **Glenn Hicks**—Detroit. **Ray Markham**—NY Rangers. **Jordy Douglas**—Toronto, Hartford, Minnesota, Winnipeg. **Larry Lozinski**—Detroit.

Leach's record-setting 87 goals and 131 points put him in second place. Meanwhile goalie Chris Worthy registered ten shutouts in 54 games, including a consecutive string of just over 265 scoreless minutes. In the playoffs Flin Flon went all the way to the finals where they were blown out by the Estevan Bruins.

The 1968–69 Bombers repeated as first overall in regular-season play, led once again by Bobby Clarke who won his second consecutive scoring race. Clarke's linemate, Reg Leach, was out for much of the season with shoulder problems but Brian Marchinko, Steve Andrascik and Wayne Hawrysh were all among the top ten scorers. Leach was healthy for the playoffs, where he scored 13 goals and the Bombers defeated Edmonton to win the league title.

Because of a dispute between the league and the Canadian Amateur

Hockey Association, the Bombers were not eligible to play in the Memorial Cup tournament in 1969. Instead they hosted the St. Thomas sBarons of the Western Ontario Junior Hockey League in a best-of-seven series to decide the champions of the short-lived Canadian Hockey Association. It was a bloody series, with St. Thomas on the losing end of most of the rough stuff, and after four games the Ontario team withdrew, trailing 3–1. Despite protests against Flin Flon's style of play, the league awarded the championship to the Bombers and expelled St. Thomas.

The following season Bobby Clarke had graduated to the NHL but it didn't seem to matter to the Bombers, as they finished first overall in regular season standings for the third straight year. Reg Leach took over as the team's, and the league's, leading scorer and Flin Flon repeated as league champions, besting Edmonton in the final series for the second year in a row. Unfortunately the league was still excluded from Memorial Cup play, and because of the controversy surrounding the previous year's series with St. Thomas there was no CHA championship, so the Bombers did not get an opporunity to test themselves against the best in the East.

During the 1970–71 season it was Chuck Arnason's turn to win the scoring title, marking the fourth time a Bomber had finished at the head of the pack. Arnason won both the regular season and the playoff scoring crowns that winter as Flin Flon advanced to the league final for the fourth straight year. The opposition was Edmonton yet again, and this time the Oil Kings, behind the scoring of Dan Spring and Dave Kryskow, finally managed to defeat Flin Flon and win a championship.

By 1971 the Bombers had been in the league for four years. During that time they had advanced to the final each season and had won the championship twice. Perhaps it was inevitable that the team would falter. In 1971–72 the franchise finished below .500 for the first time and fell victim to the Regina Pats in the first round of the playoffs. The team rallied in the next season to finish tied for second place overall, but once again bowed out early in the playoffs. The 1973–74 season was almost a carbon copy of the previous one, except that halfway through the winter Pat Ginnell left the team to move to Victoria. Every club has a cycle and during the mid-1970s Flin Flon was headed down, finishing out of the playoffs for the next three consecutive years.

The 1977–78 season marked the return of playoff hockey to Flin Flon; ironically, it also marked the end of the franchise. The Bombers finished regular-season play in second place in their division and made it all the way to a controversial round-robin semifinals in the playoffs. But at the conclusion of the season the league told the owners the franchise would have to move. Flin Flon, 870 kilometres north of Winnipeg, was simply too far off the beaten track for most of the other teams in the league. Initially the franchise was headed for Winnipeg but when the new ownership backed out the Bombers moved instead to Edmonton. The previous Oil Kings franchise had folded in 1976 and its owner, Bill Hunter, combined with restaurateur Vic Mah to bring in the Flin Flon team and give it the old Oil Kings name. The team only lasted one season in the Alberta capital. In 1979, when the WHA's Edmonton Oilers joined the National Hockey League, the junior franchise moved south to Great Falls, Montana, then later to Spokane before folding in 1982.

Meanwhile, junior hockey is still alive and well in Flin Flon, which has an successful entry in the Saskatchewan Junior Hockey League.

Bobby Clarke

Without question, the most talented hockey player born and raised in Flin Flon was the incomparable Philadelphia Flyers centre Bobby Clarke. Born in 1949, Clarke began his junior career with Flin Flon in 1966 when the Bombers were part of the Manitoba Junior Hockey League, along with teams from Brandon, Winnipeg, Selkirk and St. James. He scored 71 goals that season and won the league scoring crown for a team that went all the way to the Western Canadian Abbott Cup final.

Next season the Bombers entered the fledgling Western Canada Junior Hockey League, but it made no difference to Clarke. He won the scoring championship again, finishing 37 points ahead of his linemate, Reg Leach. It was the same story in 1968–69, Clarke's final season of junior play, when he took top scoring honours for the third year in a row, leading the Bombers to a league championship. The league has since renamed the scoring trophy the Bob Clarke Trophy. In 1968–69 Clarke also captured the Most Valuable Player award.

After such an outstanding junior career Clarke would have gone much higher in the draft if not for the fact he had diabetes. This condition scared off many teams which felt that a diabetic would not be able to endure the rigours of NHL play. But Gerry Melnyk, Philadelphia's head scout, urged the Flyers to take a chance on Clarke and the team drafted him in the second round in 1969. The Flyers never had any reason to be disappointed. Clarke developed into one of the superstars of the game. The highlight of his 15 seasons in Philadelphia came as a member of the famous "LCB" line, along with his old Flin Flon teammate Reg Leach and Bill Barber. Four times he was named to the NHL all-star team, three times he won the Hart Memorial Trophy as the Most Valuable Player in the league, and in 1983 he added the Frank Selke Trophy for best defensive forward. Clarke was the captain of the Flyers team which won back-to-back Stanley Cup championships 1974–75. He finished as the team's all-time points and assists leader.

In May, 1984, Clarke announced that he was retiring from active play to become the new general manager of the Flyers. He remained in Philadelphia for six seasons, then moved to the GM's chair in Minnesota.

Future superstar Bobby Clarke in Flin Flon Bombers colours.

In 1992 he returned to the Philadelphia organization as a senior vice-president but on March 1, 1993, he left again to become the first general manager of the new Florida Panthers NHL franchise. As the captain of the first expansion team to win the Stanley Cup, Bobby Clarke's name is in the record books a number of times, but the thing he may be most remembered for is overcoming a serious ailment to become one of the most tenacious players the game has seen.

Reggie Leach

Reggie Leach, born April 23, 1950, was a native of Riverton, Manitoba and was known during his junior hockey days as the "Riverton Rifle" because he was such a dangerous goal scorer. Leach's career with Flin Flon stretched over four seasons, from 1966 when the team was still in the Manitoba Junior Hockey League, to 1969–70 when the Bombers won the WHL championship for the second consecutive year. During most of this time, Leach teamed with Bobby Clarke to form one of the most feared goal-scoring duos the WHL has ever seen. In 1967–68 Leach finished second in the scoring race to Clarke and then, after a season plagued by injury, he bounced back to win the crown in 1969–70.

After being drafted third overall in the 1970 amateur draft by the Boston Bruins, Leach spent 41 games in the Central Hockey League with the Oklahoma City Blazers before being called up to the Bruins to finish out the season. During a lacklustre 1971–72 campaign the Bruins traded him to the California Golden Seals, where he remained for two mediocre years. However, his career did not take off until 1974 when good fortune, and a trade with Philadelphia, reunited him with his old Flin Flon linemate Bobby Clarke. The rest is hockey history. Leach flourished in Philadelphia, scoring 45 goals in 1974–75, the year the Flyers repeated as Stanley Cup champions, then notching 61 goals, still a team high, the following season. In the 1976 playoffs, Leach was sensational. Thanks in large part to his 19 goals and 5 assists, the Flyers returned to the finals. In a game against Boston he tied a playoff record with 5 goals. In the end, Philadelphia lost to Montreal, but Leach won the Conn Smythe Trophy as Most Valuable Player in the playoffs.

Leach remained with the Flyers until the end of the 1981–82 season when he was signed as a free agent by the Detroit Red Wings. After a season in Detroit, and another season in the minor leagues, he retired and started a lawn-care business near Philadelphia. In the summer the "Riverton Rifle" always comes home to his native Manitoba.

Chuck Arnason

Born in Winnipeg in 1951, Ernest "Chuck" Arnason developed his hockey skills as a young teenager in Ashern, playing in the central Manitoba senior leagues with men ten years older than he was. In 1967, on the advice of Danny Summers, a Detroit Red Wings scout, he moved to Selkirk to play in the Manitoba Junior Hockey League. During his two years with the Selkirk Steelers, Arnason's prolific goal-scoring caught the attention of Pat Ginnell, who brought him north to Flin Flon for the 1969–70 season.

In his rookie campaign with the Bombers, Arnason scored 34 goals and added 27 assists. Teammate Reg Leach led the scoring parade in the WHL that season, but come the playoffs even Leach had to take a backseat to Arnason, who collected 14 goals and 18 assists in 17 games to lead the Bombers to the championship. Arnason continued his scoring heroics the following season, this time setting a WCHL record for most goals in a season with 79 (now held by Ray Ferraro with 108), winning both the regular season (163 points) and playoff (37 points) scoring crowns. It was the fourth year in a row that a Flin Flon player had led all scorers in the league.

The Montreal Canadiens chose Arnason seventh overall in the 1971 amateur draft, but in a professional career which spanned eight seasons and eight NHL teams he did not live up to the promise of his junior years in Flin Flon. In his best season, 1974–75 with the Pittsburgh Penguins, he collected 26 goals and 58 points and he left the NHL with only 199 points in 401 games. Arnason played his final year of pro hockey, 1980–81, in Cologne, Germany, then retired to operate a driving range in Winnipeg.

Blaine Stoughton

Blaine Stoughton, a native of Gilbert Plains, Manitoba, skated onto the junior hockey scene in 1968–69 when, as a 15-year-old, he suited up with the Dauphin Kings of the Manitoba Junior Hockey League. The following year, Stoughton reached the major junior level with the Flin Flon Bombers, where he stayed for four years. His WHL career started slowly on a Bombers team that was a consistent league champion. During Stoughton's second season, as he seemed to be developing into a formidable scorer, a nasty incident resulted in his suspension. On December 5, 1970, during a game with Medicine Hat, Stoughton accidentally speared Tigers defenceman Don Dirk in the eye. Dirk was not seriously injured but Stoughton took a match penalty, his second of the season, and league commissioner Ron Butlin suspended him for 29 games.

Stoughton rebounded in 1971–72 to score a league-leading 60

goals and finish third in the scoring race behind behind Medicine Hat forwards Tom Lysiak and Stan Weir. Then, in his draft year of 1972—73, he notched 58 goals, good enough for fifth place in individual scoring. Stoughton was drafted by the Pittsburgh Penguins and spent a season getting acclimated to professional hockey with the Hershey Bears of the American Hockey League. Despite the fact that the Bears won the AHL championship, Stoughton was dissatisfied and asked to be traded. In September, 1974, in exchange for Rick Kehoe, he

Blaine Stoughton was a Maple Leaf from 1974 to 1976.

moved to the Toronto Maple Leafs but, after two indifferent seasons, he jumped to the rival World Hockey Association, signing with the Cincinnati Stingers. In 1976–77 Stoughton enjoyed his first standout season as a pro, scoring 52 goals for Cincinnati. After being traded to the Indianapolis Racers, where he played briefly with Wayne Gretzky, he wound down his WHA career with the New England Whalers, remaining with them when they moved into the NHL in 1979 as the Hartford Whalers.

In 1979–80, the Whalers' first NHL season, he recorded his best scoring totals, tying for the league lead in goals with 56 and obtaining 100 points. In his only other season of note, Stoughton scored 52 goals and 91 points for the 1981–82 Whalers. After a stint with the New York Rangers in 1985, he retired and acquired a sports bar in Boca Raton, Florida. In 1993 he rejoined the Whalers as assistant coach with their American Hockey League farm team, the Springfield Indians.

KAMLOOPS

The Kamloops Chiefs, Junior Oilers & Blazers

Heading into the 1991–92 season, Kamloops enjoyed the dubious distinction of being the winningest franchise in the WHL never to have won a Memorial Cup. After coming into the league in 1981, the Blazers won the West Division title seven times, and the league crown three times, but always the national championship eluded them. Until 1992, that is, when Kamloops, playing in its fourth Memorial Cup tournament, finally brought home the trophy, defeating the Sault Ste. Marie Greyhounds 5–4 in a thrilling finale.

The Blazers team that dominated the WHL through the 1980s was not the first major junior franchise to call Kamloops home. In 1973 the short-lived Vancouver Nats were in disarray, having managed to win just ten games during the previous season. A group of Kamloops business people, headed by Ephraim Steinke, Ernie Rempel and Andy Berna, bought the Nats and moved the team to the interior city, renaming it the Chiefs. The franchise remained in Kamloops for four seasons, enjoying respectable on-ice success, before majority owner Steinke, dissatisfied with the local arena, decided to move the team to Seattle in 1977.

That left the field open for another junior franchise, and one appeared in 1981 in the form of the New Westminster Bruins. Once the proud flagship of the WHL West Division, the Bruins had fallen on hard times. With the backing of the NHL Edmonton Oilers, the franchise relocated to Kamloops, and the Junior Oilers were born. It was a unique situation—Kamloops was the only WHL team to enjoy direct support

GRADUATES TO THE NHL

Kamloops Chiefs

1975: **Brad Gassoff**—Vancouver. **Terry McDonald**—Kansas City.

1976: **Barry Melrose**—Montreal, Winnipeg, Toronto, Detroit. **Rob Flockhart**—Vancouver, Minnesota.

1977: **Reg Kerr**—Cleveland, Chicago, Edmonton. **Dan Clark**—Philadelphia, NY Rangers. **Jamie Gallimore**—Minnesota. **Tim Watters**—Winnipeg (drafted from Michigan Tech in 1979), Los Angeles.

Kamloops Junior Oilers

1982: **Jan Ludvig**—New Jersey, Buffalo. **Dean Evason**—Washington, Hartford, San Jose, Dallas.

1983: **Richard Hajdu**—Buffalo. **Gord Mark**—New Jersey. **Mark Ferner**—Buffalo, Washington. **Jim Camazzola**—Chicago (drafted in 1982 from Penticton of the BC Junior Hockey League).

1984: **Doug Bodger**—Pittsburgh, Buffalo. **Daryl Reaugh**—Edmonton, Hartford.

1985: **Ryan Stewart**—Winnipeg. **Rudy Poeschek**—NY Rangers, Winnipeg.

1986: **Ron Shudra**—Edmonton. **Rob Brown**—Pittsburgh, Hartford, Chicago. **Greg Hawgood**—Boston, Edmonton, Philadelphia. **Mark Kachowski**—Pittsburgh.

1987: **Robin Bawa**—Washington, Vancouver, San Jose. **Dave Marcinyshyn**—New Jersey, Quebec, NY Rangers.

1988: **Mark Recchi**—Pittsburgh. **Glen Mulvenna**—Pittsburgh.

1989: **Dave Chyzowski**—NY Islanders. **Pat MacLeod**—Minnesota, San Jose. **Mike Needham**—Pittsburgh. **Geoff Smith**—Edmonton.

1990: **Darryl Sydor**—Los Angeles. **Paul Kruse**—Calgary.

1991: **Scott Niedermayer**—New Jersey. **Corey Hirsch**—NY Rangers.

from an NHL club—and it did not last long. In 1984 the Oilers ended their involvement with the franchise and the team, renamed the Blazers, became community-owned.

Kamloops inherited a massive rebuilding job with the Bruins franchise, as evidenced by its 18–53–1 record in 1981–82. But it did not take long to turn the franchise around, thanks largely to coach Bill LaForge, who used his Edmonton-area contacts to bring a wealth of good, young talent to the team, and to the signing of an unheralded, 16-year-old named Dean Evason. Obtained from the defunct Spokane Flyers midway through 1981–82, Evason turned out to be a franchise player. In 1982–83 he scored 71 goals to finish second in the scoring race and won the WHL Player-of-the-Year award. Evason had considerable help with the scoring chores in 1983–84 as LaForge coached Kamloops to its first Memorial Cup appearance. Fans were treated to the play of two phenomenal 15-year-old defencemen—Rob Brown and Greg Hawgood—called up from the St. Albert Saints of the Alberta Junior Hockey League. Brown in particular, his modishly long blond hair trailing behind him, was a gifted offensive defenceman who patterned himself after his boyhood idol, Bobby Orr. He even wore the same number, 4, on his jersey. In just 50 games he scored 16 goals and 42 assists as one of the two youngest regulars in the league. Hawgood added 10 goals and 23 assists. While Hawgood remained a free-wheeling defenceman with a cannonading slapshot, Brown made his mark when he converted to the centre-ice position. In 1985–86, with Kamloops once again winning the league championship, Brown led all scorers with 173 points and was named West Division MVP. Then, in 1986–87, he established single-season assists and points scoring records which still stand, 76 goals and 136 assists for 212 points.

By this time, Bill LaForge had left Kamloops for an NHL coaching stint with the Vancouver Canucks and the "Big Man," Ken Hitchcock, was at the helm. Hitch, as he was commonly called, was assisted by general manager Bob Brown, the father of team superstar, Rob Brown. Two-time winner of the Coach-of-the-Year award, Hitchcock was an affable giant who laughingly shed the taunts of those who made light of his appearance. He almost always had the last laugh. In six years with the Blazers (1984–1990), he took the team to two more WHL titles and Memorial Cup appearances, and posted a career record in league play of 291–125–15, the best winning percentage of any WHL coach with three or more years service in the league.

Boasting high-powered offensive play, and always coached with a philosophy of aggressive forechecking and a grinding physical game, Kamloops has averaged 45 wins a season over the past decade and has never descended below the .500 mark. A wealth of hockey talent has passed through the city on the way to the NHL. Ryan Walter, Barry Melrose and Reg Kerr all played for the Kamloops Chiefs during the 1970s. More recently, the Blazers have produced many first-round draft picks and NHLers, among them Dean Evason, Robin Bawa, Rob Brown, Mark Recchi, Doug Bodger, Craig Berube, Dave Chyzowski, Scott Niedermayer, Darryl Sydor and David Wilkie. The team has retired the numbers of four star graduates: Evason, Brown, Hawgood and Greg Evtushevski, a high scorer with the Blazers 1984–86.

The 1992 Memorial Cup win in Seattle broke what was beginning to look like a jinx for the Blazers franchise. With the losses of top players

Scott Niedermayer, Darryl Sydor, Corey Hirsch, Zac Boyer and head coach Tom Renney, the Blazers weren't expected to have a successful 1992–93 season, but under new head coach Don Hay, the team finished with 86 points and made it to the West Division finals in the playoffs. With a long tradition of excellence, and a new 5000-seat arena, Kamloops seemed well positioned to continue its winning ways.

Bob Brown

One of the most successful general managers of the Western Hockey League in the mid-1980s has been Bob Brown of the Kamloops Blazers. A native of Kingston, Ontario, Brown was an executive with a financial services company in Toronto for 17 years before taking his management skills into the hockey arena. Not that he was a stranger to the game; Brown played professionally in the International and the Eastern Professional leagues, and at the Senior A level with the Kingston Aces.

Brown, the father of Blazers scoring sensation Rob Brown, has watched Kamloops win five West Division titles, three league championships and one Memorial Cup in the years he has occupied the front office. The Blazers' great achievement cannot be attributed to tradition or luck. The team has always been loaded with excellent coaches and talented players, so the team's consistent success can be accredited to the great

Bob Brown----Kamloops GM.

decision-making and personnel recruitment of Bob Brown. Following the 1990–91 season, when coach Tom Renney was chosen WHL Coach of the Year, Brown won the Lloyd Saunders Trophy as the league's top executive. When the position of director of hockey operations for the Vancouver Canucks became open in 1992, Brown was originally keen on getting the job. He was one of the finalists, but he didn't attain the appointment. "After I was out of the running, I wondered why I was in it in the first place," Brown said. "I realized I was happy with what I was doing."

Doug Bodger

Doug Bodger played all of his minor hockey in and around Chemainus, BC, where he was born in 1966. In 1982 he graduated from the midget league to Kamloops, where he played for two seasons with the Junior Oilers. A good-sized defenceman at 6'2" and 195 pounds, Bodger had a sensational rookie season, scoring 26 times, adding 66 assists, and earning a place on the WHL all-star team.

In his second season, 1983–84, Bodger played on defence along with Rob Brown, and the duo was a major reason, along with the scoring heroics of Dean Evason, that the Junior Oilers topped the league and went on to the Memorial Cup tournament that spring. Bodger produced 98 points during the year and was back on the all-star team. Pittsburgh drafted him ninth overall and, even though he still had two years of junior eligibility remaining, Bodger made the jump to the NHL for the 1984–85 season. He has been a solid NHL defenceman ever since, consistently scoring in the 45–55 points range. After four seasons with the Penguins he was traded to Buffalo, where he soon established himself as the team's top defenceman.

Rob Brown

Born in Ontario in 1968, Rob Brown, the Kamloops Blazers all-time points leader, moved with his family to Alberta and played his bantam and minor junior hockey in the Edmonton suburb of St. Albert. It was while he was starring on defence for the St. Albert Saints of the Alberta Junior Hockey League that he attracted the attention of WHL scouts and he began his career with Kamloops in 1983–84. During that first major junior season, Brown blossomed as a rushing defenceman and the next year the team began experimenting with him at the centre-ice position. By 1985–86 he had completed the adjustment to the forward line, winning his first scoring title and making the West Division first all-star team. He was also named the division's Most Valuable Player. Far from resting on his laurels, Brown returned the next season to repeat as scoring champion with 212 points, still a WHL single-season record, including 136 assists, another record. His point total was 66 ahead of the second-leading scorer, Craig Endean, the largest winning margin in the history of the league. Once again he was an MVP and an all-star, and he was named the outstanding major junior hockey player in Canada.

The Pittsburgh Penguins drafted Brown and, in his second NHL season, 1988–89, he blossomed into a leading scorer, notching 49 goals and 115 point in only 68 games. However, his point production fell off over the next two seasons and, when he had scored just 6 goals in 25

Rob Brown, the Blazers' all-time points leader.

games during the 1990–91 campaign, the Penguins traded him to Hartford. Early in 1992 he was on the move again, this time to Chicago where he reached the low-point of his career. Brown only played 15 games for the Hawks during the 1992–93 campaign, spending the rest of the season with the Indianapolis Ice of the International Hockey League, where he scored 33 points in 19 games. Brown's play seemed to have hit rock-bottom, but the Dallas Stars, signed him to a multi-year contract in 1993, hoping that he could regain his scoring touch of the past.

Greg Hawgood

One of the many discoveries the Kamloops franchise has made in the Edmonton area over the years, defenceman Greg Hawgood belonged to that vanishing breed of junior-age players who managed to spend five years in the WHL. He joined the league as a 15-year-old in 1983, when the team was still called the Junior Oilers, and helped Kamloops capture five consecutive divisional pennants. These were teams that featured prolific scorers like Dean Evason, Mark Recchi, Rob Brown, Ken Morrison and Greg Evtushevski, but, back on the blue line, Hawgood turned in season after season of outstanding play. Three years in a row he made the all-star team, and in 1987–88 he was named top defenceman in the WHL. He also contributed his share of goals, finishing among the league's top-ten scorers in his final two seasons and establishing himself as one of the finest offensive defencemen in the history of the league.

Drafted by Boston, Hawgood played regularly for the Bruins for two seasons. In his rookie year, he scored 40 points in 56 games and threatened Ray Bourque's goal-scoring record for a Bruin rookie defenceman. The 1990–91 campaign was a troubled one, however. He began the year playing in Italy, then returned to the Bruins, who quickly dispatched him to the Maine Mariners of the American Hockey League. Then, at the end of October, he was traded to the Edmonton Oilers and spent the rest of the season with the AHL's Cape Breton Oilers. Hawgood was back in Cape Breton for the 1991–92 season, though he was called up by Edmonton late in the year. Even though he didn't play the entire season in Cape Breton, he earned the Eddie Shore Plaque for being the league's most outstanding defenceman.

Hawgood seemed to get back on track in 1992–93, when he was traded to the Philadelphia Flyers after playing 29 games for the Oilers. In 69 NHL games that season, he picked up a career-high 46 points. Unlike his previous NHL teams, the Flyers seemed to recognize Greg Hawgood's great talent.

Blazers captain Greg Hawgood was one of the finest offensive defencemen in league history.

Mark Recchi

Mark Recchi was a hometown boy who almost got away. Born in Kamloops in 1968, he played his minor hockey in the city but when it came time to graduate to the junior level, for some reason the WHL Blazers overlooked him. In 1984 young Recchi decided to join the New Westminster Bruins franchise and he headed down to the coast, where he played for one season with the Bruins' Tier II affiliate, the Langley Eagles. In

1985–86 he joined the senior club and, under the tutelage of coach "Punch" McLean, Recchi scored 21 goals and finished the season with 61 points, pretty respectable numbers for a rookie. So respectable, in fact, that Kamloops finally took notice and traded for the hometown hero.

A broken ankle limited Recchi's production during his first season back in Kamloops, but in 1987–88 he exploded for 61 goals and a league-leading 93 assists in 62 games. This was just 6 points behind Joe Sakic and Theoren Fleury, who tied for the scoring crown that season. In the playoffs, the Blazers went all the way to the finals, which they lost

Kamloops Blazer Mark Recchi breaks away from the tight check of a member of the Spokane Chiefs early in the 1987–88 season.

to the eventual Memorial Cup winners, the Medicine Hat Tigers. Recchi tied the Tigers' Rob Dimaio for the playoff scoring title with 31 points in 17 games.

Despite his success at the junior level, Recchi was drafted 67th overall in 1988, the Pittsburgh Penguins' fourth pick, because of his size, 5'10". "I don't think anybody looked at Recchi to be a scorer in the NHL," said the Blazers general manager, Bob Brown. At first he had trouble breaking in, spending most of 1988–89 at Muskegon of the International Hockey League. But in 1989–90 Recchi emerged from the minor leagues to score 30 goals for the Penguins. The next season, 1990–91, he led the Penguin scoring parade with 40 goals and 113 points, fourth in the entire league.

Pittsburgh won the Stanley Cup that year and Recchi figured to be part of the team for a few years to come, but on February 19, 1992, the Penguins traded him to Philadelphia in a complicated, multi-player deal involving Rick Tocchet going to Pittsburgh. He finished the season with 43 goals and in 1992–93, his first complete year with the Flyers, once again finished among the league's top ten scorers. Recchi racked up a career-high 53 goals and 123 points, but playing on one of the best young lines in the league with Eric Lindros, it seemed likely that he would break his high in the future. Overlooked twice in his hockey-playing days, Mark Recchi silenced any doubts that he belonged in the NHL.

Scott Niedermayer

Scott Niedermayer, a solid defenceman drafted by the New Jersey Devils, began his hockey career in his hometown of Cranbrook, BC. He reached the WHL as a 16-year-old in 1989 and played three standout seasons with the Kamloops Blazers, twice helping them reach the Memorial Cup tournament. During his sophomore season, 1990–91, Niedermayer made the West Division first all-star team and was chosen the top student athlete in major junior hockey. A straight-A scholar in high school, Niedermayer wants to become a doctor once his playing career is over. New Jersey picked him third overall in the spring draft, but after playing four games with the Devils he returned to Kamloops early in the 1991–92 campaign. Hampered by injuries, he only played in 35 regular-season games, but come playoff time his gifted scoring touch returned as he notched 9 goals and 14 assists in 17 games.

Kamloops reached the Memorial Cup tournament for the second time in three years in 1992, and in the final game it was defenceman Niedermayer who beautifully set up Zac Boyer's game-winning goal with only 15 seconds left in regulation time to defeat Sault Ste. Marie and finally bring the national championship to Kamloops. Niedermayer was selected the tournament's Most Valuable Player, and was named to the

*Cranbrook native Scott Niedermayer was an all-star Blazer defenceman
and top student athlete in junior hockey.*

all-star team along with fellow Blazers Corey Hirsch in goal and Mike Mathers on left wing. In his rookie season with the Devils, Niedermayer was part of the team's first-string defensive tandem with Scott Stevens. He scored 11 goals and 40 points and drew comparisons to a young Ray Bourque or a more defensive-minded Paul Coffey.

LETHBRIDGE

The Lethbridge Broncos & Hurricanes

Major junior hockey came to Lethbridge, Alberta, in the summer of 1974. Bill Burton, owner of the Swift Current Broncos franchise in the WHL, was considering a move to a bigger community with a larger arena. Lethbridge hockey fans were hungry for a WHL team, and the city boasted a spanking new 5100-seat facility, the Sportsplex, which was being built for the 1975 Canada Winter Games. Burton and his partners decided to make the leap to the southern Alberta city and on October 6, 1974, in front of an enthusiastic crowd, the Lethbridge Broncos made their home-ice debut, a 5–1 victory over the Regina Pats.

Initially, Burton was the team's general manager, while Earl Ingarfield, former coach of the New York Islanders and part-owner of the Bronco franchise, was head coach. During the year Burton sold his majority share to Dennis Kjeldgaard. The on-ice leader of the Broncos that first year was Bryan Trottier, soon to be a star in the NHL with the Islanders. New York sent him back to the WHL for one more year of seasoning. He finished second in the scoring race and was named the Most Valuable Player in the league. Ron Delorme joined Trottier from Swift Current and contributed with 87 points and tough play. One of Trottier's teammates with Lethbridge was Brian Sutter, a young, hard-nosed forward who could not skate very well but made up for it with the tenacity of a bulldog. Sutter was the first of six brothers who played starring roles for the Broncos.

After its successful inaugural season, Lethbridge slumped badly,

GRADUATES TO THE NHL

Lethbridge Broncos

1975: **Ron Delorme**—Kansas City, Colorado, Vancouver. **Alex Tidey**—Buffalo, Edmonton.

1976: **Brian Sutter**—St. Louis. **Darcy Regier**—California, Cleveland, NY Islanders.

1977: **Rocky Saganiuk**—Toronto, Pittsburgh. **Rollie Boutin**—Washington.

1978: **Steve Tambellini**—NY Islanders, Colorado, New Jersey, Calgary, Vancouver. **Darryl Sutter**—Chicago.

1979: **Duane Sutter**—NY Islanders, Chicago. **Lindy Ruff**—Buffalo, NY Rangers. **Doug Morrison**—Boston. **Gord Williams**—Philadelphia. **Earl Ingarfield Jr.**—Atlanta, Calgary, Detroit.

1980: **Mike Moller**—Buffalo, Edmonton. **Troy Murray**—Chicago, Winnipeg. **Brent Sutter**—NY Islanders, Chicago.

1981: **Randy Moller**—Quebec, NY Rangers, Buffalo. **Marc Magnan**—Toronto. **Dave Barr**—Boston, NY Rangers, St. Louis, Hartford, Detroit, New Jersey.

1982: **Ron Sutter**—Philadelphia, St. Louis. **Rich Sutter**—Pittsburgh, Philadelphia, Vancouver, St. Louis. **Vern Smith**—NY Islanders. **Ken Wregget**—Toronto, Philadelphia, Pittsburgh. **Troy Loney**—Pittsburgh, Anaheim.

1983: **Gerald Diduck**—NY Islanders, Montreal, Vancouver.

1984: **Darin Sceviour**—Chicago.

1985: **Mike Berger**—Minnesota. **Trent Kaese**—Buffalo. **Steve Nemeth**—NY Rangers.

1986: **Warren Babe**—Minnesota.

Lethbridge Hurricanes

1989: **Wes Walz**—Boston, Philadelphia.

1990: **Mark Greig**—Hartford. **Jason Ruff**—St.Louis, Tampa Bay. **Doug Barrault**—Minnesota, Florida.

1991: **Brandy Semchuk**—Los Angeles (drafted in 1990 from Canadian National Team).

finishing with under 20 wins for the next three years. But over the years the team featured many fine players who went on to have noteworthy careers in the NHL. The Sutters were not the only brother act. There was also the Mollers—Randy, a first-round draft pick of the Quebec Nordiques, and Mike—and the Ruff boys—Lindy, who played for the Buffalo Sabres for ten seasons, Marty, a first-round pick of the St. Louis Blues, and eldest brother Randy. Smooth-skating Steve Tambellini, Rookie of the Year in 1975–76, notched 75 goals, finished third in the scoring race in 1977–78 and twice was named most sportsmanlike player. Doug Morrison and Gord Williams were two high-scoring forwards, while Bob Rouse won WHL Defenceman-of-the-Year honours in 1983–84. And all Lethbridge fans recall the blazing speed and booming slapshot of diminutive Rocky Saganiuk.

It was the 1981–82 season before Lethbridge established itself as a power in the league. That year, under the coaching of John Chapman, the Broncos featured not just one Sutter but three. Brent starred down the middle; he was the key figure on the ice and in the dressing room. But whenever he grew tired of playing club leader, brothers Rich and Ron emerged to carry the gauntlet. Not to forget Mike Moller, who began the season by scoring 67 points in the first 17 games. Ivan Krook, Marty Ruff, Randy Moller, Troy Loney, Gerald Diduck and goalie Ken Wregget rounded out a roster that had seven future NHLers. Bronco fans began to talk about a championship. Which is just about when Buffalo called up Mike Moller to the NHL and the Islanders called up Brent Sutter. The Broncos managed to overcome these losses to finish atop the standings with their first-ever 100-point season. But in the playoffs, even with Moller back to lead the team in scoring, they fell to Regina in the deciding game of the East Division Finals.

The next season began with Lethbridge heavy favourites to win it all. They got off to a terrible start and by Christmas there was some question whether the Broncos would even make the playoffs. Bob Rouse was brought in from Nanaimo to stabilize the defence and suddenly the team jelled. Another defenceman was rookie Mark Tinordi, who scored only four points that season but went on to become a star in the NHL. After Christmas they did not lose a home game and despite a fifth-place finish in their division they romped through the playoffs, defeating Portland in the final series 4–1. Ron Sutter led all scorers in the playoffs, ably supported by brother Rich, Ivan Krook and Rick Gal. The one sour note was the loss of goaltender Ken Wregget, considered by many to be the top netminder in the country that year. He twisted his ankle during one of the final games and was lost to the Broncos for the Memorial Cup. With the goaltending situation unsettled, Lethbridge made a disappointing show in the round-robin tournament, winning only one game before being eliminated.

That 1982–83 season proved to be the highwater mark for the franchise. Something seemed to go out of the team after the thrill of the Memorial Cup appearance. They began to finish well down in the standings and for three straight seasons did not advance beyond the first playoff round. Attendance at the games declined, leaving owner Dennis Kjeldgaard little choice. In 1986 he sold the franchise back to Swift Current; the Lethbridge Broncos were defunct.

As it turned out, Lethbridge only endured one winter without a WHL team, thanks to a group of local enthusiasts who were determined to resuscitate major junior hockey in the city. The difference was that the second time around the team was community owned, not privately owned. Shares were sold for $100 each and in 1987 the group purchased the Calgary Wranglers and moved them south to Lethbridge. A contest came up with the name Hurricanes for the new franchise, a reference to the famous Chinook winds of southern Alberta. The first season's talent was pretty thin and the Hurricanes failed to blow up much of a storm, but by 1989–90 they were the class of their division. Four Hurricanes—Corey Lyons, Wes Walz, Bryan Bosch and Mark Greig—were among the league's top scorers and the team finished first with a record of 51–17–4. In the playoffs they were twice extended to seven games but managed to win their division, then lost to Kamloops in the league final.

The Hurricanes graduated most of their top scorers in 1990 and no one expected them to repeat the magic of the previous season. But coach Bob Loucks went to work, adding scoring punch with players like Czechoslovakian-born Radek Sip, former Canadian National team member Brandy Semchuk, and rookies Rob Hartnell and Jamie Pushor. At the same time, the fine young defence that included Pushor, Shane Peacock and Darcy Werenka matured quickly with the addition of veteran Terry Hollinger. Jason Ruff finished fifth in league scoring, Brad Rubachuk was close behind him, Kevin St. Jacques earned over 100

Classy 5100-seat Lethbridge Sportsplex, home of the Broncos, was built for the 1975 Canada Winter Games.

points and strong goaltending was provided in the form of Jamie McLennan. Putting it all together, the Hurricanes claimed their second straight division title, defeating Medicine Hat in a hard-fought seven-game series. Once again, however, the league crown was denied them, this time by Spokane.

The next season, the team had an excellent roster with the league's leading scorer St. Jacques and stars Sip, Hartnell, Hollinger, Pushor, Peacock, Werenka, Brad Zavisha and Brad Zimmer. Unfortunately for Lethbridge, the team only finished fourth in the East and was eliminated in the first round of the playoffs. After another disappointing season in 1992–93, Bob Loucks was fired and replaced by Rob Daum.

In their first three seasons, the Hurricanes went from the bottom to the top. Attendance is up, and the franchise is sending its fair share of young players to the NHL. It looks like junior hockey is back in Lethbridge to stay.

The Sutters

There have been several prominent families in hockey history—the Richard brothers, Dennis, Bobby and Brett Hull, the Hextalls, the Howes—but the Sutters from Viking, Alberta, have a fair claim to being considered the First Family of Hockey. Never before, and likely never again, will one family produce six NHL-calibre players. The eldest of the boys, Brian, turned professional in 1976, while the twins, Rich and Ron, were still playing with St. Louis during the 1992–93 season. Not forgetting that Brian and Darryl became coaches with Boston and Chicago respectively, that is a 17-year association the family has had with the NHL, and still counting.

Along the way, all the brothers played their major junior hockey in Lethbridge with the Broncos. Brian was with the franchise as it struggled through the early years. St. Louis drafted him twentieth overall in 1976 and he spent his entire 12-year NHL playing career with the Blues before having his number retired and becoming their head coach. After his surprise firing in 1992, he was quickly hired to the same position with the Boston Bruins. Darryl graduated from Lethbridge in 1978 and after a season in the American Hockey League jumped to the Chicago Blackhawks where he played for eight seasons, five of them as the team captain. After serving as the head coach of Chicago's International Hockey League farm team and an assistant with the big club, he replaced Mike Keenan as the Blackhawks' head coach in 1992.

Duane Sutter played one full season in Lethbridge, 1978–79, scoring 50 goals and finishing fourth in the WHL scoring race, making him the most prolific goal scorer of all the brothers at the junior level. The New York Islanders made him their number one draft pick in 1979 and he won four Stanley Cup rings as part of the Islanders' dynasty of the early 1980s. Duane finished his playing career with Chicago, spent a couple of years as a scout for the Hawks and then returned to the WHL to coach the Medicine Hat Tigers.

Brent Sutter was the fourth in the long line of Sutter brothers who passed through Lethbridge on their way to the National Hockey League. Brent played Tier II junior hockey with the Red Deer Rustlers under coach John Chapman. In 1980 he led a Rustlers team which included his

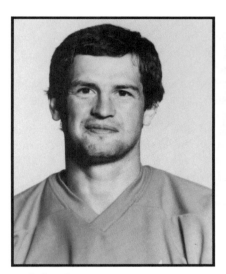

Brian Sutter

Darryl Sutter

Duane Sutter

Rich Sutter

younger twin brothers Rich and Ron to the Centennial Cup national championship. He scored 70 goals in just 59 games that season, and in the championship game against North York he notched the tying and winning goals to bring the Cup to Red Deer. So impressive was Sutter's performance all season that the New York Islanders selected him 17th overall in the 1980 draft, the first player ever drafted in the first round from the Tier II level.

For the 1980–81 season Sutter moved up to the Lethbridge Broncos, along with his Red Deer coach, John Chapman. He finished with 108 points, including 54 goals, and also got his first taste of the NHL when the Islanders called him up for a three-game stint. When the 1981–82 season began the Broncos were geared up for a run at the league championship. Right off the bat they put together a 17-game unbeaten string. Through the first half of the season there was no stopping Sutter, who scored 46 goals in the first 34 games. Unfortunately for Lethbridge, the Islanders were paying attention, and they brought up the star centre for the rest of the season. In New York he joined his brother Duane, whom he would play with for six years. Lethbridge's hopes for a WHL title more or less died with Sutter's departure.

The Sutters——Brian, Gary, Louis, Darryl, Duane, Brent, Ron and Rich. This photo was taken during the 1993 Sutter Charity Golf Tournament in Lethbridge.

Sutter instantly became an integral part of the Islanders, contributing 43 points in 43 games as New York won its third consecutive Stanley Cup. The following season his point production fell off, but he had an outstanding playoff, helping the Islanders win an incredible fourth Stanley Cup in a row. His performance earned him an invitation to try out for Team Canada as it prepared for the 1984 Canada Cup. He ended up playing on a line with New York teammates Mike Bossy and John Tonelli. Sutter turned the experience of playing with the world's best to good effect and in 1984-85 he had his best NHL season ever, scoring 42 goals and finishing with 102 points.

As a junior Brent was a high-scoring centre, but in the pros he gradually turned into more of a role player. He didn't pile up the points like the superstars but he was reliable and tireless, working the corners and tiring out the opposition. A highly motivated player, he has been a leader on any team to which he belonged. It may not have been spectacular, but his hard-working style of play won Sutter invitations to the 1985 NHL all-star game and to the 1987 and 1991 Canada Cup teams. In 1991-92, he was traded to Chicago, where he surpassed Brian as the NHL career scoring leader of the six brothers.

Ron and Rich Sutter played together in Lethbridge for most of three seasons 1980-83. Their final junior campaign saw the Broncos win the WHL championship and advance to the Memorial Cup for the first and only time. In the playoffs that season, Ron led all scorers with 22 goals in 20 games, while brother Rich added 14. Philadelphia drafted Ron fourth overall in 1982 and he played several seasons in the City of Brotherly Love. When the Flyers named him captain during the 1989-90 season he became the fourth Sutter to captain an NHL team. Rich is the most travelled of the brothers. He was drafted by Pittsburgh in 1982, tenth overall, and has played in Philadelphia and Vancouver. Both twins now suit up for the St. Louis Blues.

Add up all the scoring, and no family in NHL history has lit up more goal lights than the Sutters. Going into the 1993-94 season, the "Six Shooters" had 1230 goals and 1452 assists in regular season play. But those are just the cold statistics. What they do not show is the intense competitive drive shared by all the brothers and the leadership they provide on and off the ice. What they lack in finesse they have always made up for with hard work and sheer determination.

The Sutters have not forgotten their roots. All the brothers have homes in Alberta, and in Lethbridge the annual Sutter Brothers Charity Golf Classic is one of the most successful pro-hockey celebrity golf tournaments anywhere.

John Chapman

The Broncos' head coach during their one and only appearance at the Memorial Cup tournament was John Chapman, a native of Stettler, Alberta, who is now head scout with the Tampa Bay Lightning. Chapman's introduction to the WHL came in the 1960s when he played for the Estevan Bruins, a team coached and owned by Scotty Munro and Ernie McLean. From Estevan he bounced around the minor leagues for a few years until a serious knee injury cut short his playing career and he decided to get into coaching.

Chapman learned his coaching style from Munro and McLean. He emphasized hard work, sound defence and lots of physical contact. His first job was with a senior B team in his hometown of Stettler, but he was fired after eight games because the team was too physical. He ended up in Lethbridge coaching the Sugar Kings of the Alberta Junior Hockey League. From 1970 to 1972 he nurtured many fine young hockey talents, including Len Frig, Lanny McDonald, Dave Shardlow, Randy Andreachuk, John Davidson, Terry Tarnow and Mike Rogers. The Sugar Kings were a farm club for Scotty Munro's Calgary Centennials and following a disagreement between Munro and Lethbridge officials the team moved to Blairmore, Alberta, to be reborn as the Pass Red Devils. For the next several seasons Chapman moved back and forth between Calgary, where he was briefly head coach, and the Red Devils.

After retiring briefly from coaching, Chapman was back behind the bench with the Red Deer Rustlers in 1979–80, when three of the Sutter brothers—Brent, Rich and Ron—powered the team to the Canadian Tier II junior championship. Following that successful season, Chapman returned to the WHL, and to Lethbridge, with the Broncos. He remained in Lethbridge for five seasons and worked on his reputation for being an intense, temperamental, colourful coach. (In Red Deer, while under suspension, he once showed up wearing a gorilla suit.) After one game in Billings, Montana, during the 1981–82 season he was convicted of assault for grabbing a fan by the collar. But as well as fines and suspensions, Chapman also got results. Each season the Broncos improved their play until in 1983 they won the WHL championship. They only fared so poorly in the Memorial Cup tourney because standout goalie Ken Wregget could not play due to an injury.

In 1985–86 the Broncos finished well below .500, the franchise moved back to Swift Current, and Chapman lost his job. He went to Calgary as general manager of the Wranglers for a year, then moved into scouting with the New York Rangers. It was Phil Esposito who offered him the Rangers job, and when "Espo" left New York and became involved with the Tampa Bay franchise it didn't take much convincing for Chapman to follow.

Ken Wregget

The key to any championship hockey team is good goaltending, and the Lethbridge Broncos squad which won the WHL crown in 1983 was no exception. The league has produced some top goalies over the years—Grant Fuhr, Mike Vernon, Mark Fitzpatrick, Kelly Hrudey, Ed Staniowski, Bill Ranford, and Andy Moog to name a few—but any list would have to include Lethbridge's Ken Wregget somewhere near the top.

Born in Brandon, Manitoba, Wregget arrived in Lethbridge in 1981 as a 17-year-old with all the earmarks of a great one. Coach John Chapman had an eye for talent, and he was convinced Wregget had the potential to star in the NHL. In his first season in Lethbridge the team finished first overall, and Wregget split the goaltending chores with Cleo Rowein. His performance was good enough to attract the attention of the Toronto Maple Leafs, who selected him in the third round of the 1982 entry draft. Wregget had a superb second junior season, posting a 3.49 goals-against average, second in the league to Mike Vernon of the Calgary Wranglers. The Broncos finished a disappointing fifth in their division, but caught fire in the playoffs where Wregget improved to a 3.02 average, best of any netminder. Fans still speculate how well Lethbridge might have done at the Memorial Cup tourney that year if the young goalie had not twisted his ankle in one of the playoff games and been forced out of action.

Wregget returned to the Broncos for his third season in 1983–84 and was the workhorse of the WHL. He played a league-leading 3053 minutes over 53 games, recording a 3.16 average. He made the first all-star team and was also a member of Canada's national junior team. Called up by the Maple Leafs, he made his NHL debut in a *Hockey Night in Canada* telecast against the Calgary Flames. The game went into overtime and Wregget was selected the first star.

After five seasons with Toronto, Wregget was dealt to Philadelphia in 1989, then to the Pittsburgh Penguins, whom he won a Stanley Cup with, in 1992. After ten NHL seasons, he has established himself as one of the senior netminders in the league.

Gerald Diduck

In this age of point-conscious, puck-rushing defencemen, Gerald Diduck, the former Lethbridge Broncos blueliner, is a rare breed. You won't see any rink-length dashes from this defender. Diduck is most comfortable in front of his own net, letting his forwards make the rushes, and he'll punish anyone who dares step into his territory. He is the prototype stay-at-home defenceman.

Diduck learned his style of play from some of the best coaches in the business, coaches who believe that good defence wins hockey games. As a midget playing in Sherwood Park, outside his hometown of Edmonton, he was coached by Ken Hitchcock, later the skipper of the WHL's Kamloops Blazers and an assistant coach with the Philadelphia Flyers. Hitchcock instilled the importance of defence in Diduck very early. Then, when he graduated to the Lethbridge Broncos as a 16-year-old in 1981, he became a project for John Chapman, another coach who preached defence first. Chapman coached some of the best defenders the WHL has produced, including Randy Moller, Bob Rouse, Mark Tinordi and Gerald Diduck.

During Diduck's three seasons in Lethbridge, the franchise enjoyed its greatest success. In 1981–82 the team completed the regular season in first place overall, then extended Regina to the limit in the East Division Finals before bowing four games to three. The next year, despite finishing well back in the standings, the Broncos came on strong in the playoffs, overwhelming Portland 4–1 to win the league championship. Diduck especially recalls beating Saskatoon in the divisional semi-finals. The Blades had finished 26 points ahead of Lethbridge in the standings. "Out of all the series, that was the hardest one we played," he says. "Anytime you can knock off the top team in the league, it feels good." The Broncos' trip to the Memorial Cup that year was a bit of a disappointment. With regular goalie Ken Wregget injured, Lethbridge floundered and finished last in the tournament.

Personally, Diduck's best season in Lethbridge was his last, 1983–84. He scored a junior-career-high 34 points, including 10 goals, and, along with fellow defender Bob Rouse and the WHL's top goalie Ken Wregget, anchored a defensive corps which allowed the fewest number of goals in the league. He also played for Canada at the World Junior Championships.

The New York Islanders picked Diduck 17th overall in the 1983 NHL entry draft. He joined the Islanders as a 19-year-old for the 1984–85 season and spent six years on Long Island before being traded to Montreal after the 1989–90 season. Diduck was not happy with the Canadiens, however, and early in 1991 they dealt him to Vancouver where he found new life with a Canucks team on the verge of developing into a league powerhouse. In his first full season in Vancouver he was chosen the most aggressive player on the team, as Diduck continued to excel at the stay-at-home style of defensive play that has been his trademark throughout nine NHL seasons and over 500 games.

Wes Walz

The 1989–90 version of the Lethbridge Hurricanes boasted one of the most potent offences in all of major junior hockey. The free-wheeling

Hurricanes posted a record of 51 wins, 17 losses and 4 ties, while outscoring opponents 465–270. The team featured the so-called "Super Six," six players who scored 100-plus points during the season. Corey Lyons set team single-season records for most goals and most points, and finished eighth in the league scoring race. Bryan Bosch, with 48 goals and 90 assists, established a team record for assists in a season. Mark Greig had 55 goals and 80 assists, and was selected in the first round of the NHL draft by the Hartford Whalers. Kelly Ens fired 62 goals, and Jason Ruff had 55 goals and 64 assists. And in the nets, Dusty Imoo set new team marks for single-season goals-against average (3.58) and shut-outs (3).

The sparkplug of this powerful offence, however, was Wes Walz, a 5'10", 180-pound centre from Calgary. Walz finished the season with 54 goals and 86 assists, despite having missed 16 games due to injury. He joined the rest of the "Super Six" on the East Division all-star team and was named the WHL's Outstanding Player of the Year. It was a spectacular season for a young player, who only a few years earlier had been so discouraged that he considered giving up hockey.

Walz played midget hockey with the Calgary North Stars of the Alberta Major Midget Hockey League. In his first year he and Corey Lyons played on a team that finished dead last, and Walz began to have serious doubts about his own ability. That was when Bob Loucks appeared on the scene to coach the North Stars. The subsequent season Loucks engineered a startling turnaround. The team, led by Walz and Lyons, went all the way to the national championship before losing to Regina. Walz scored 47 goals in just 35 regular-season games, and was named Most Valuable Player in the championship tourney. Whatever questions anyone had about his ability were answered.

Loucks, Walz and Lyons all graduated to the WHL at the same time. As an 18-year-old rookie, Walz fired 29 goals, set up 75 others, and earned Rookie-of-the-Year honours in 1988–89. But no matter what happens the rest of his hockey career, Walz will have the memories of a lifetime from his second season of junior hockey in 1989–90. First of all, he was a member of the national team which won a gold medal at the World Junior Hockey Championships in Helsinki in January. Walz scored the winning goal in a critical game against the Soviet Union and assisted on another goal in the title-clinching 2–1 victory over Czechoslovakia. In February the Boston Bruins called him up to the NHL for his first professional games and in front of a hometown crowd in Calgary he scored a goal and an assist in a 5–3 Boston win. Then, in April, Walz and the rest of the "Super Six" carried the Hurricanes all the way to the WHL final before falling to Kamloops. In 19 post-season games, Walz scored 13 goals and added 24 assists to tie for the playoff scoring lead.

The transition to the NHL was not an easy one for Walz. He was certainly a talented offensive player, but his back-checking was weak and some people questioned his desire. He split the 1990–91 season between Boston and the American Hockey League and the next season saw less and less ice time until early in 1992 the Bruins dealt him to Philadelphia. In 1992–93 Walz scored 80 points for the Flyers' farm team in Hershey, and in September, 1993 was signed to a contract by his hometown team, the Calgary Flames.

MEDICINE HAT

The Medicine Hat Tigers

The Medicine Hat Tigers joined the WHL in 1970. The league was expanding and Medicine Hat, with its brand new 5000-seat Arena Convention Centre, looked like a sure bet for a new junior operation. Three local businessmen—Rod Carry, Joe Fisher and George Maser—came up with the $2000 franchise fee and hired Jack Shupe as the franchise's first head coach and general manager.

A native of Ceylon, Saskatchewan, Shupe was no stranger to Medicine Hat. For eight seasons (1948–56) the Gas City had hosted a franchise in an earlier western junior league and for three of those seasons Shupe played defence for the team. The coach at the time was Joe Fisher, a former Stanley Cup winner and Detroit Red Wing defenceman who was now one of the three owners of the new Tigers. After his junior days were over, Shupe played senior hockey in Saskatoon, Yorkton and Moose Jaw. He was coaching in the Saskatchewan Junior League when the new owners lured him back to Medicine Hat with the challenge of building a team from the ground up.

In their first season the Tigers finished 22–43–1, good enough for last place in the five-team West Division. But Shupe was busy off the ice. In the original expansion draft the new Medicine Hat franchise selected the rights to Henry Van Drunen from Edmonton. When Van Drunen refused to report, Shupe struck a deal with Edmonton that brought a kid named Tom Lysiak to the team instead. Likewise Shupe acquired the rights to Lanny McDonald when another draftee, John Senkpiel, preferred to play for Calgary. Lysiak and McDonald would turn out to be two of the finest hockey players the franchise ever produced.

GRADUATES TO THE NHL
Medicine Hat Tigers

1972: **Stan Weir**—California, Toronto, Edmonton, Colorado, Detroit.

1973: **Tom Lysiak**—Atlanta, Chicago. **Lanny McDonald**—Toronto, Colorado, Calgary. **Bob Gassoff**—St.Louis. **Jim McCrimmon**—Los Angeles, St. Louis.

1974: **Ed Johnstone**—NY Rangers, Detroit.

1975: **Barry Dean**—Kansas City, Colorado, Philadelphia. **Bryan Maxwell**—Minnesota, St. Louis, Winnipeg, Pittsburgh. **Greg Vaydik**—Chicago.

1976: **Don Murdoch**—NY Rangers, Edmonton, Detroit. **Greg Carroll**— Washington, Detroit, Hartford. **Morris Lukowich**—Pittsburgh, Winnipeg, Boston, Los Angeles. **Ken Holland**—Detroit.

1977: **Brian Hill**—Atlanta, Hartford. **Ron Areshenkoff**—Buffalo, Edmonton. **John Hilworth**—Detroit. **Pete Peeters**—Philadelphia, Boston, Washington.

1978: **Merlin Malinowski**—Colorado, New Jersey, Hartford. **Jim Nill**—St.Louis, Vancouver, Boston, Winnipeg, Detroit.

1980: **Ken Solheim**—Chicago, Minnesota, Detroit, Edmonton. **Kelly Hrudey**—NY Islanders, Los Angeles.

1981: **Rod Buskas**—Pittsburgh, Vancouver, Los Angeles, Chicago.

1982: **Murray Craven**—Detroit, Philadelphia, Hartford, Vancouver.

1983: **Kevin Guy**—Calgary, Vancouver. **Al Pedersen**—Boston, Minnesota, Hartford.

1985: **Troy Gamble**—Vancouver. **Shane Churla**—Hartford, Calgary, Minnesota. **Gord Hynes**—Boston, Philadelphia. **Bob Bassen**—NY Islanders, Chicago, St. Louis.

1986: **Neil Brady**—New Jersey, Ottawa. **Mark Pederson**—Montreal, Philadelphia, San Jose. **Craig Berube**—Philadelphia, Toronto, Calgary, Washington.

1987: **Wayne McBean**—Los Angeles, NY Islanders. **Dean Chynoweth**—NY Islanders. **Mark Fitzpatrick**—Los Angeles, NY Islanders, Florida. **Rob Dimaio**—NY Islanders, Tampa Bay. **Dale Kushner**—NY Islanders, Philadelphia.

1988: **Trevor Linden**—Vancouver. **Neil Wilkinson**—Minnesota, San Jose, Chicago.

1989: **Jason Miller**—New Jersey. **Brent Thompson**—Los Angeles Kings.

1990: **Dan Kordic**—Philadelphia.

In their second season of play, the Tigers finished 35–30–3, a modest improvement. More important for the future, they had four of the top ten scorers in the league: Lysiak in first place, Stan Weir right behind him, Jeff Ablett in sixth and McDonald tied for seventh.

The next year, 1972–73, in just their third season, the Tigers climbed all the way to the top of the league behind the formidable offensive play of Lysiak, McDonald and newcomer Boyd Anderson. For the second year in a row Lysiak led the league in scoring, with 58 goals and 96 assists in 67 games. Jack Shupe later marvelled that he was "the best hockey player I ever had."

However, not even the talented Lysiak was enough for the Tigers to win that year's Memorial Cup. Held at the Montreal Forum, the tournament was a round-robin affair and even though the Tigers defeated the Toronto Marlboros in an early round, it was the Marlies who went home with the cup.

The hangover from the celebrated 1972–73 season lasted a long time. It was 14 years before another Medicine Hat team won a WHL championship. Meanwhile the fans had something to cheer about in Don Murdoch, a young right-winger who later starred with the New York Rangers. His first season with the Tigers, 1974–75, Murdoch scored 82 goals in 70 games, still the WHL record for most goals by a rookie. The next season he bettered this mark by netting 88 goals, 16 more than his nearest rival.

The Jack Shupe era came to an abrupt end in 1977 when the owners removed him as coach and general manager. Shupe went to Victoria where he coached from 1977 to 1982. In 1981 he took the Cougars all the way to the Memorial Cup, making him one of the few coaches to have taken two teams from the same league to the prestigious tournament.

After Shupe's departure, the Tigers floundered under a series of coaches—Jim McCrimmon, Vic Stasiuk, and Sheldon Ferguson—none of them lasting two full seasons. Then, in 1979, George Maser took over sole ownership of the club and hired Pat Ginnell to call the shots behind the bench.

The new coach seemed to breathe new life into the franchise. With Kelly Hrudey sparkling in goal and Steve Tsujiura enjoying a 102-point season, the Tigers made a run at it, reaching the finals of the East Division before falling to the Regina Pats in five games.

The next year, 1980–81, left-winger Ken Solheim led the league in goals with 68 and Tsujiura added 139 points to finish fourth in scoring. Hrudey was brilliant enough to be named the second team all-star netminder, behind Victoria's Grant Fuhr. But it was not enough. The Tigers were eliminated in the first round of the playoffs.

The Ginnell era reached its low point early the next season when the coach was charged with assaulting a linesman during a bench-clearing brawl in a game with Lethbridge. Ginnell, who pleaded guilty, received a fine from the court and a 36-game suspension from the league, the longest suspension in WHL history. The Tigers finished out of the playoffs for only the second time in their existence.

It came as no surprise when Ginnell did not return as general manager or coach for the 1982–83 season.

The rest of the 1980s was the Farwell era in Medicine Hat. Russ Farwell was coach of the Billings Bighorns when he was hired away to become general manager of the Tigers. During his six years with the team he orchestrated a stunning turnaround that resulted in Memorial Cup championships in 1987 and 1988. Under coaches Ray McKay (1982–84) and Doug Sauter (1984–86), the Tigers rose steadily from also-rans to league finalists. These teams featured the high scoring of Al Conroy, Mark Lamb, and Mark Pederson, the defensive play of Kevin Guy, Al Pedersen, and Dean Chynoweth, and the goaltending of Gary Johnson and Troy Gamble.

When Sauter moved to Regina in 1986, Farwell picked a former journeyman NHL defenceman, Bryan Maxwell, to continue the comeback. The Tigers under Maxwell went 48–19–5 to top the East Division with a balanced attack. In each of the playoff series they fell behind, facing elimination four times, but managed to defeat Portland in the finals for a berth in the Memorial Cup, their first visit to the tournament since 1973.

Five Tigers went to the tournament all-star team—goaltender Mark Fitzpatrick, defenceman Wayne McBean, the tournament's Most Valuable Player, and forwards Jeff Wenaas, Guy Phillips and Dale Kushner. But it was the strapping 17-year-old Trevor Linden, now a standout with the Vancouver Canucks, who turned out to be the team leader. Linden scored the first goal of the final game less than two minutes after play began, then netted another before the first period was over. The Tigers went on to defeat Oshawa 6–2 and bring the Memorial Cup to Medicine Hat.

When Maxwell left Medicine Hat that summer to sign as assistant coach with the Los Angeles Kings, a lot of people wrote off the Tigers' chances to repeat as national champions. But Farwell hired Barry Melrose, a veteran NHLer, as coach and the team responded by winning its second consecutive league title.

The Memorial Cup was played in Chicoutimi, Quebec that year, home of the legendary goaltender Georges Vezina, so it was fitting that the Tigers' Mark Fitzpatrick was selected the top netminder for the second year in a row.

In the final game Medicine Hat faced the heavily favoured Windsor Spitfires, riding a 21-game winning streak. The Tigers fell behind by three goals in the early going but came roaring back behind the play of Linden,

Mark Pederson and Rob Dimaio, the tournament MVP. With less than three minutes left in regulation time, Pederson scored his second goal of the game to break a 6–6 tie and bring Medicine Hat the 1988 championship. In 69 seasons of competition for the coveted trophy, the Tigers were only the sixth team to win back-to-back Memorial Cups.

Despite their success on the ice, the Tigers experienced upheaval in the front office the following summer. Four people quit the team, including Farwell and Melrose who both jumped to the Seattle Thunderbirds. By the time the 1988–89 season began, Tim Speltz was general manager and Ron Kennedy was behind the bench. Kennedy, a native of North Battleford, had played and coached for several years in Europe before coming to Medicine Hat. During his two seasons with the club the Tigers fell to fifth place in their division and did not win a single playoff game.

George Maser decided on a dramatic change. Firing both Speltz and Kennedy, he turned to none other than Jack Shupe, the Tigers' first coach and general manager back in 1970. The 60-year-old Shupe had spent the previous year coaching the Medicine Hat Cubs to the Central Alberta Junior B championship and was operating a gas station in the city. He hired on as general manager in May 1990 and a month later signed Tim Bothwell, a former NHLer from Vancouver, as coach.

Howard Bradley, Bob Gassoff and Ken Gassoff.

The Tigers were poised to jump back into contention in the East Division, but the season was overshadowed suddenly when a fatal heart attack struck down George Maser on November 29, 1990. Maser was one of the people involved in bringing junior hockey to Medicine Hat in the first place. He had been with the franchise since its inception, and his death left a gaping hole in the organization.

The Tigers responded by going all the way to the division final where they lost to Lethbridge in a thrilling seven-game series. The highlight of the season was the superb goaltending of Chris Osgood who joined defenceman Brent Thompson and centre Jason Miller on the league's second all-star team.

Following the 1990–91 season there was a lot of speculation that the Maser family would sell the franchise. George's son Darrell put an end to all the talk when he replaced his father on the league board of governors. As junior hockey entered its third decade in Medicine Hat, a Maser was still at the helm.

With stars Kevin Riehl, Rob Niedermayer, Clayton Norris, David Cooper, Mike Rathje and Sonny Mignacca playing in the 1991–92 season, the Tigers managed to finish third in the WHL with 96 points. Cooper made the league's first all-star team and Norris, Rathje and Mignacca were second team all-stars. Despite the team's fine players and regular season success, it was swept in the first round of the playoffs by Swift Current, a team that only recorded 78 points over the course of the season. Following the upset, Jack Shupe was fired.

With Niedermayer, Norris, Cooper, Rathje and Mignacca returning to the club in 1992–93, most WHL watchers predicted that the Tigers would finish first or second in the East and be one of junior hockey's finest teams. Instead, the Tigers surprised everyone by totalling a disappointing 69 points, and only managing to capture the final playoff spot in the East Divison. But in 1993, it was the Tigers' turn to be the spoilers. In the first round of the playoffs, Medicine Hat upset the fourth best team in the WHL's regular season, the Brandon Wheat Kings, winning three games to one in a best-of-five series. The Tigers could not continue their winning ways against the champions of the WHL, the Swift Current Broncos, losing the second-round best-of-seven series 4–2. Bobby Loucks was named as the new coach of the Medicine Hat Tigers for the 1993–94 season.

Tom Lysiak

Tom Lysiak, a classy scorer who starred with the Tigers from 1970 to 1973, was one of the finest centres to ever play in the Western Hockey League. Certainly his former coach Jack Shupe thought so. "I think talent-wise, size-wise and everything else, Tommy was a great hockey

The Atlanta Flames chose Tigers all-star Tom Lysiak second overall in the 1973 NHL entry draft, but he never quite achieved the stardom his skills promised.

player," says Shupe, whose long career included coaching stints in Medicine Hat and Victoria. "Grant Fuhr is the best goaltender I've ever seen or ever coached. But Tommy was the most talented player."

A native of High Prairie, Alberta, a small town up near the Peace River country, Lysiak was born April 22, 1953. He began playing hockey when he was seven years old and he starred at both the midget and junior levels. During 1969–70 Lysiak divided his season between the High River juniors of the Peace Junior Hockey League and the High Prairie Midgets, leading both teams in scoring.

Still, the Edmonton Oil Kings were willing to surrender his rights in a three-for-one trade with Medicine Hat. Along with Lysiak, right-winger Leif Jacobsen and goalie Ken Ruptash went to the Tigers in return for Henry Van Drunen. It is interesting to look back on that trade now. Van Drunen's best season in the WHL was 1971–72 when he scored 30 goals. That same year Lysiak tallied 46 goals and led the league in scoring. While Van Drunen never made it to the NHL, Lysiak was a standout for several years, first with the old Atlanta Flames, then with Chicago.

None of this future success seemed likely during Lysiak's first season in Medicine Hat, 1970–71, when he scored only 14 times. But the young centre justified coach Shupe's confidence in him the following two seasons as he emerged to terrorize WHL netminders and lead the league in scoring twice.

Lysiak was named all-star centre in both seasons. On December 30, 1971, he set a WHL record, which he still shares today, by scoring 10 points in a 10–6 romp over the Oil Kings. He also led the scoring during the Tigers' run to the league championship in 1973. During the playoffs he scored 12 goals and had 27 assists for a total of 39 points in 17 games, as the Tigers won the right to represent the WHL in the Memorial Cup. Medicine Hat made it all the way to the final game before losing to the Toronto Marlboros.

Overall Lysiak collected 327 points in his three years in the Gas City.

The Atlanta Flames made Lysiak their first pick in the 1973 amateur draft, second overall behind New York Islanders defenceman Denis Potvin. The Medicine Hat graduate did not disappoint the Flames. After his rookie season, he finished a close second to Potvin in the voting for Rookie-of-the-Year honours. It was some consolation when rival players voted him top rookie in the NHL's West Division in a poll sponsored by *The Sporting News*.

Tom went on to play six seasons of good hockey for Atlanta. He was popular in the city, was named team captain at one point, and never contributed less than 58 points in a season. But all good things come to an end, and on March 10, 1979, he was part of a huge trade involving eight players that sent him to Chicago.

Lysiak played seven complete seasons in Chicago, 1979 to 1986. One incident for which Blackhawk fans will always remember him occurred on October 30, 1983 at Chicago Stadium. In a game against the Hartford Whalers, Lysiak tripped linesman Ron Foyt. The league took immediate action and suspended Lysiak for 20 games. It seemed that the graceful centreman never fully recovered from this unfortunate incident and he was never again the same kind of hockey player. He retired at the end of the 1985–86 season with final NHL scoring statistics that read: 292 goals, 551 assists and 843 points in 919 games.

On retirement Lysiak moved back to Georgia,where he took up ranching.

Lanny McDonald

The Medicine Hat Tigers of the early 1970s were blessed with a one-two scoring punch seldom seen in the Western Hockey League before or since. Flashy centreman Tom Lysiak led the league in scoring for two seasons, but right behind him came linemate Lanny McDonald.

In the 1971–72 season, while Lysiak fired 46 goals and 96 assists, McDonald also finished in the top ten in scoring, with 50 goals and 64 assists. The next season the Tiger duo finished first and third in the scoring race, lifting Medicine Hat to the league championship and a trip to the Memorial Cup final. McDonald led the playoffs with 18 goals that spring and capped off a banner season by capturing the right-wing position on the league all-star team.

As a youngster, McDonald played bantam and midget hockey in his hometown of Hanna, Alberta, about 150 kilometres east of Calgary. The Calgary Centennials added him to their protected list, and when he was 16 the Centennials sent him to play for their Tier II junior franchise in the Alberta Junior Hockey League, the Lethbridge Sugar Kings. In his second year at Lethbridge, 1970–71, McDonald found his scoring touch, finishing second in the league in total points and winning Most-Valuable-Player honours.

Ready to graduate to the WHL, McDonald would, in the normal course of things, have gone to play in Calgary. But when the dust from the expansion draft settled, his rights belonged to Medicine Hat and as a result he ended up playing his junior hockey in a Tigers uniform and on the same line as Tom Lysiak.

The WHL scoring heroics of Medicine Hat's twin terrors did not go unnoticed by pro scouts, who wore a path to Medicine Hat to watch them perform. In the 1973 June draft, Lysiak went second overall and two picks later the Toronto Maple Leafs chose McDonald.

With his trademark handlebar mustache, McDonald patrolled right wing for the Leafs for five full seasons during the turbulent years when

Tigers star Lanny McDonald would go on to distinguish himself as an NHL Hall-of-Famer----and owner of hockey's most famous moustache.

the late Harold Ballard owned the team. But whatever fireworks were going off in the front office, McDonald and linemate Darryl Sittler provided the kind of scoring punch that made them fan favourites in Toronto.

Therefore it came as a shock, during the 1979–80 season, when Leaf general manager Punch Imlach shook up his team by dealing McDonald, along with young defenceman Joel Quenneville, to the expansion Colorado Rockies for Pat Hickey and star forward Wilf Paiement.

In the 1980–81 season McDonald led the Rockies in scoring and was named Colorado Athlete of the Year. But his stay in Colorado turned out to be brief. The Calgary Flames were rebuilding the old Atlanta franchise and general manager Cliff Fletcher was looking for a player who could combine on-ice leadership with a positive community presence off the ice. Just 16 games into the 1981–82 season, he gave up veterans Don Lever and Bob MacMillan to bring McDonald back to his home territory.

McDonald played perhaps the best hockey of his career in Calgary. In 1982–83 he scored 66 goals and added 32 assists, his own personal best and still the most goals scored by a Calgary player in a single season. He capped off the year by making the NHL second all-star team and winning the Bill Masterton Memorial Award for the player showing most dedication to the game.

At the same time as he was winning honours inside the arena, McDonald gave up many hours to work with a variety of charities, including the Special Olympics, Ronald McDonald House and the Children's Miracle Network Telethon. In 1988 he won the King Clancy Award recognizing the player most combining commitment and service to hockey on and off the ice.

And the best was yet to come.

McDonald planned to retire at the close of the 1988–89 season, regardless of the outcome. As co-captain of the team, he entered his final year needing just 11 goals to reach the magic 500 mark for his career. Early in March he tallied his 1000th career point, but he was playing only part-time and with 20 games to go he was still 7 goals shy of 500. It didn't look as if he would make it.

Then, in a memorable rush of seven games in March, he went over the top. It began with a pair of goals in a 10–3 shelling of the Pittsburgh Penguins and culminated on March 21 with the last regular season goal of his career, magic number 500 against New York Islanders rookie goalie Mark Fitzpatrick.

Still, the season was far from over. The Flames were hot that year, finishing first overall and powering their way to the Stanley Cup final against Montreal. Unintimidated by the Habs' long tradition of winning, the upstart Flames knocked off the Canadiens. Not only did Calgary win, they won in Montreal, becoming the first visiting team ever to win a Stanley Cup in the Montreal Forum.

Always the master of the theatrical moment, McDonald closed out his career by scoring his final NHL goal in his final NHL game. Stepping from the penalty box, he took a pass and whistled a high shot past Habs goalie Patrick Roy. It was the go-ahead goal in a game the Flames went on to win to help clinch the cup.

After such a season, it was only fitting when McDonald was honoured as the NHL's Man of the Year.

On retirement McDonald stayed in Calgary doing front office work for the Flames. In 1992 he was inducted into the NHL Hall of Fame.

Don Murdoch

Don "Murder" Murdoch was born October 25, 1956 in Cranbrook, British Columbia. In BC, he developed into an excellent young hockey player and was quickly made property of the Brandon Wheat Kings. Before playing a game in the Wheat Kings uniform, he was dealt to the Kamloops Chiefs in a multi-player swap.

Murdoch, a right-winger, appeared in four games for the Chiefs but played most of the 1973–74 season with the Junior A Vernon Vikings. He scored 50 goals on the season, but was not expected to be star player for the Chiefs, and was traded to the Medicine Hat Tigers for Brad Gassoff. Murdoch played two seasons in Medicine Hat and led the league in goals twice. In his WCHL rookie season he scored 82, enough to easily lead the league and establish a long-standing rookie record that may never be broken.

The next season, 1975–76, Murdoch struck for 88 goals, setting a 15-year record for goals by a right-winger and outdistancing Saskatoon Blades' Bernie Federko, the WCHL's scoring king, by 16. He was WCHL Rookie of the Year in 1974–75, and made the first all-star team in 1974–75 and 1975–76.

Murdoch was the New York Rangers' first pick, sixth overall, in the NHL's 1976 draft. Few players, if any, have experienced a more spectacular debut in the National Hockey League than Murdoch. He scored eight goals in his first three games, including five in a single game against the Minnesota North Stars. The five goals tied an NHL rookie record, originally set by the famous Howie Meeker.

Murdoch continued the torrid pace with 16 goals in his first 16 games, including five game-winning goals. With 32 goals in 59 games, he was forced to complete his season when shoulder problems and a torn tendon in his ankle sidelined him. He bounced back with 27 goals the following season, but once again suffered another serious injury, a

Don Murdoch's 82 goals in 1975 set a league record for rookies.

Tigers backstop Kelly Hrudey became a top NHLer.

vertebrae problem, before he could finish one full season. His injuries on the ice led to deeper wounds off the ice.

While the team was on the road, he was left alone with the nightclubs, bright lights and fast talkers of New York. "I loved New York," Murdoch said. "It was a 24-hour-a-day city, seven days a week. I would go to a bar and people recognized me. They were always around me. They would buy me a drink, then another one." Murdoch unfortunately became hooked on the lifestyle.

"I was a kid with a drinking problem and I became one with a drug problem. I knew it, but I didn't know where to go for help. I needed help and I really didn't get it. I went through a hard time emotionally. It's a black mark for the rest of your life." By now, Murdoch had acquired the nickname "Cocaine Kid" and his career was in jeopardy. While passing through Toronto International Airport in August 1978 on his way home to Cranbrook, 4.8 grams of cocaine was found concealed in a pair of socks. He was eventually fined $400 in court and suspended from play for a year by NHL President John Ziegler, who later reduced it to 40 games. Murdoch was the first NHL player suspended for drug use. Many of his so-called friends vanished from him at this time. Murdoch claims the Ranger management left him twisting in the wind. What was thought of as a brilliant career was imperilled. After returning to the Rangers in

1978–79 his hockey career was in deep trouble. He was dealt to the Edmonton Oilers in March 1980 for Cam Connor and a third-round draft selection. But by this time, his reputation was permanently scarred and virtually destroyed. Finally Murdoch was dealt to the Detroit Red Wings where his career soon drifted into the depths of the minor leagues.

Murdoch soon began to tour the minor league cities and had to learn how to ask directions to cities instead of jumping on airplanes to NHL destinations. One by one the cities began to multiply to include Toledo, Muskegon, Glens Falls, Wichita and Billings as his career slipped further into despair.

Murdoch decided that he had had enough and launched a career in scouting with Phil Esposito's New York Rangers. Later he followed Esposito south to the Tampa Bay Lightning.

Kelly Hrudey

Kelly Hrudey's career began when he was 12 years old, playing road hockey in the streets of Edmonton. To that point he had shown no interest in strapping on the blades and giving ice hockey a whirl. But the father of one of his friends noticed the young goaltender playing in the street and encouraged him to try the real thing.

As he made his way through the Edmonton minor hockey system, it became apparent that young Hrudey had the potential to become a gifted goalie. When he made the jump to the major junior level in the fall of 1978, he joined a Medicine Hat team under coach Vic Stasiuk which was in a rebuilding mode.

"We were a pretty bad team," Hrudey says looking back. "We took our fair share of beatings. I played a lot so it turned out pretty good for me. I went there and I got a lot of action and I had an opportunity to improve." For a young goalie who had started playing relatively late, getting lots of ice time was the best thing possible.

The 1978–79 Tigers finished 15–50–7, the worst record in the WHL. Hrudey played in 57 games and posted a 6.17 goals-against average, which still meant that he was stopping almost 86% of the shots that came his way.

The next season the fiery Pat Ginnell was coaching in Medicine Hat and managed to engineer a dramatic turnaround. From last place the Tigers climbed all the way to the East Division final. Once again Hrudey played over 3000 minutes but lowered his goals-against average to 4.17. In the final the Tigers fell to the powerful Regina Pats. Led by Doug Wickenheiser, Ron Flockhart, Darren Veitch and Brian Varga, the Pats went on to win the league championship.

Hrudey's third and last season with Medicine Hat was his best yet. His goals-against average dropped to 3.97, good enough to win him a place on the league's second all-star roster. And the team improved its record slightly. But in the playoffs, the Tigers dropped the first round to an upstart Lethbridge club, ending Hrudey's WHL career on a bit of a sour note.

Hrudey's pro career began slowly. He was drafted by the New York Islanders, but missed the glory days of the team that won four consecutive Stanley Cups (1980–83). Unable to crack a lineup which included goaltenders Billy Smith and Chico Resch, Hrudey toiled for two seasons with the Indianapolis Checkers of the International Hockey League. By the spring of 1984, however, he was up with the Islanders, just in time to be part of another rebuilding program.

Hrudey put in four very respectable seasons with New York before being traded to the Los Angeles Kings in February, 1989. Kings owner Bruce McNall had stunned the hockey world the previous summer by acquiring Wayne Gretzky from Edmonton and he was looking for a goaltender to anchor his Stanley Cup contending "dream team." The 28-year-old Hrudey was it.

"He's a great goalie," said Los Angeles general manager Rogie Vachon. "One of the top three or four goalies in the league."

Medicine Hat fans had a special interest in that trade. Not only was Hrudey a Tiger alumnus, but two of the players the Kings gave up to get him were goalie Mark Fitzpatrick and defenceman Wayne McBean, both of whom also had played their major junior hockey in the Gas City.

In the 1993 Stanley Cup Playoffs, Hrudey fulfilled the important role that McNall dreamed of for him, by taking Los Angeles to the Stanley Cup Finals. After backup goalie Robb Stauber won the Kings' first series against Calgary, Hrudey backstopped the team past Vancouver and Toronto and started every game in the Cup Finals, playing 20 games in all. Unfortunately for Hrudey, the Kings lost the Stanley Cup in five games to Patrick Roy and the Montreal Canadiens.

Trevor Linden

Born in Medicine Hat on April 11, 1970, Trevor Linden played his entire amateur career in his hometown. During his two seasons with the WHL Tigers, he tasted championships not once or twice but three times. In the 1986–87 season he scored two goals, including the game winner, in a 6–2 victory over the Oshawa Generals, to bring the Memorial Cup to Medicine Hat for the first time. The following year he scored 25 points in 16 playoff games, helping the Tigers win their second national championship in a row. On top of these two huge accomplishments, he was a part of the Canadian team that won the World Junior Hockey Championship in Moscow in January 1988.

After such a successful junior career, Linden was bound to go high in the NHL entry draft. Sure enough, Vancouver picked him second overall. He was the type of player around whom the Canucks hoped to build a winner.

"There's no doubt that one of the things we liked about Trevor was that he had that winning background," said Vancouver coach and general manager Pat Quinn. "A player who has tasted a championship knows what it's like to win."

As an NHL player, Linden was compared in his style of play to Philadelphia standout Bobby Clarke. But Linden himself claims his boyhood idol was another Medicine Hat alumnus, Lanny McDonald, whom he used to watch play for the Calgary Flames back in McDonald's glory days in the 1980s.

During his rookie season in the NHL, Linden was the youngest player in the league. That did not stop him from becoming the first

Future Vancouver Canucks captain Trevor Linden skates hard in the uniform of the WHL Medicine Hat Tigers.

Vancouver rookie to net 30 goals in a single season, and the first rookie to win the Cyclone Taylor Trophy as the team's Most Valuable Player. Although he finished second to Brian Leetch of the New York Rangers in the voting for the Calder Trophy as the NHL's outstanding first-year player, *The Hockey News* chose him Rookie of the Year for 1988–89 in its own poll.

In his second year with the Canucks, Linden suffered a bit of a letdown, scoring the fewest points of his professional career to date. However, he did become the first teenager to score 100 career points in a Vancouver uniform. He returned to top form in 1990–91 as he led the team in scoring, won MVP honours for a second time, and was the youngest player to appear in the all-star game. In 1991–92 he won team scoring honours again, and played in the all-star game for the second consecutive season. Linden, who hasn't missed a game in the last three seasons, played all 84 in 1992–93 and scored 72 points. He displayed his true value in the 1993 playoffs though, scoring 13 points in 12 games, playing physically, and proving to his critics that he can be a dominant force in the NHL.

MOOSE JAW

The Moose Jaw Canucks and Warriors

Junior hockey in Moose Jaw, Saskatchewan, has a history dating back to World War One. Teams like the Maple Leafs, the Wanderers and the Moose made the prairie city one of the earliest hockey hotbeds in Western Canada. During the depression the Moose Jaw Canucks were formed, and in 1945 they moved into the national limelight with their first-ever visit to the Memorial Cup tournament. Coached by Reg Bentley, the Canucks travelled east to Toronto, where they fell victim to a powerful St. Michael's College squad in Maple Leaf Gardens. That Moose Jaw team graduated several players into the NHL, including Metro Prystai, Dick Butler, Frank Ashworth, Bert Olmstead, Ralph Nattrass and Clarence "Mark" Marquess.

In 1947 the Canucks were back in the hunt for the Memorial Cup, coached this time by Ken Doraty, famous for having scored the only goal in a triple-overtime game for the Maple Leafs during the 1933 Stanley Cup playoffs to eliminate Boston. Once again Moose Jaw lost to St. Michael's College from Toronto. During the final game in Regina, a group of Moose Jaw fans began hurling bottles onto the ice surface. Some of the players fled to the dressing rooms, while others took refuge in the nets. When the rioters would not stop, the game was forfeited to the Toronto team, which at that point was already leading 8–1 with only six minutes left to play.

During the 1940s and 1950s several prominent NHLers performed for the Canucks: goaltender Emile "The Cat" Francis, a builder in the

GRADUATES TO THE NHL

Moose Jaw Canucks

1967: **Garth Rizzuto**—Chicago, Vancouver. **Ray McKay**—Chicago, Buffalo, California.

1968: **Barry Long**—Chicago, Los Angeles, Detroit, Winnipeg. **Ken Brown**—Chicago. **Lynn Powis**—Montreal, Chicago, Kansas City.

1969: **Larry McIntyre**—Toronto.

1970: **Jerome Mrazek**—Philadelphia. **Duane Wylie**—NY Rangers, Chicago.

Moose Jaw Warriors

1985: **Kelly Buchberger**—Edmonton.

1986: **Lyle Odelein**—Montreal.

1987: **Theoren Fleury**—Calgary. **Mike Keane**—Montreal.

1989: **Blair Atcheynum**—Hartford, Ottawa.

Hockey Hall of Fame; Larry Popein, a New York Rangers standout; and Fred Shero, coach of the Philadelphia Flyers team which won back-to-back Stanley Cups 1974–75, who coached in Moose Jaw during the 1958–59 season.

The Canucks belonged to the Saskatchewan Junior Hockey League until 1966, when the franchise joined the newly-formed Canadian Major Junior Hockey League, the forerunner of the WHL. Coached by Brian Shaw, the Canucks finished fourth in the seven-team league but caught fire in the playoffs, eliminating Edmonton and Regina to win the inaugural league title. Because of disagreements between the CMJHL and the Canadian Amateur Hockey Association, Moose Jaw was unable to compete for the Memorial Cup.

Moose Jaw only remained in the league for one more season before they withdrew back to the SJHL. In the brief time that the franchise was part of the WCJHL, however, several players wore the Canucks uniform who later went on to perform in the NHL: Lynn Powis, Ray McKay, Barry Long, Garth Rizzuto, and netminder Kenny Brown.

Throughout the 1970s and early 1980s there was no Moose Jaw franchise in the WHL. Meanwhile, a young American on his way to the University of Wisconsin and later NHL stardom played for Moose Jaw's SJHL team in the late seventies and early eighties. Chris Chelios went on to win first-all-star recognition, a Norris Trophy for being the NHL's top defenceman, a Stanley Cup with the Montreal Canadiens, and another Norris Trophy along with both first-team and second-team all-star honours for the Chicago Blackhawks. A couple of years after Chelios left, during the winter of 1983–84, the Winnipeg Warriors ran into trouble on the ice and at the box office, prompting rumors of a franchise shift. In December a consortium consisting of Lorne Humphries, Barry Webster and a group of Moose Jaw business people purchased the Winnipeg franchise and moved it west to the Saskatchewan city in time for the 1984–85 season. Moose Jaw was once again a part of the WHL, and it has remained so ever since.

Under coach Graham James, the relocated Warriors showed an immediate improvement. The previous season in Winnipeg they had managed to win just nine games; in 1984–85 the Moose Jaw club registered 21 victories and featured future NHLers Theoren Fleury, Mike Keane and Kelly Buchberger. In the 1986–87 season the Warriors, led by general manager Harvey Roy and coach Greg Kvisle, climbed above the .500 mark and made the playoffs for the first time, losing in the second round to the eventual Memorial Cup champions, the Medicine Hat Tigers.

Through its first decade in the WHL, Moose Jaw was unable to produce a consistent team, though it produced some excellent hockey players, including Blair Atcheynum, fourth-leading scorer in the league in 1988–89; Vancouver Canucks goaltending prospect Jason Fitzsimmons; Chris Schmidt, the team's leading scorer in 1991–92, and Chris Armstrong, a third-round draft choice of the Florida Panthers in 1993. Meanwhile Warriors fans kept hoping that Moose Jaw's proud junior hockey tradition, stretching back 75 years, would translate into success in the future.

Theoren Fleury

Oxbow is a lonely prairie town down in the southeast corner of Saskatchewan, a farming community which takes its name from a nearby bend in the Souris River. Probably the most famous person to come out of Oxbow was the late Ralph Allen, author, war correspondent and legendary editor of *Maclean's* magazine and the *Toronto Daily Star*. But hockey fans, at least, know Oxbow for an entirely different reason, as the birthplace of Theoren Fleury, the tiny perfect scoring machine with the Calgary Flames.

Because of his small size—he stands 5'6" and weighs about 160 pounds—no one gave young Fleury much of a chance of making it as a professional hockey player. One of those who did was Graham James, then a scout for the Winnipeg Warriors of the WHL, who first saw Fleury play at the bantam level in Russell, Manitoba. James added the youngster to the Warriors' protected list, and in 1983 placed him on the St. James Canadians for a season of midget hockey.

Fleury joined the Moose Jaw Warriors in 1984, when he was 16, for the team's first season in its new home. In four WHL seasons he turned into a prolific scorer, finishing fifth in the league in 1986–87, then tying Joe Sakic for the scoring championship in 1987–88. While Sakic won official Major-Junior-Player-of-the-Year honours that season, *The Hockey News* decided to give its version of the award to Fleury. He was also a starter on the East Division all-star team in 1986–87, and played on Canada's world junior hockey team twice—in Prague in 1987 and in Moscow in 1988, where he was captain of the gold-medal-winning team.

Little Theoren Fleury had four big seasons in Moose Jaw.

Because of his size, Fleury was chosen well down in the NHL draft, but Calgary has never had any reason to regret its decision. Unlike other small skaters who have trouble making it to the big league, Fleury wasn't exclusively a finesse player. He was very aggressive, hard-working, tenacious and feisty; in his final year of junior, he picked up 235 penalty minutes. Fleury began the 1988–89 season in Salt Lake City of the International Hockey League, and moved up to Calgary at mid-season, in time to contribute to the Flames' triumphant run to the Stanley Cup. In 1990–91 he broke the 50-goal barrier, leading the team with 51 goals and 104 points. He also played in the 1991 all-star game and the Canada Cup tournament.

Fleury has been called one of hockey's most charismatic players; some people love him, and some people hate him. As the smallest 50-goal scorer in NHL history, he has proven to everyone that there is still a place in the professional game for small players with quickness, speed and a lot of guts.

Tiny perfect Warrior Theoren Fleury became smallest 50-goal scorer in NHL history.

NEW WESTMINSTER

Ernie McLean and the Estevan / New Westminster Bruins

Certain Western Hockey League franchises are linked forever with a coach or general manager who led the team to its greatest successes. Scotty Munro in Calgary, for example, or Bill Hunter in Edmonton.

Another of these league legends was Ernie "Punch" McLean, one of the founders of the WHL and owner of the Estevan, later the New Westminster, Bruins. A coach for 16 years, he remains the only skipper to win four consecutive WHL championships, and one of only six to take home back-to-back Memorial Cups.

Born and raised in Estevan, McLean played in the Saskatchewan Junior Hockey League with the Humboldt Indians in the early 1950s. That's where he and Scotty Munro got together. Later the two men ended up in Estevan running the Bruins franchise. In 1961 Munro left Estevan temporarily and McLean took over behind the bench, starting a long coaching career.

It wasn't too long before Munro was back on the scene, in time to join McLean and a few other junior hockey people in the West who were unhappy with the way the Canadian Amateur Hockey Association was running things. At a meeting in Clear Lake, Manitoba, in the summer of

GRADUATES TO THE NHL

Estevan Bruins

1966: **Barry Gibbs**—Boston, Minnesota, Atlanta, St. Louis, Los Angeles. **Ross Lonsberry**—Boston, Los Angeles, Philadelphia, Pittsburgh. **Ted Hodgson**—Boston.

1967: **Morris Stefaniw**—Atlanta. **Grant Erickson**—Boston, Minnesota. **Gregg Sheppard**—Boston, Pittsburgh.

1968: **Danny Schock**—Boston, Philadelphia. **Jim Harrison**—Boston, Toronto, Chicago, Edmonton.

1969: **Dale Hoganson**—Los Angeles, Montreal, Quebec.

1970: **Greg Polis**—Pittsburgh, St. Louis, NY Rangers, Washington.

New Westminster Bruins

1972: **Lorne Henning**—NY Islanders. **Bernie Lukowich**—Pittsburgh, St. Louis. **Don Martineau**—Atlanta, Minnesota, Detroit.

1973: **Terry Richardson**—Detroit. **Vic Mercredi**—Atlanta. **Bob Stumpf**—Philadelphia, St. Louis, Pittsburgh. **Gord Lane**—Pittsburgh, Washington, NY Islanders.

1974: **Bob Hess**—St. Louis, Buffalo, Hartford. **Ron Greschner**—NY Rangers.

1975: **Gord Laxton**—Pittsburgh. **Barry Smith**—Boston, Colorado. **Alan Cameron**—Detroit. **Rick Shinske**—California, Cleveland, St. Louis.

1976: **Harold Phillipoff**—Atlanta, Chicago. **Clayton Pachal**—Boston, Colorado. **Steve Clippingdale**—Los Angeles, Washington. **Fred Berry**—Detroit. **Kevin Schamehorn**—Detroit, Los Angeles.

1977: **Barry Beck**—Colorado, NY Rangers, Los Angeles. **Brad Maxwell**—Minnesota, Quebec, Toronto, Vancouver, NY Rangers. **Miles Zaharko**—Atlanta, Chicago. **Mark Lofthouse**—Washington, Detroit.

1978: **Stan Smyl**—Vancouver. **Brian Young**—Chicago. **Ken Berry**—Edmonton, Vancouver.

1979: **John Paul Kelly**—Los Angeles. **John Ogrodnick**—Detroit, Quebec, NY Rangers. **Larry Melnyk**—Boston, Edmonton, NY Rangers, Vancouver. **Dave Orleski**—Montreal.

1984: **Cliff Ronning**—St.Louis, Vancouver. **Todd Ewen**—Edmonton, St. Louis, Montreal.

1985: **Bill Ranford**—Boston, Edmonton. **Brian Noonan**—Chicago.

1987: **Jayson More**—NY Rangers, Minnesota, Montreal, San Jose. **Alan May**—Boston, Edmonton, Washington.

1966, several club owners decided to form a new league, even if it meant breaking away from the CAHA, which it did. Thus the Canadian Major Junior Hockey League, later the Western Hockey League, was born.

McLean, Munro and a longtime friend of McLean's, Bill Shinske, represented the Estevan franchise and in the new league's second season of play, 1967–68, the Bruins won the championship and went on to the Memorial Cup tournament. In the aftermath of that season, Munro sold his share in the club and moved to Calgary, taking half of the roster with him. McLean molded the remainder of the team into a top contender and in three subsequent seasons it never finished lower than second place in its division. Some of the future NHL players who profited from McLean's coaching included: Greg Polis, twice runner-up in the Western League scoring race; Lorne Henning, nine-year veteran with the New York Islanders, Greg Sheppard, ten years with Boston and Pittsburgh; Jim Harrison, Barry Gibbs, Danny Schock, Dale Hoganson, Willie Brossart and Brian "Spinner" Spencer.

Coach Ernie McLean hypnotized players and fans.

In April 1971, McLean almost died when a light plane he was flying from The Pas, Manitoba, to Yorkton, Saskatchewan, crashed into a clump of trees near Kamsack. McLean, who was alone on board, was found wandering a rural road and was rushed to a Regina hospital where he was treated for a broken jaw and lacerations. Ultimately he lost his left eye. After the crash McLean decided to give up his construction business in order to devote full-time to his hockey club.

Whether or not the crash had anything to do with it, that summer McLean moved the Estevan franchise to New Westminster, ushering in the era of the big, bad, brawling Bruins of the 1970s. The franchise flourished on the coast, where the team played in the 4900-seat Queen's Park Arena and acquired a reputation for playing a bruising brand of hockey. Beginning with the 1974–75 season, the Bruins rang up four consecutive league titles. In 1975–76 McLean was named WHL Coach of the Year. Twice, in 1977 and 1978, his teams won the Memorial Cup. The 1977 club was led by the multi-talented Barry Beck, the highest NHL draft pick ever to wear a Bruins uniform. He was chosen the Most Valuable Player of the tournament that year, and joined fellow Bruins defenceman Brad Maxwell and right-winger Mark Lofthouse on the all-star team. Eight Bruins from the Memorial Cup winning team were selected in the 1977 NHL amateur draft: Barry Beck, Bryan Maxwell, Miles Zaharko, Mark Lofthouse, Bruce Andres, Randy Rudnyk, Ray Creasy and Carey Walker.

The next season, 1977–78, the Bruins were supposed to be rebuilding, but they won the final four games of the season to squeak into the playoffs, then stunned the hockey world by marching to their second straight Cup win. Standouts during the tournament included team captain Stan Smyl, rookie centre Scott McLeod, who had a hat trick in the championship game, John Ogrodnick and defenceman Brian Young.

Through all the success, McLean had a notorious sense of humour that sometimes got him into hot water. During a 1976 playoff game in Saskatoon, with his team losing 9–3, Coach McLean reacted to what he believed was a missed off-side call. "I reached out to tap him [linesman Harv Hildebrandt] on the head and my hand caught in his hair," McLean

The New Westminster Bruins 1976–77 Memorial Cup champions:
Back row: Doug Sauter, John Paul Kelly, Carl Van Harrewyn, Doug Derkson, Don Hobbins, Randy Rudnyk, Ray Creasy, Larry Dean.
Middle row: Jack Mitchell, Miles Zaharko, Randy Betty, Jerry Bell, Bruce Andres, Dave Orleski, Mark Lofthouse, Brian Young, Dr. Peter Wodynski.
Front row: Blaine Peterson, Brad Maxwell, Ernie McLean, Barry Beck, Bill Shinske, Stan Smyl, Carey Walker.

recalled. "He was wearing a toupee which came off in my hand, so I just dropped it on the ice. The funny thing is that Harv reached down and put it on . . . backwards." The league was not amused and ordered McLean to post a $5000 personal performance bond. On another occasion McLean, an accomplished hypnotist who sometimes used his powers to relax players before a game, hypnotized the unsuspecting president of the Calgary Centennials booster club and had him cheering for the Bruins throughout the game, to the outrage of his own fans.

In New Westminster McLean built up one of the fiercest rivalries in western Canadian sports history, between his Bruins and Brian Shaw's Portland Winter Hawks, coached by Ken Hodge. Some of the incidents were funny. For instance, the night the Bruins were playing in Portland and, with the score tied 1–1, Winter Hawks defenceman Blake Wesley was tagged with a penalty. The team benches being side by side, McLean reached around, grabbed a Portland water bottle and, when no one was looking, threw it at the referee. The Winter Hawks name was all over the bottle. Naturally enough the referee handed out another penalty, leaving Portland two players short. The Bruins scored on the power play and won the game.

Other incidents weren't so funny. At Queen's Park one night in March, 1979, the Bruins emptied their bench to beat up on the Winter Hawks. It was a period when the league was cracking down on violence in the game. Seven players ended up in court and received two-month suspensions. On another occasion McLean was taken from the Portland Coliseum in handcuffs after shoving a fan. Shaw had to bail the Bruin coach out of jail, but the fan eventually dropped charges.

By this time the fight had gone out of the Bruins and their coach. The team went 10–61–1 in 1979–80, finishing out of the playoffs for the first time in McLean's long career. He decided he had worn out his welcome and sold the team to Vancouver entrepreneur Nelson Skalbania who in turn sold it to Peter Pocklington, owner of the Edmonton Oilers. In 1981 Pocklington moved the franchise to Kamloops.

New Westminster was back in the league for the 1983–84 season. Vancouver businessman Ron Dixon bought the one-year-old Nanaimo Islanders franchise and moved it to Queen's Park. And who showed up a couple of years later but Ernie McLean. McLean joined the Bruins front office, even did a little coaching, but he did not see eye-to-eye with Dixon and in 1987 he retired for good. He now works a small gold mine near Atlin, BC, and keeps a close eye on the local hockey scene from his home in North Vancouver.

As for the battling Bruins, a year after McLean left New Westminster, so did the team. The franchise moved south to Kennewick, Washington, in 1988 and became the Tri-City Americans.

Jim Harrison

Jim Harrison was born July 9, 1947 in Bonnyville, Alberta, northeast of Edmonton. He got his start in junior hockey in 1963, playing with the Kamloops Central Rockets. Kamloops had a player development arrangement with the Estevan Bruins, which is why Harrison ended up back on the prairies in 1964 playing in the Saskatchewan Junior Hockey League for coach Ernie McLean's Bruins.

Harrison played four seasons in Estevan, two of them in the SJHL and two more in the newly-organized Western Canada Hockey League. He really came of age in the 1966–67 campaign, Estevan's first in the new circuit. In one home game against the Regina Pats he scored 3 goals in 24 seconds during the final minute of play, propelling the Bruins to a 6–5 victory. It is a record that is not likely to be equalled.

The 1967–68 season was Harrison's finest in a Bruins uniform. Although he finished just one point better than the previous season with 75 scoring points, he was voted the league's Most Valuable Player and enjoyed a splendid post season. Playing on a line with Ernie Moser and Danny Schock, he led all scorers in the playoffs with 13 goals and 22 assists. The Bruins captured the league championship that season but lost in the Memorial Cup final to Niagara Falls.

Harrison began his NHL career in 1968 with Boston. The Bruins traded him at the end of 1969 to Toronto, where he had three inconsistent seasons. Harrison believed the Maple Leafs were interested in him only as an intimidator, and in 1972 he jumped to the Alberta Oilers of the World Hockey Association. He played four years in the WHA, with Alberta and then with the Cleveland Crusaders. In that time he established several records. On one memorable night in 1973 in a game against the New York Raiders Harrison scored 3 goals and added 7 assists, setting records for the most points by a player in a single game—10—and the most assists by one player in a game. On another occasion he set the record for most points in a period with five, four goals and one assist.

In 1976 Harrison returned to the NHL with the Chicago Blackhawks, but injuries to his back and hand reduced his effectiveness and he was traded to Edmonton for the final season of his career, 1979–80. His final NHL statistics were 67 goals and 86 assists in 324 games.

Since hanging up his skates, Harrison has coached at the junior level in Moose Jaw and Estevan, and served as general manager of the Kelowna Spartans in the BC Junior Hockey League. He is now retired once again from hockey and operates a restaurant in Kelowna.

Greg Polis

One of Ernie McLean's brightest junior stars in Estevan was Greg Polis, a product of Dapp, Alberta—population 75. As a youngster out skating on the frozen ponds, Polis used to practise stick handling around his black Labrador retriever, a habit which turned him into a tireless skater and a nifty puck handler.

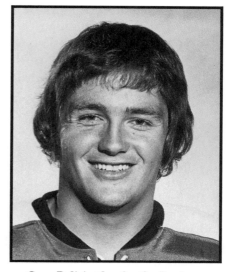

Polis arrived in Estevan in 1966 for the first season of the new Canadian Major Junior Hockey League, and remained with the franchise for four seasons. For three of those campaigns he was a league all-star at his customary left-wing position. A prolific goal scorer, he twice finished second in the scoring race, once to Bobby Clarke and once to Reggie Leach.

Although Polis never became the NHL superstar many hockey observers expected, he enjoyed a solid, ten-year professional career. He was the seventh player drafted overall in 1970, just ahead of Maple Leaf great Darryl Sittler, and played three and a half years for Pittsburgh, where he appeared in the league all-star game three times, once winning the game's Most-Valuable-Player award.

Greg Polis's play for the Bruins fueled superstar expectations.

Polis finished out the 1974 season with the St. Louis Blues, then moved to the New York Rangers where he began experiencing the knee problems which would end his career. His final season was 1979–80 when he played with the Washington Capitals, his fourth NHL team. He later became an automobile salesman in Prince George, BC.

Lorne Henning

A native of Melfort, Saskatchewan, Lorne Henning showed his hockey promise early. By the time he was old enough to leave home to play in the WHL, he had already led his bantam and midget teams to five provincial titles. No wonder Ernie McLean signed up the young centre for his Estevan Bruins club. It was 1968, the year Scotty Munro sold his share of the Estevan franchise and moved to Calgary with half the roster.

Henning was just in time to fill one of the empty spots created by this shakeup.

Henning played four seasons for the Bruins, proving himself a hard-working two-way player and an outstanding penalty killer. Of course, he could score goals as well. In 1969–70 he finished fourth in league points scoring, and the next year he moved up to third. McLean transferred the franchise to New Westminster for the 1971–72 season, when Henning was captain. In spite of missing part of the year with hepatitis, he still managed to collect 114 points, tied for seventh overall in the league with Medicine Hat's Lanny McDonald. Henning stood out as one of the few junior players to wear a helmet before it became mandatory at the end of 1971.

Henning spent nine seasons in the NHL, 1972–1981, all with the New York Islanders. He was not a high-scoring centre, but he filled a valuable role as a penalty-killing specialist. The highlight of his pro career was the Islanders' two Stanley Cup championships in 1980 and 1981.

When he retired from active play, Henning turned to coaching. From 1981–84 he served as an Islanders assistant coach under Al Arbour. After a year coaching with the Islanders' AHL affiliate, the Springfield Indians, he joined the ranks of NHL head coaches in Minnesota. During the 1986–87 season he was replaced in Minnesota, and returned to the Islanders to work as an assistant.

Barry Beck

Back in the mid-1970s when the biggest, most belligerent junior hockey franchise in all of Canada was the New Westminster Bruins, the biggest, most belligerent Bruin was Barry Beck.

As a youngster in his hometown of Vancouver, Beck took boxing lessons and gained a reputation as a tough individual as well as a skilled hockey player. When he reached his 16th birthday the Kamloops Chiefs placed him on their protected list and sent him to play in 1973–74 for the Langley Lords in the Tier II BC Junior Hockey League. Beck racked up 329 penalty minutes in Langley, which is probably what caught the attention of Ernie McLean, New Westminster's hard-nosed coach. It cost McLean and the Bruins four players, but they managed to obtain Beck. "I have never regretted the deal," McLean said afterwards. "Barry is as fine a junior defenceman as I've ever seen."

Beck spent three seasons in New Westminster, and each season the Bruins went to the Memorial Cup. In 1975 they lost to the Toronto Marlboros, and in 1976 they lost to the Hamilton Fincups. Beck came of age as a player during that second season, scoring 99 points, accumulating 325 penalty minutes and earning a place on the WHL all-star team. The next year he was the top defenceman in the league, as well as the

Most Valuable Player and a first team all-star for the second time. But best of all the Bruins went back to the Memorial Cup tournament and this time brought home the national championship. Beck's three-year totals with New Westminster were 44 goals, 159 assists and 654 penalty minutes.

In 1977 the Colorado Rockies drafted the strapping defenceman (6'3", 215 pounds) in the first round, second overall. His rookie season with the Rockies turned out to be his best in the NHL. He scored 22 goals, setting a rookie defenceman record that stood for 11 years, added 38 assists, reduced his penalty minutes to 89 in 75 games and finished second to Mike Bossy for Rookie-of-the-Year honours.

Barry Beck was the WHL's top defenceman in 1977.

When Don Cherry took over coaching duties in Colorado, he wanted to change the team's style, so early in the 1979–80 season Beck was traded to the New York Rangers for five players. In seven seasons with New York he continued the rugged play which had earned him a reputation as one of the top defenceman in the NHL. But his output was hampered by persistent shoulder problems which cut down on his playing time. He finally retired at the end of the 1985–86 season. With help from Wayne Gretzky, Beck came out of retirement briefly to play for the Los Angeles Kings in 1989–90, but it was an experiment that did not work, and he hung up his skates permanently, moving back to Horseshoe Bay, BC where he became part owner of the Big Bam Boo Club, a Vancouver disco.

Brad Maxwell

As much as any other player, big Brad Maxwell was responsible for the run of championship teams that played in New Westminster in the mid-1970s. At 6'2" and 190 pounds, Maxwell was a defenceman in the mold of Bobby Orr, able to control a game single-handed. A tremendous rushing defenceman, he set up almost 200 Bruins goals during his three years in the WHL. When paired with Barry Beck on power plays and in shorthanded situations, they were probably the top defensive duo ever to play in the league.

The Bruins under coach Ernie McLean were synonymous with rough, tough hockey. "We definitely had a big team," recalled Maxwell, "and we were very tough. But I don't think we were goons. Thinking back over all the hockey games I've played in, and all the games I've watched, I've never seen anybody hurt bad in a fight. We did a lot of fighting in those years, but it was because Ernie foresaw the changing scene. He knew that big tough players were the next NHLers and that's how he built his great teams."

Maxwell's formative years were spent in his birthplace of Brandon, Manitoba. The son of Ron Maxwell, a former player, coach and manager for the Brandon Wheat Kings, Brad used to help out on the bench from 1968–70, when his father coached the team. In 1970, Ron Maxwell moved his family to Victoria, BC so that he could continue his coaching career with the Victoria Cougars of the BC Junior Hockey League. As Brad's minor hockey career progressed through the Victoria midget ranks, he was placed on the New Westminster Bruins' protected list.

After playing for the Bellingham Blazers of the BC Junior Hockey League in 1973–74, he joined the Bruins for the 1974–75 season and helped the franchise win the first of its four consecutive league championships. In the playoffs that year, the rookie defenceman notched 20

points in 18 games, fifth-best among all scorers. In 1975–76 the Bruins overpowered the league, losing only two games in their march through the playoffs to a second championship. The Hamilton Fincups won the Memorial Cup that year, but Maxwell contends that the 1975–76 side was the strongest of the Bruins teams for which he played. In 1976–77 the Bruins once again romped through the playoffs with only two losses, then defeated Ottawa to win the Memorial Cup. He provided the heroics in the tournament, scoring a scintillating goal on a rink-length dash to break a tie in the sudden-death final, and give New Westminster a 6–5 victory.

Brad Maxwell set up 200 Bruin goals.

Drafted seventh overall by

Minnesota in 1977, Maxwell immediately went on to spend ten years in the big leagues, eight of those with the North Stars. He split the last two and a half years of his stay among Quebec, Toronto, Vancouver and the Rangers. No doubt the highlight of his 1977–1987 professional career was making it to the 1980–81 Stanley Cup Finals with the Minnesota North Stars, despite being beaten there in five games by the powerful New York Islanders.

Stan Smyl

Every city, it seems, has a sporting hero who can be identified easily by a nickname. "The Babe," "The Rocket," "The Golden Jet." In Vancouver during the 1980s the most familiar nickname in town was "The Steamer" and belonged to the captain of the Canucks, Stan Smyl. The 13-year veteran of the Canucks came by his name while playing in the WHL for the New Westminster Bruins. He wasn't big, and he didn't skate like the wind or have a booming shot. What he had was a lot of desire, tenacity and perseverance. "Stan's biggest quality was his hockey sense," recalled his junior coach, Ernie McLean. "You could put him on the ice in any situation and you knew he was never going to make a bad play. He never got himself in trouble. I don't think I ever had a player, and I had a lot, who came to play every night like Stan."

A native of Glendon, Alberta, Smyl moved to the West Coast in 1974 to play in the BC Junior A Hockey League for the Bellingham Blazers, a New Westminster farm team. He joined the Bruins at the end of the 1974–75 season when the franchise was beginning a run of four consecutive WHL championships. The Steamer was part of every one, along with the two Memorial Cup victories in 1977 and 1978. In the 1978 final-game win over Peterborough he scored a goal and three assists and afterwards was named tournament MVP.

Drafted by the Canucks, it did not take Smyl long to develop into a productive offensive threat. When he retired in 1991 he was the team leader in games played (896), goals scored (262), assists (411) and points (673). During his long career he led the Canucks in scoring twice, was the team MVP three times, and was captain from 1982 to 1990. He stayed in West Vancouver as an assistant coach with the Canucks.

John Ogrodnick

Born on June 20, 1959, John Ogrodnick, the soft-spoken Ottawa native, played his midget hockey in Edmonton before crossing the mountains to launch a starry Junior A career in 1976 with the Maple Ridge Bruins of the BC Junior Hockey League. That season, Ogrodnick led his team in scoring and was rewarded with an invitation to finish out the year in the WHL with the New Westminster Bruins. Ogrodnick arrived just in time to accompany the Bruins on their march to the 1977 Memorial Cup championship.

Ogrodnick was a left-winger during his minor career until the 1977–78 season, when the Bruins shifted him to the right side to form the exciting "Maple Ridge Line" with Randy Irving and Terry Kirkham at centre. During his first complete season in New Westminster he rifled 59 goals, and shared Rookie-of-the-Year honours with Keith Brown, a defenceman with the Portland Winter Hawks. The Bruins did not have a single player in the top ten in scoring that year, but their balanced attack carried them back to the Memorial Cup tournament which they won for the second year in a row, defeating Peterborough in the final game.

After another season in New Westminster, Ogrodnick was disappointed not to be picked until the fourth round in the 1979 NHL entry draft. Detroit sent him to their Adirondack affiliate in the American Hockey League to begin the 1979–80 season, but he was soon up with the parent club and played a total of seven full seasons with the Red Wings. His best NHL campaign was 1984–85, when he finished with 55 goals and 50 assists and made the first all-star team.

After a brief stint with Quebec, Ogrodnick joined the New York Rangers in 1987. Banished to the minor leagues briefly in 1988–89 after a personality clash with coach Michel Bergeron, he rediscovered his scoring touch under new coach Roger Neilson the next season and sniped 43 goals, his second-highest total in his tenth season.

The 1992–93 season found Ogrodnick playing a limited role back in Detroit, finishing his NHL career where it began. Interestingly, he is the last New Westminster Bruin from the Ernie McLean era still playing in the NHL.

Cliff Ronning

In the 1990s, smaller players are no longer the rarity they once were in the National Hockey League. One of the players who helped bring about this change is Vancouver native Cliff Ronning. Throughout his career, the 5'8" Ronning has had to overcome doubts about his size. Along with other WHL graduates Brian Propp, Pat Conacher, Kelly Kisio, Ray Ferraro, Kevin Todd, Mark Recchi and Theoren Fleury, Ronning has proven that there is room at the top for the small hockey player with a big heart.

Born on October 1, 1965, Ronning played his midget and bantam hockey in Vancouver. Late in the 1982–83 season the Nanaimo Islanders, a short-lived entry in the WHL's West Division, acquired the rights to Ronning. The following season the Islanders, newly-acquired by Ron

Dixon, moved to New Westminster, where they became a born-again version of the Bruins, and their rights to Ronning went with them.

Ronning's first year in a Bruins uniform was one of the most phenomenal rookie years in league history. He scored 69 goals and added 67 assists in 71 games, good enough for seventh place in the scoring race and selection as WHL Rookie of the Year. That summer the St. Louis Blues made him their ninth selection in the NHL entry draft, showing confidence that in spite of his size he could stand up to the heavy hitting in the big league.

Ronning was back in New Westminster for his second and final season in the WHL in 1984–85. It was another unforgettable campaign. His 89 goals, combined with 108 assists, set a new WHL individual scoring record of 197 points. This mark is now second on the all-time list since Rob Brown of the Kamloops Blazers topped it in the 1986–87 season with 212 points. Ronning left New Westminster with a roomful of trophies from that last season, winning the Most Valuable Player Award, the Most Sportsmanlike Player Trophy and the Bobby Clarke Trophy as league scoring champion. As well, he started at centre for the West Division all-star team.

Pint-sized Cliff Ronning shredded WHL scoring records.

Instead of jumping right to the NHL, Ronning opted to skate with the Canadian Olympic Team in 1985–86. In 71 games with the Olympians he scored 55 goals and added 63 assists. In 1986 he joined St. Louis, where he played for most of the next three years. His best season in a Blues uniform was 1988–89, when he finished fourth on the team in scoring and tied Brett Hull for most power-play goals. The following year he decided to play in Italy, where he averaged almost two goals per game.

Ronning's big break came on March 5, 1991. He was back playing for St. Louis when the Blues traded him to Vancouver, along with Robert Dirk, Sergio Momesso and Geoff Courtnall. This trade brought Ronning home and seemed to turn the season around for the Canucks, who surprised everyone by playing so well in the opening playoff round against the heavily favoured Los Angeles Kings. Ronning scored six goals in the series' six games to solidify his place on his new team. In 1991–92, his first full season with the Canucks, he played in every game and finished second on the team in scoring with 71 points. The next season, Ronning scored a career-high, 85 points in 79 games. Cliff Ronning established himself as an important part of Vancouver's continuing quest for a Stanley Cup, proving along the way that small players can make big contributions.

Bill Ranford

Bill Ranford was born in Brandon, Manitoba on December 14, 1966 and later moved west to Red Deer, Alberta, where most of his formative hockey was played as a goaltender.

Advancing through the levels of hockey, Ranford found himself on the player's list of the New Westminster Bruins, after spending the 1982–83 season in midget hockey with the Red Deer Chiefs.

Ranford graduated to the Western Hockey League in the colours of the re-born New Westminster Bruins in 1983–84. After another season of hockey with New Westminster, the Boston Bruins were satisfied enough with his progress in junior hockey to select him as an underage junior in the 1985 NHL entry draft. The following season, in 1985–86, he joined the Boston Bruins for four games but played the balance of the season with New Westminster, where he was a second team all-star under the coaching of Ernie "Punch" McLean.

He joined the Boston Bruins as a regular in the 1986–87 season and had an outstanding rookie season, playing in 41 games and recording a 3.33 goals-against average.

After being sent down to the Maine Mariners of the American Hockey League in 1987–88 and spending the whole season in the minors, he was traded to the Edmonton Oilers in March. He was shipped west to Edmonton with wingers Geoff Courtnall and Petro Koivunen for netminder Andy Moog, a trade that the Oilers never regretted making and that proved its worth in a little over two years time, with a Stanley Cup victory on May 24, 1990.

As goaltender Grant Fuhr began to experience injuries and to encounter off-ice problems with drug use, Ranford gained more confidence in the Oilers net. He took over the regular goaltending assignment in the 1989–90 campaign and promptly led the Oilers to their fifth Stanley Cup that season. He won the Conn Smythe Trophy for the Most Valuable Player in the Stanley Cup playoffs, as the Oilers eliminated the Boston Bruins in five games. Ranford also shared the NHL single season playoff record for most wins by a goaltender with 16.

Ranford was a member of the Campbell Conference All-Star team which played in Chicago on January 19, 1991, and later that year he played on the gold medal Team Canada team at the 1991 Canada Cup series. He played all eight games for Canada, completed a 6–0–2 win-loss-tie record and led all goaltenders with a 1.75 goals-against average, a .939 save percentage and one shutout.

Ranford continued his fine play for the Oilers in the 1992–93 season, with a 3.84 goals-against average. When the Oilers missed the playoffs in 1992–93, he was selected to play for Team Canada at the 1993 World Hockey Championships in Munich, Germany.

Ex-Bruin all-star Bill Ranford defied the odds by beating Grant Fuhr out of the starting job in Edmonton.

PORTLAND

The Portland Winter Hawks

When the Edmonton Oil Kings franchise moved to Portland for the 1976–77 season, it was a big gamble for Brian Shaw, general manager of the team. Shaw was taking a chance that the hockey market in the United States was ready for major junior play. As things turned out, the gamble was more like a windfall, triggering a growing movement of Canadian-based teams to the US. Today, Portland, Seattle, Spokane, Tacoma and the Tri-City area all boast top-drawing teams in the Western Hockey League, not to mention the addition of Detroit to the Ontario Hockey League.

Portland inherited a franchise with a long and celebrated history. While based in Edmonton, the Oil Kings went to the Memorial Cup tournament in 1962, 1963, 1966, 1971 and 1972, the last time with Brian Shaw making his debut as coach. Edmonton only won the Cup once, in 1966, but the franchise was the most respected in Western Canada during the early years of the WHL.

Shaw was involved with the league for more than two decades and, along with Scotty Munro, Ernie McLean and Pat Ginnell, belongs in the pantheon of junior hockey legends. In 1973 he joined forces with coach Ken Hodge in Edmonton and the tandem continued working together for 20 years, with Shaw acting as the president and governor of the franchise, Hodge being the head coach and the two men sharing the duties of general manager.

The franchise moved to Portland because of the advent of profes-

GRADUATES TO THE NHL
Portland Winter Hawks

1977: **Jeff Bandura**—Vancouver, NY Rangers. **Dave Hoyda**—Philadelphia, Winnipeg. **Randy Ireland**—Chicago, Buffalo. **Tony Currie**—St.Louis, Vancouver, Hartford.

1978: **Mark Messier**—Edmonton, NY Rangers. **Wayne Babych**—St.Louis, Pittsburgh, Quebec, Hartford. **Brent Peterson**—Detroit, Buffalo, Vancouver, Hartford. **Larry Playfair**—Buffalo, Los Angeles. **Paul Mulvey**—Washington, Pittsburgh, Los Angeles. **Doug Lecuyer**—Chicago, Winnipeg, Pittsburgh.

1979: **Perry Turnbull**—St.Louis, Montreal, Winnipeg. **Keith Brown**—Chicago, Florida. **Blake Wesley**—Philadelphia, Hartford, Quebec, Toronto. **Tim Tookey**—Washington, Quebec, Pittsburgh, Philadelphia, Los Angeles. **Jim Dobson**—Minnesota, Colorado. **Mike Toal**—Edmonton.

1980: **Dave Babych**—Winnipeg, Hartford, Vancouver. **Ed Cooper**—Colorado. **Darrell May**—Vancouver, St. Louis. **Randy Turnbull**—Calgary. **Robert Geale**—Pittsburgh. **Florent Robidoux**—Chicago.

1981: **Jim Benning**—Toronto, Vancouver. **Gary Yaremchuk**—Toronto. **Clint Malarchuk**—Quebec, Washington, Buffalo. **Perry Pelensky**—Chicago.

1982: **Gary Nylund**—Toronto, Chicago, NY Islanders. **Ken Yaremchuk**—Chicago, Toronto. **Jim Playfair**—Edmonton, Chicago. **Brian Curran**—Boston, NY Islanders, Toronto, Buffalo. **Richard Kromm**—Calgary, NY Islanders. **Grant Sasser**—Pittsburgh.

1983: **Cam Neely**—Vancouver, Boston. **Alfie Turcotte**—Montreal, Winnipeg, Washington. **Randy Heath**—NY Rangers. **Gord Walker**—NY Rangers, Los Angeles. **John Kordic**—Montreal, Toronto, Washington, Quebec.

1984: Brian Benning—St.Louis, Los Angeles, Philadelphia, Edmonton, Florida. **Jeff Rohlicek**—Vancouver. **Ray Podloski**— Boston.

1985: **Jeff Finley**—NY Islanders.

1986: **Dan Woodley**—Vancouver.

1987: **Glen Wesley**—Boston. **Dave Archibald**—Minnesota, NY Rangers, Ottawa. **James Latos**—NY Rangers.

1989: **Byron Dafoe**—Washington. **James Black**—Hartford, Minnesota. **Roy Mitchell**—Montreal, Minnesota.

1991: **Steve Konowalchuk**—Washington.

sional hockey in Edmonton. The Oilers had joined the World Hockey Association and the junior team was fighting a losing battle for fan dollars. It was the same situation in other WHL cities, notably Calgary and New Westminster, but Edmonton was the first franchise to make the move and Portland greeted the team with open arms. The city had been hungry for top-level hockey entertainment since the demise of the Portland Buckaroos of the professional West Coast Hockey League. The Buckaroos had been a powerhouse in the WCHL, with talented and rugged clubs that boasted such players as Art Jones, Andy Hebenton and Connie Madigan, clubs that could fill the 10,400-seat Memorial Coliseum. It was an open question whether the Winter Hawks would fill those seats with the same regularity.

Once Portland fans became sold on major junior hockey, however, the club began to set attendance records. In good years the team came near to filling the building for games, and even in the down years Portland led the league in ticket sales. Attendance peaked in 1986–87 as Portland and Kamloops fought a sizzling battle for the West Division title. Portland sold out Memorial Coliseum seven times that season. But already the success of the franchise at the gate had convinced other owners to make the move south of the border; in 1977–78 the Kamloops Chiefs moved to Seattle, while the Kelowna Wings moved to Spokane in 1985–86.

The Winter Hawks not only filled the seats; they played some standout hockey. In the early years the team featured solid defensive play. In 1977–78 Bart Hunter was the league's top goaltender, and then for four consecutive seasons Portland produced the WHL's best defencemen: Keith Brown (1978–79), Dave Babych (1979–80), Jim Benning (1980–81) and Gary Nylund (1981–82). The roster of star defensive players was topped off in the mid-1980s by Glen Wesley, who was the West Division's best defenceman two years in a row.

Portland has won the WHL crown once, in 1981–82, when it defeated Regina 4–1 in the final series. Curiously, its only Memorial Cup win came not that year but the next, when the Winter Hawks lost the league championship to Lethbridge but were permitted to enter the tournament by virtue of being the host team. It was the first time the tourney was held in an American city and the Winter Hawks celebrated by pulling an upset, hammering the Oshawa Generals 8–3 in the final game. The Cup-winning team was led by Ken Yaremchuk (160 regular-season points to finish fifth in the league), Randy Heath (151 points), Alfie Turcotte (127), Cam Neely (120), Grant Sasser (119), Richard Kromm (103) and Brad Duggan (100). In all, seven Winter Hawks tallied 100 or more points, a WHL single-season record.

In the next decade, the team had its ups and downs, and always failed to make it to the Memorial Cup. The Hawks came close in 1986–87, when they took the Memorial Cup–bound Medicine Hat Tigers to the seventh and final game in the league final; in 1988–89, when they made it to the championship series again but were swept by the powerful Swift Current Broncos; and in 1992–93, when they lost to the Broncos again, this time four games to three. The 1992–93 team didn't feature any future NHL superstars, but with players like Jason McBain, Colin Foley, Adam Deadmarsh, Nick Vachon, the team's playoffs leading scorer Lonny Bohonos, CHL Rookie of the Year Jason Wiemer and goalies Joaquin Gage and Scott Langkow, it managed to finish first in the West Division with 93 points.

Over the years the Portland franchise has been noted for some exceptional brother acts. For example, the Babych brothers, Dave and Wayne, who played for the Winter Hawks in the late 1970s. Wayne, drafted by St. Louis, posted a 54-goal season with the Blues in 1980–81, the highlight of a nine-year NHL career. Dave, drafted by Winnipeg second overall in 1980, has played in the NHL all-star game twice and in 1993 completed his 14th NHL season in a Vancouver uniform. Other brother acts include Edmonton natives Ken and Gary Yaremchuk, Blake

Portland Winter Hawks Memorial-Cup-winning 1982-83 team:
Back Row: Rick Davidson, Grey Holomay, Brian Curran, Kelly
Hubbard, Jim Playfair, Bryan Walker.
Middle Row: Ken Yaremchuk, Brian Shaw (GM), Curt Brandolini,
Brad Duggan, Terry Jones, Gordon Walker, Bruno Campese, Derek
Laxdal, John Kordic, Tim Lorenz, Cam Neely, Ken Hodge (coach).
Front Row: Mike Vernon, Ray Ferraro, Rich Kromm, Ian Wood, Alfie
Turcotte, Grant Sasser, Randy Heath.

and Glen Wesley (Glen is still a mainstay of the Boston Bruin defence), Jim and Brian Benning, and the Turnbull boys from Bentley, Alberta: Perry, the WHL Most Valuable Player in 1978–79, and Randy, holder of the Winter Hawks' single-season and career records for penalty minutes.

Portland is also notable for being major junior hockey's first "international" team, combining players from all over the continent and even one, Kevin Griffin, from London, England. Fans fell in love with Grant Sasser during the surprising 1982–83 season, since he was the first name player born and raised in Portland. Other American players were Dan Woodley, born in Oklahoma City, and Jeff Rohlicek from Illinois, both drafted by the Vancouver Canucks. And then there was defenceman Keith Brown, all the way from Cornerbrook in Newfoundland. An NHL veteran of 15 seasons, he tied for WHL Rookie of the Year in 1977–78 and was the league's top defenceman the next season.

An era ended for the Portland franchise on July 27, 1993 when Brian Shaw died of cancer.

Ken Hodge

Although Portland Winter Hawks coach Ken Hodge never played professional hockey, he has established himself as the winningest coach in the history of the Western Hockey League. A native of Jasper Place, Alberta, Hodge played his minor hockey in the Edmonton area, then headed to the Moose Jaw Canucks of the Saskatchewan Junior Hockey League for the 1964–65 season. The Chicago Blackhawks had Hodge ticketed for an NHL career, even inviting the youngster to training camp in the fall of 1965, but his dream of playing professionally ended with a nasty incident involving Regina Pats left-winger Ernie Hicke at Regina's Exhibition Stadium during the 1965–66 junior season. Hodge sustained a serious injury to his left eye and had to retire from the game he loved so much. Forced to leave the playing ranks behind, Hodge turned his ambitions to coaching. He started out as Brian Shaw's assistant with the Moose Jaw Canucks in 1967–68, then headed east to coach in the Chicago farm system, first with the Sorel Blackhawks of the Quebec Junior Hockey League, then for five years with the Flint Generals of the International Hockey League. Hodge led the Generals to a divisional pennant in 1972–73. He returned to his native Alberta the next year when Bill Hunter, general manager of the Edmonton Oil Kings, handed him the coaching reins. When the franchise was sold to Don Scott and Doug Messier after the 1974–75 campaign, Hodge was out, but 11 games into the new season the team was back in the hands of Brian Shaw and Hodge has coached the team ever since, moving with the franchise to Portland in 1976.

Hodge's career as coach of the Winter Hawks has been sparkling.

He has coached more seasons, and won more games, than any other person, has captured a league title and a Memorial Cup championship, and was named WHL Coach of the Year in 1980–81. Hodge added all-time winningest coach in playoff history to his list of accomplishments in the spring of 1992, surpassing New Westminster's Ernie McLean.

Wayne Babych

Ken Hodge and the Edmonton Oil Kings took notice of Wayne Babych's exceptional skills when he displayed them in the uniform of the Edmonton Mets in 1973–74. During one Mets game, Babych fired 3 goals in 24 seconds.

Babych, who was born on June 6, 1958 in Edmonton, moved up to the Oil Kings for the end of 1973–74 and became a regular in the next season. He started his WCHL career slowly, but was just getting going on an elongated career of four seasons. After another season of play in Edmonton, the franchise moved to Portland, Oregon and Babych's career took off simultaneously. He represented the Western Division in the all-star game in Brandon and recorded the first of two consecutive 50-goal seasons in the league's regular scheduled games. In 1977–78 he prepared for professional hockey by earning 121 points, making the WCHL first all-star team and also compiling 218 penalty minutes. By the time he had left the Winter Hawks, his brother Dave joined the team and later proved that the Babychs were one of the most talented sibling duos in the WHL and NHL.

In the amateur draft, Wayne was chosen third overall and immediately stepped into the National Hockey League with the St. Louis Blues in 1978–79. Babych, a natural athlete who excelled at numerous sports, was also offered a chance to play professional baseball with the Montreal Expos.

He decided to stay with hockey and went on to play six seasons in St. Louis. Without a doubt his career highlight was the 1980–81 season. He rifled in 54 goals, piled up 96 points, and never came close to equalling the feat in all his days in the NHL.

Babych had a very unusual experience during his professional career while playing for St. Louis. During September 1984 he was conditionally traded by St. Louis to Edmonton for future considerations and then in October of the same year he was returned by Edmonton to the St. Louis organization to cancel the trade. The Oilers were worried about his previously injured right shoulder that was not responding to therapy. A few days later, at the National Hockey League waiver draft, the Pittsburgh Penguins were happy to select Babych. Wayne had the pleasure of playing with a young Mario Lemieux but had a hard time enjoying it, with injuries taking a toll on his skills and career. He lasted

Wayne Babych started off his major junior hockey career with his hometown team, the Edmonton Oil Kings, from 1974–1976.

just one year in the steel city and was on the move to Quebec City by the time the 1985–86 season began. After another trade, the Alberta native closed out his career in the 1986–87 season with the Hartford Whalers.

Wayne's final career scoring statistics during his nine NHL seasons were 519 games played, 192 goals, 246 assists and 438 points. Since leaving hockey, Wayne moved to Winnipeg where he coached the Southeast Thunderbirds of the Manitoba Junior Hockey League and became owner of Larter's St. Andrews Golf and Country Club..

Cam Neely

Cam Neely, whose great 50-goal seasons with the Boston Bruins in 1989 and 1990 confirmed him as the NHL's outstanding power forward, is the biggest star ever produced by the Winter Hawks—and if you asked before 1991 when a devastating injury placed his career in doubt, many would have said he was the biggest current NHL star produced by the Western Hockey League.

Neely was born on June 6, 1965, in Comox, BC, but learned to play hockey in Moose Jaw, Saskatchewan. Cam's family later moved back to British Columbia and he played midget hockey at Maple Ridge, outside Vancouver. In the 1981–82 season Neely had a sensational year, scoring 73 goals and adding 68 assists for 141 points. The Portland Winter Hawks scouted him and the rest is history. His rookie season in the WHL was 1982–83—and what a season it was. He scored 56 goals and added 64 assists for 120 points and 13th place in the regular-season scoring race. In the playoffs he added 9 goals and 11 assists in 14 games. Portland finished first in the West Division, five points behind the overall leader, Saskatoon.

This was the year that the Winter Hawks became the first US-based team to have its name inscribed on the Memorial Cup. Neely scored three goals in the championship game against the Oshawa Generals and was chosen most outstanding player. "That was the greatest part of my (amateur) career," he said. "Coming out of midget and having only one year of junior, just being in the Memorial Cup, winning it and getting the hat trick . . . it was just something you can only dream of."

After his sensational year the Vancouver Canucks made Neely their first choice and ninth overall selection in the 1983 entry draft. Neely started the 1983–84 campaign with Portland, but was called up to the Canucks in December and remained in the professional ranks for good, scoring 16 goals and 15 assists in 56 games during his freshman year. His second season was decent, with 21 goals, and his trademark aggressiveness on the ice began to show as he racked up 137 penalty minutes.

Neely's goal production dropped off significantly in the 1985–86 season, which prompted the Canucks to trade him to the Boston Bruins for ex-Victoria Cougar centre Barry Pederson. "The trade only took about two hours," said Boston general manager Harry Sinden. "The Canucks wanted to sign Pederson and they made him an offer that we weren't prepared to match. Our priority was then to salvage as much as possible from the deal. Neely was the guy we wanted. To be perfectly honest, I was surprised to get him. I don't think he would have been available if he had had a good year in 1985–86."

Cam Neely's high-impact play made power forwards the hockey fashion of the nineties.

Neely made Sinden look brilliant by becoming the Bruins' most dangerous player offensively, as well as the most physical player on the roster and one of the best body-checkers in the game. In 1988 and 1990 he played a major role in helping get Boston to the Stanley Cup finals. Then came the injury. Neely hurt his thigh and knee in a playoff game against Pittsburgh Penguins on May 11, 1991, but the seriousness of the injury was not realized until the following January when he experienced severe inflammation. Neely was able to dress for just nine games before undergoing arthroscopic surgery.

PRINCE ALBERT

The Prince Albert Raiders

Junior hockey got its start in Prince Albert, Saskatchewan 40 years ago, with the Prince Albert Blackhawks. During the 1950s, the franchise turned out future NHL players like Orland Kurtenbach, Dave Balon, Jim Neilson, and Hall-of-Fame goalkeeper Johnny Bower. Prince Albert fans were die-hard, and when the Minto Arena burned to the ground in 1961, leaving no place for the local team to play, it was just a matter of time before another junior franchise rose from the ashes.

In the late 1960s, the Civic Facilities Association began raising money for the construction of a new all-purpose arena in Prince Albert. By the summer of 1971 the Northern Hockey Development Association was ready to apply to the Saskatchewan Amateur Junior Hockey League for an expansion franchise, and when play got underway that fall the Prince Albert Raiders were part of the action. The first games had to be played on the road while the team waited for its new home to be completed, but on December 12 the Communiplex officially opened and junior hockey was back in Prince Albert.

Alf Poulin was the Raiders' original coach and general manager, and directed the team to the second round of the playoffs during 1971–72. Early the next season he was replaced by Terry Simpson, a former professional player in the Eastern Hockey League, who was coaching the nearby Shellbrook Elks of the North Saskatchewan Junior Hockey League. Simpson's long association with the Raiders was marked by astonishing success. Between 1972 and 1982 Prince Albert won the league championship eight times and the Centennial Cup, emblematic of Tier II junior hockey supremacy, four times. From 1980 to 1982, the

GRADUATES TO THE NHL

Prince Albert Raiders
SJHL Franchise

1981: **Greg Paslawski**—Montreal, St. Louis, Winnipeg, Buffalo, Quebec, Philadelphia, Calgary. **Dave Tippett**—Hartford, Washington, Pittsburgh, Philadelphia. **James Patrick**—NY Rangers.

1982: **Bill Watson**—Chicago. **Todd Bergen**—Philadelphia.

Prince Albert Raiders
WHL Franchise

1983: **Dan Hodgson**—Toronto, Vancouver. **Al Stewart**—New Jersey, Boston.

1984: **Dave Pasin**—Boston, Los Angeles. **Emanuel Viveiros**—Edmonton, Minnesota.

1985: **Dave Manson**—Chicago, Edmonton. **Steve Gotaas**—Pittsburgh, Minnesota. **Rod Dallman**—NY Islanders, Philadelphia. **Ken Baumgartner**—Buffalo, Los Angeles, NY Islanders, Toronto.

1986: **Pat Elynuik**—Winnipeg, Washington. **Kim Issel**—Edmonton. **Dean Kolstad**—Minnesota, San Jose. **Kevin Todd**—New Jersey, Edmonton. **Richard Pilon**—NY Islanders.

1987: **Gord Kruppke**—Detroit.

1988: **Mike Modano**—Minnesota, Dallas. **Darin Kimble**—Quebec, St. Louis, Boston, Chicago.

1989: **Reid Simpson**—Philadelphia, Minnesota. **Todd Nelson**—Pittsburgh. **Frederic Chabot**—Montreal.

1991: **Dean McAmmond**—Chicago, Edmonton.

team included future NHL players Greg Paslawski, Dave Tippett, James Patrick and Bill Watson.

Having proven their mettle at the Tier II level, Prince Albert jumped to the major junior level in 1982, joining the East Division of the Western Hockey League. The team won just 16 games in its inaugural season and failed to advance to the playoffs, something it wouldn't do again for ten years. The next season saw a mild improvement, enough to win Terry Simpson Coach-of-the-Year honours. But nothing prepared Prince Albert fans for the storybook season of 1984–85. In only their third year in the WHL, the Raiders finished atop the league with a record of 58–11–3. They were led by their brilliant centre, Dan Hodgson, later voted the best player in junior hockey that year, along with Tony Grenier and Dave Pasin, both of whom scored 60-plus goals. In the playoffs they only lost one game as they methodically disposed of Calgary, Medicine Hat and Kamloops to win the championship and advance to the Memorial Cup tournament. After dropping their first game to the Shawinigan Cataracts, the Raiders won three straight to earn a berth in the final, then defeated Shawinigan 6–2 in a rematch to win the Cup and the national championship.

The Memorial Cup year has been the high point for the Prince Albert franchise, though there has been lots of good hockey played in the Communiplex since. After winning his second Coach-of-the-Year award in 1985–86, Terry Simpson left to become head coach of the New York Islanders. He was succeeded in Prince Albert by his longtime assistant, Rick Wilson, and the Raiders maintained their winning ways, posting 43 victories in each of Wilson's two seasons behind the bench. In 1988, Wilson rejoined Simpson as an assistant coach in New York, and for the next four seasons Prince Albert changed its head coach annually. Even Simpson returned for one season while he was in between jobs in the NHL.

Meanwhile, on the ice, the Raiders continued to play competitive hockey, advancing to their division final in 1990 and again in 1992. They reached a low point in 1992–93, falling to last place in the East Divison, but the organization's success over the years indicates that they won't stay there for long. One positive move was the appointment of Donn Clark, a local from Kelvington and Wendel Clark's brother, to the position of head coach. During the team's WHL years, it has produced talent like Hodgson, Al Stewart, 1985–86 East Divison MVP Emanuel Viveiros, Dave Manson, Ken Baumgartner, Pat Elynuik, Kevin Todd, Rich Pilon, Mike Modano, Darin Kimble, Scott Allison, Dean McAmmond, Jeff Nelson, Denis Pederson and Shayne Toporowski. Since its inception in 1971, the club has won five Canadian championships at two different levels, making Prince Albert one of the most successful junior hockey franchises in the history of the sport in Western Canada.

Terry Simpson

For 16 seasons, through the most successful years of the franchise, the name Terry Simpson was synonymous with hockey in Prince Albert. The Brantford, Ontario, native first took up the sport in 1953 as a ten-year-old in Shellbrook, Saskatchewan, just down the road from Prince Albert. Simpson's talent developed quickly and by the time he was 16 years old the lanky right-winger was playing Junior A hockey in the Saskatchewan Amateur Hockey League with the Estevan Bruins. During his junior career, Simpson decided he was better suited to playing defence and he remained at that position when he jumped to the semi-pro level in 1963 with the Jacksonville Rockets of the Eastern Hockey League. After a season of senior hockey in Alberta, Simpson began his coaching career as player/coach back home in Shellbrook with an Intermediate B team. That squad won two provincial titles, indicating that Simpson had a promising future in the coaching profession.

Simpson hung up his skates in the mid-1960s, but he kept on coaching, by this time at the Junior B level in Shellbrook where he attracted the attention of the new Prince Albert Raiders franchise. Not long into the 1972–73 season, Prince Albert wanted to make a coaching change and decided that Terry Simpson was the leader who could turn the team around. And that is exactly what he did, coaching the Raiders to nine straight victories in his first nine games. Ultimately the team reached the division final that season, but that turned out to be only the beginning. From 1972 to 1982 Prince Albert captured eight provincial titles, seven in a row, and four national championships.

Following the 1981–82 season, Simpson spearheaded a move that saw the Raiders join the Tier I Western Hockey League. It took them just three seasons to get the measure of the new league, and in 1985 Simpson and his Prince Albert team were back on the top of the junior hockey world, winning the Memorial Cup in Shawinigan, Quebec. At the same time, Simpson was making a name for himself at the international level. An assistant coach with the national junior program in 1984, he became head coach of the team for the 1985 world championship in Helsinki, where he guided Canada to a gold-medal finish. He was also coach of the national team in 1986 when it finished second to the Soviet Union.

By 1986 it was becoming evident that Simpson, twice named WHL Coach of the Year, was ready to take on a new challenge. In June he jumped to the NHL, signing as head coach with the New York Islanders. In his first year in New York the Islanders captured their division title, but the 1987–88 campaign was not as successful as an aging team finished well back in the standings. Part way through the 1988–89 season, the Islanders fired Simpson and brought back Al Arbour, the coach who had led the team to four Stanley Cups early in the decade.

The firing was the first real setback of Simpson's coaching career. He moved back to Prince Albert and the 1989–90 hockey season found him back behind the bench for the Raiders, leading them to the second round of the playoffs. It wasn't long before the NHL came knocking on his door once again. This time it was the Winnipeg Jets and Simpson served as an assistant coach in the Manitoba capital for two seasons. However, junior hockey seemed to be in Terry Simpson's blood and, as the 1992–93 season got underway, he was the owner of a brand-new WHL expansion franchise in Red Deer, Alberta. But he was too talented to stay out of the NHL for long. On May 24, 1993 Simpson was named as the new head coach of the young, up-and-coming Philadelphia Flyers.

Rick Wilson

Rick Wilson's hockey career came full circle in 1980. He joined the Prince Albert Raiders as an assistant coach under Terry Simpson. Wilson had learned how to play the game during his youth in Prince Albert, and even spent one year in the North Saskatchewan Junior Hockey League with the Prince Albert Junior Knights in 1967–68, before heading off to the University of North Dakota. Wilson enjoyed a fine university career on defence with the UND Fighting Sioux, once winning a place on the all-American second team. Following graduation he turned pro and spent four seasons in the NHL with Montreal, St. Louis and Detroit. In 1977–78 he was an all-star defenceman for the Philadelphia Firebirds of the American Hockey League, then left his playing career on a highnote and returned to UND as assistant coach of the Fighting Sioux. The team won a national championship while he was there.

When Wilson returned home to join the Prince Albert Raiders in 1980, the team was the powerhouse of the Saskatchewan Junior Hockey League, in the middle of a string of seven straight league championships. With Wilson as assistant coach the franchise continued its winning ways, capturing the Tier II national championship in 1981 and again in 1982. He remained with the Raiders when they made the jump to the WHL, helped them to their Memorial Cup championship in 1985, then stepped in to fill the head coach position in 1986–87 when Terry Simpson left for the New York Islanders.

In 1988, after eight successful seasons with Prince Albert, Wilson accepted an offer from New York to become Simpson's assistant once again, this time in the NHL. Since Simpson was fired that season, Wilson didn't last more than a year in New York, but he managed to keep the assistant's capacity elsewhere in the NHL, filling the role in Los Angeles from 1989–92 and then in Minnesota for 1992–93. He gained another NHL career to follow when his son, Landon Wilson, was drafted in the first round, 19th overall, by the Toronto Maple Leafs in the 1993 NHL entry draft.

Dan Hodgson

The same year that Prince Albert entered the Western Hockey League, 1982, the franchise welcomed a 17-year-old rookie centre from northern Alberta named Dan Hodgson. That first year the Raiders managed to win only 16 games, but Hodgson served notice that he was going to be a real force in the league before his junior career was over. He netted 56 goals, accumulated 130 points, finished ninth in the scoring race and was named WHL Rookie of the Year.

Hodgson, who is part Cree, came to Prince Albert almost by

accident. Raised in Fort McMurray, he moved to Edmonton in the late 1970s to play bantam hockey. Two of his linemates were right-winger Dave Pasin and centre Al Stewart; together these three would make a formidable unit when they teamed up again at the junior level with the Raiders.

Hodgson moved from the Edmonton bantam leagues to Duncan on Vancouver Island and the British Columbia Junior Hockey League. From 1980 to 1982 he played for the Cowichan Valley Capitals, where he developed into one of the top scorers in the league. His rights belonged to the Spokane Flyers of the WHL but 26 games into the 1981–82 season the Flyers franchise folded. The players active with Spokane at that time were dispersed around the league in a special draft but this arrangement did not affect Hodgson, who was still playing for the Cowichan Valley team. Before the beginning of the 1982–83 season, his rights, and the rights of other players on the Spokane list, went to the Prince Albert franchise which was just coming into the league. It was one of the best deals that Prince Albert ever made.

Following his rookie season in the WHL, Hodgson continued to pile up the scoring points. In 1983–84 he finished second in the scoring race to Brandon's Ray Ferraro, scoring 62 goals, adding a league-high 119 assists in 66 games, and winning a spot on the second all-star team. His final season of junior play, 1984–85, was astonishing. He was the captain of the Raiders and also captain of the 1985 gold-medal winning National Junior team. He scored a team-record 70 goals and finished runner-up in the scoring race again, this time to Cliff Ronning of the New Westminster Bruins. He set individual records for the Prince Albert team for most goals, assists and points in a season and in a career. In the playoffs he led all scorers and at the Memorial Cup tournament, won by Prince Albert, he was selected to the tournament's all-star team at centre and won the Stafford Smythe Trophy as the Most Valuable Player. To top things off, he was chosen the best junior hockey player in Canada.

Hodgson was drafted by the Toronto Maple Leafs but he never fulfilled his promise at the professional level. After a season and a half the Leafs traded him to Vancouver. Things seemed to be looking up for him in 1987 when he began the season in Fredericton and was leading the league in scoring after 13 games. The Canucks recalled him and in his first four games he collected ten points. But his season came to a sudden end late in November when he broke his leg in a collision with Brad McCrimmon of the Calgary Flames. The next season he saw action with the Canucks and Milwaukee of the International Hockey League and then he left for Europe where he played for teams in Switzerland and Germany.

Pat Elynuik

Like so many other top hockey prospects, Pat Elynuik, right-winger with the Washington Capitals, began his journey to the NHL at the famous Athol Murray College of Notre Dame in the small town of Wilcox, Saskatchewan. When he was 16 years old he headed north to Prince Albert, attracted by the Raiders' winning reputation and the chance to play in the WHL. After a season with the midget Raiders, Elynuik graduated to the major junior level in 1984–85, just in time to join the Prince Albert team which went all the way to the Memorial Cup championship. His point total was low that year, but the experience of being on a national champion was unforgettable.

In his next two seasons with the Raiders, Elynuik posted all-star numbers, scoring more than 50 goals per year and, in 1987, being part of the national team that was suspended from the World Junior Hockey Championship in Czechoslovakia after a brawl with the Soviets.

During his junior career, Elynuik was drafted by the Winnipeg Jets. He began his professional career in 1987 with the Moncton Hawks of the American Hockey League, but before the season was over he was up in the NHL with the Jets. In 1989–90 and 1990–91 he developed into a 30-plus goal scorer and one of the Jets' top point-producers, teaming on a line with centre Thomas Steen.

The Hockey Scouting Report has called Elynuik "a 40- or 50-goal scorer waiting to happen," but it hasn't happened yet. Before the 1992–93 season he was traded by the Jets to Washington for right-winger John Druce. Scoring only 22 goals and 57 points that season, it remained to be seen whether the young native of Foam Lake, Saskatchewan, would realize his true potential with the Capitals.

Mike Modano

Without question, Mike Modano, from Livonia, Michigan, is the best American hockey player to graduate from the Western Hockey League. Born in 1970, he played his midget hockey in Detroit but when the time came to graduate to the junior level, he was somehow overlooked by the neighbouring Ontario Hockey League. Instead he was free to take up Prince Albert's offer of a place on the Raiders for the 1986–87 season.

Playing on a line with Pat Elynuik, the young rookie fired 32 goals. Gaining in maturity and size, Modano improved his point production to 47 goals and 80 assists during his sophomore year, finishing tenth in the league scoring race and attracting a lot of attention from NHL scouts. At 6'3" and 190 pounds, he combined good size with outstanding skating ability, a dynamite combination in a centre. As a result, the Minnesota North Stars picked him first overall in the 1988 entry draft. But Modano could not come to an agreement with Minnesota and decided to return to Prince Albert for his last year of eligibility. It turned out that the season ended prematurely for Modano. Playing in the WHL all-star game, he suffered a broken wrist and had to sit out the rest of the year. Even so, he led the Raiders in scoring.

Modano broke into the NHL in 1989–90 and immediately established himself as one of the league's rising young stars. He scored 29 goals, added 46 assists, was second in the league in rookie scoring and finished runner-up to Calgary's Sergei Makarov in the voting for Rookie of the Year. He scored 93 points in 1992–93, but many hockey observers believed that as one of the most skilled players in the league, he would surpass even that total to become an NHL superstar.

RED DEER

The Red Deer Rebels

The expansion Red Deer Rebels franchise of 1992–1993 was among the most successful first-year teams in WHL history. The team was operated by the Simpson brothers, Terry as owner and Wayne as the general manager. They selected former Prince Albert and Seattle coach Peter Anholt to run the bench.

The squad had a remarkable first year, finishing in sixth place in the East Division with a 31–39–2 record for 64 points, one ahead of the seventh-place Medicine Hat Tigers. The Rebels met the Saskatoon Blades in the East Division playoffs and after winning the first contest 2–1 in overtime they dropped the round in four games in a best-of-five series to the Blades.

Three Rebels made the voting for the 1992–93 WHL East Division all-star team: defenceman Darren Van Impe; former Tri-City Americans centre Dean Tiltgen and Winnipeg-born Brian Loney, a 1992 Vancouver Canucks draft choice. Van Impe also made the NHL entry draft, as did Manitoba right-winger Peter Le Boutillier—both selections of the New York Islanders—and Sean Selmser, an eighth-round choice of the Pittsburgh Penguins.

The previous junior franchise in town, the Red Deer Rustlers of the Alberta Junior Hockey League, had earier formed an enviable junior hockey record. Twice they captured the Centennial Cup as the Tier II Junior A champions of Canada, first in 1970–71 and again in 1979–80 with coach John Chapman and a trio of Sutters—Ron, Rich and Brent—in uniform. The city of Red Deer is host to the 1994–1995 World Junior Hockey Championships.

REGINA

The Regina Pats

The year was 1916 and the world was at war. Senior hockey, the most popular level of play in the Regina area, was decimated as player after player answered the call to arms. As it turned out, this was the opportunity that the younger players were looking for, and prior to the 1916–17 season junior hockey became an official classification in Saskatchewan for the first time.

By 1917–18 there were 12 junior teams operating, including three in Regina. One of the Regina clubs was the newly-formed Patricia Hockey Club, soon known as the Pats. Most hockey historians agree that it is the oldest junior franchise in existence.

Since 1916, this tradition-laden franchise has made 14 visits to the Memorial Cup tournament and has brought home the cup on four occasions. Those original Pats started off the franchise's history gloriously, defeating Weyburn 21–9 in a two-game, total-goal, home-and-home series to win the Corbeau Cup as provincial champions.

Other great achievements of the pre-WCHL Pats were representing the West in the first Memorial Cup ever in 1919 and other times in 1922, 1925, 1928 as the Regina Monarchs, 1930, 1933, 1950, 1952, 1955, 1956 and 1958. Of those years, they managed to win the hardware in 1925, the first time a team from Western Canada claimed the Cup, in 1928 when they united with the Regina Falcons under the name Monarchs and in 1930. Those teams featured players like Johny Gottselig, Ken Doraty, Frank Ingram, Buzz Boll, Gordon Pettinger, Ed Wiseman, Earl Ingarfield, Bob Turner and Lorne Davis.

In 1966 Regina became one of the seven franchises which broke away from the CAHA to form the Canadian Major Junior Hockey League, later the WHL. The Pats finished third in league play but fought their way to the finals behind the scoring of Rick Sentes, Barry Meissner and Brian Lavender before bowing to their old rival Moose Jaw.

With the CAHA refusing to sanction the new league, the Pats withdrew back to the Saskatchewan Junior Hockey League for two seasons and it was during this time, in 1969, that the team, coached by Bob Turner, advanced yet again to the Memorial Cup, losing to the Montreal Junior Canadiens.

In 1970 Regina rejoined the WHL for good and by 1973–74 the league was back in the good graces of the CAHA and eligible for Memorial Cup play once again. The Pats didn't lose any time. Led by centre Dennis Sobchuk, they whipped Calgary in the league championship, then defeated St. Catharines and Quebec City to win the national championship for the first time since 1930.

The rest of the 1970s saw the Pats descend into a deep slump. The worst season was 1976–77 when the team only managed to win eight games. At one point they went 36 games without a victory. The coach changed, then changed again, but things were pretty desperate in the summer of 1979 when Bob Strumm took over as general manager and hired future Detroit Red Wings general manager Bryan Murray to coach. Miracle of miracles, the club rebounded with 47 victories during 1979–80 to finish atop the East Division, then beat Victoria to win the league championship. It was the first time in league history that a last-place team in one season emerged the champion in the next. The dream season ended in the Memorial Cup round robin, however, where the Pats lost three out of four games.

Although they did not win another league crown, the Regina teams of the 1980s enjoyed enormous success. And there was one year, 1983–84, when the Pats came within seconds of the championship. Leading the Kamloops Junior Oilers 3–2 in games and by one goal in the dying seconds of the sixth game, the Pats saw it slip away when Kamloops scored with 12 seconds left in the third period, won the game in overtime and went on to a seven-game series victory. The Pats had some quality players during this period. In fact, Regina players won four consecutive WHL scoring championships from 1979–80 through 1982–83—in order, they were Doug Wickenheiser, Brian Varga, Jock Callander and Dale Derkatch. Other notable team members were Dave Michayluk, Rookie of the Year in 1980–81 and the 1982 playoffs' leading scorer, Gary Leeman, the Montreal Canadien forward who was top defenceman in the WHL in 1982–83, and other all-star defencemen Darren Vietch and Garth Butcher.

But undoubtedly the most famous member of the Regina Pats organization is a player who never even made the team. A 16-year-old

GRADUATES TO THE NHL

Regina Pats
WCHL Franchise

1967: **Brian Lavender**—St. Louis, NY Islanders, Detroit, California. **Ernie Hicke**—California, Atlanta, NY Islanders, Minnesota, Los Angeles. **Barrie Meissner**—Minnesota.
1968: **Ron Snell**—Pittsburgh.

Regina Pats
SJHL Franchise

1970: **Rich Preston**—Chicago, New Jersey.

Regina Pats
WCHL Franchise

1971: **Larry Wright**—Philadelphia, California, Detroit. **Rod Norrish**—Minnesota. **Eugene Sobchuk**—NY Rangers, Vancouver. **Gary Bromley**—Buffalo, Vancouver.
1972: **Dwight Bialowas**—Atlanta, Minnesota.
1974: **Greg Joly**—Washington, Detroit. **Clark Gillies**—NY Islanders, Buffalo. **Glen Burdon**—Kansas City. **Dennis Sobchuk**—Philadelphia, Detroit, Quebec. **Robbie Laird**—Pittsburgh, Minnesota.
1975: **Ed Staniowski**—St. Louis, Winnipeg, Hartford.
1976: **Drew Callander**—Philadelphia, Vancouver. **Rob Tudor**—Vancouver, St. Louis.
1977: **Greg Tebbutt**—Minnesota, Quebec, Pittsburgh.
1978: **Gord Wappel**—Atlanta, Calgary. **Gerry Minor**—Vancouver. **Kevin Krook**—Colorado.

goaltender from Maple Ridge, BC named Larry Walker tried out for the Pats at the 1983 training camp. When Walker was cut from the team, he made a very wise decision, opting to give up on his dream of becoming a professional hockey goalie and concentrate on another sport, baseball. In 1990, he became the starting rightfielder for the Montreal Expos and has since become an all-star, one of the best all-around players in the game.

Despite the success of the team on the ice, the Regina franchise ran into serious problems during the 1985–86 season. Owner Herb Pinder Jr. feuded with the Regina Exhibition Association, the group that runs the Regina Agridome, and at one point the franchise was on the verge of being sold to a group from Swift Current, when the league stepped in

1979: **Dirk Graham**—Vancouver, Minnesota, Chicago. **Sandy Beadle**—Winnipeg.

1980: **Doug Wickenheiser**—Montreal, St. Louis, Vancouver, NY Rangers, Washington. **Darren Veitch**—Washington, Detroit, Toronto, St. Louis. **Mike Blaisdell**—Detroit, NY Rangers, Pittsburgh, Toronto. **Ron Flockhart**—Philadelphia, Pittsburgh, Montreal, St. Louis, Boston.

1981: **Garth Butcher**—Vancouver, St. Louis. **Todd Strueby**—Edmonton. **Dave Michayluk**—Philadelphia, Pittsburgh. **Bruce Holloway**—Vancouver. **Al Tuer**—Los Angeles, Minnesota, Hartford. **Jock Callander**—Pittsburgh

1982—**Gary Leeman**—Toronto, Calgary, Montreal. **Lyndon Byers**—Boston, San Jose. **Taylor Hall**—Vancouver, Boston. **Wally Schreiber**—Washington, Minnesota. **Esa Tikkanen**—Edmonton (drafted in 1983 from HIFK of Finland), NY Rangers.

1983: **Nevin Markwart**—Boston, Calgary. **Stu Grimson**—Detroit, Calgary (re-drafted), Chicago, Anaheim. **John Miner**—Edmonton. **Dave Goertz**—Pittsburgh.

1984: **Selmar Odelein**—Edmonton. **Doug Trapp**—Buffalo. **Robert Dirk**—St. Louis, Vancouver.

1985: **Brent Fedyk**—Detroit, Philadelphia. **Brad Lauer**—NY Islanders, Chicago.

1986: **Mark Janssens**—NY Rangers, Minnesota, Hartford. **Shawn Byram**—NY Islanders, Chicago.

1987: **Brad Miller**—Buffalo, Ottawa.

1989: **Mike Sillinger**—Detroit. **Kevin Haller**—Buffalo, Montreal. **Jim Mathieson**—Washington. **Scott Daniels**—Hartford.

1992: **Jason Smith**—New Jersey.

and purchased it. The league, in turn, sold the Pats to four Regina businessmen, Bill Hicke—a star with the Pats in the 1950s, Jack Nicol, Ted Knight and Morley Gusway. They hired Doug Sauter, one of the winningest coaches and most colourful personalities in WHL history, to serve as general manager and head coach, and Sauter brought in Dennis Sobchuk, arguably the most popular of all Pats players, as his assistant.

The Hicke group's main objective was to put fun back into junior hockey in Regina. But the franchise was devastated by two tragic accidents during the 1986–87 season. First of all, on December 30, a bus carrying the Swift Current Broncos to Regina for a game rolled off the highway, killing four players. Next, on March 1, 1987, star centre Brad

Hornung was checked head-first into the boards and ended up paralysed below the neck.

The Pats rebounded from these tragedies as they have rebounded from other setbacks during their 64 seasons of junior hockey. The franchise made it to the East Divison Finals in the 1993 WHL playoffs, but lost in four straight games and is still seeking to reach the performance level of the 1983–84 Pats. Since the 1985–86 season the Pats have developed four fine hockey players who have reached the National Hockey League. Brent Fedyk, a first-round draft choice of the Detroit Red Wings, played left wing on the "Crazy Eights" line for the Philadelphia Flyers in 1992–93. Playing alongside superstars Mark Recchi and Eric Lindros, Fedyk picked up 59 points in 74 games. Robert Dirk, a third-round draft pick of the St. Louis Blues, has shaped into a prominent stay-at-home defenceman while playing in Vancouver the last two years. Kevin Haller, the WHL's top defenceman in 1989–90, played regularly and won the Stanley Cup as a member of the Montreal Canadiens in 1992–93. Mike Sillinger, a first-round draft pick of the Detroit Red Wings in 1989, played 51 games for the club in a part-time role during the 1992–93 season, but will be given a full opportunity to become a regular in '93–94.

The 1992–93 Pats lineup also harboured some choice talent—defenceman Jason Smith, a 1992 first-round New Jersey pick; forward Jeff Shantz, a 1992 second-round Chicago pick who joined Smith on the 1993 world champion Canadian Junior Team and Jeff Friesen, a highly-touted centre who was the Canadian Hockey League Rookie of the Year.

Bob Turner

Before Bob Turner joined the Pats as coach in 1965, the Regina native was part of another hockey dynasty. As a young defenceman noted for his skating ability, Turner joined the Montreal Canadiens for the 1955–56 season, back when the NHL was still a six-team league and the Canadiens were the pick of the crop. For five seasons, 1955 to 1960, the Canadiens dominated the NHL, winning five consecutive Stanley Cups. And Bob Turner was there for every one of them.

Turner played defence the way it was supposed to be played back in those days. By modern standards his offensive numbers were anaemic—19 goals and 51 assists in 478 regular-season games, 1 goal and 4 assists in 68 playoff games. He was a stay-at-home defenceman who concentrated on keeping his own zone clear. And in the end the most important number was five—five Stanley Cups. Only 12 players wore the red, white and blue for all those cups. Along with Turner there were the Richard brothers—Maurice and Henri, the Rocket and the Pocket Rocket—Jean Beliveau, Boom Boom Geoffrion, Dickie Moore, Tom Johnson,

Jean-Guy Talbot, Donnie Marshall, Claude Provost, goaltender Jacques Plante, and Doug Harvey. The list reads like its own hall of fame.

Then, as suddenly as it began, it was over, for Turner at least. In June, 1961, he was traded to Chicago, just two months after the Blackhawks had broken Montreal's string and won the Stanley Cup. Back then the Cup champions faced off against the all-star team so Turner got to play in his sixth all-star game. And after two seasons with the Blackhawks, he retired.

He was only 30 years old and his playing days were over. He returned to his home in Regina and tried selling beer for a living. But hockey was still in his blood. So when the opportunity came to get back into it, he jumped, and on September 17, 1965, the Regina Pats of the Saskatchewan Junior Hockey League announced the signing of Bob Turner as their new head coach. (An interesting footnote: back then, NHL teams had a direct hookup with junior teams and the Pats were sponsored by the Canadiens, Turner's former team.)

Turner played all his minor hockey in Regina, including a stint with the Pats in the early 1950s. Indeed, he patrolled the blueline for the team that went to the Memorial Cup Championship in 1952. "While I have never coached a team I am confident I can do a good job," he said when he took over as coach. "I've learned my hockey from three of the best coaches in the business and am sure that much of their knowledge has rubbed off on me." Those three were Murray Armstrong, who coached the Pats during Turner's junior career; Roger Leger, who coached Shawinigan Falls when Turner was there in 1954–55; and, of course, Hector "Toe" Blake, behind the bench during the Canadiens' glory days.

As it turned out, Turner had been an attentive student. Over the next nine seasons in Regina, he guided the Pats to three league finals. Twice his teams won the championship and moved on to the Memorial Cup. In 1969, as the representative of the Saskatchewan Junior Hockey League, Regina lost the Cup to the Montreal Junior Canadiens in four straight games. But then came 1974.

In Regina, those are remembered as the glory days, the days of Dennis Sobchuk, Clark Gillies, Greg Joly and Ed Staniowski. Who was the best player he coached with the Pats? "It'd be between Greg Joly and Dennis Sobchuk," Turner later said. "Joly was a good puck carrier, he could shoot, he made the power play tick, he could do everything. Sobchuk had the shot, he could stickhandle and he brought in the big crowds. Ed Staniowski was the best goaltender by far."

In the WHL playoffs in the spring of 1974 the Pats swept Calgary in four straight games to advance to the Memorial Cup. It was the tenth Regina team that Turner had coached and it was the best. In the final game of the tournament the Pats fell behind 3–0 to the Quebec Remparts. "When it was 3–0 I was shook up pretty good," recalled Turner.

But suddenly Sobchuk got untracked, scoring three goals and leading the Pats to a 7–4 come-from-behind victory and the national championship. Turner later admitted that winning the Memorial Cup as a coach was a greater thrill than his five Stanley Cups. "You live with these players and you work with them and you know that a lot of them are going to go somewhere. And maybe, just maybe, what you did played a small part in it."

All good things come to an end, particularly when your profession is coaching. In January 1977, with the Pats floundering, the owners replaced Turner as coach with Lorne Davis, bringing to an end a Regina hockey career that had spanned most of three decades. Bob Turner stayed in his hometown and started a new career selling real estate.

Greg Joly

A husky defenceman who patrolled the blueline for the Regina Pats for three seasons, Greg Joly broke into the WHL in 1971, in the same rookie class as teammate Dennis Sobchuk. Joly quickly developed a reputation as an offence-minded defenceman, and in the 1972–73 season he accumulated 68 points and won a place on the all-star team. The next year he was back on the all-star team but a greater thrill was the Pats' Memorial Cup championship, won in Joly's hometown of Calgary.

So much was made of his offensive talents, that the Washington Capitals selected Joly first overall in the entry draft in May, 1974. Arriving in Landover, Maryland that autumn, he was mentioned as the cornerstone to the Capitals expansion franchise. But, again like Dennis Sobchuk, Joly did not mature into a consistent NHL performer. After less than two seasons Washington gave up on him and traded him to the Detroit Red Wings in 1976. He spent the rest of his career shuffling between the Motor City and the Adirondack Red Wings of the American Hockey League. In 1977–78, Joly's only full season in the NHL, he scored just 27 points.

Joly retired from hockey following the 1985–86 season. He lives in Glens Falls, New York, home of the Adirondack team, where he is manager of a radio station.

NHL dropout Greg Joly was an all-star with Regina.

Dennis Sobchuk

A native of Lang, Saskatchewan, Dennis Sobchuk was the pioneer of teenage million-dollar hockey stars. In April, 1973, when he was just 19 years old and still playing junior hockey for the Regina Pats, he signed a million-dollar contract with the Cincinnati Stingers of the World Hockey Association. Two things were odd about that contract. First of all, Sobchuk remained in Regina for another year of junior seasoning. Secondly, when he graduated to the WHA the next year, it was to play on loan for the Phoenix Roadrunners because the Cincinnati franchise was not yet ready to ice a team.

Despite his fabulous contract, Sobchuk turned out to have a disappointing professional career, surprising more than a few Regina fans who had predicted a great future for him. Certainly his three seasons with the Pats seemed to mark him out for hockey greatness. He joined the club for the 1971–72 season in a trade with Estevan and recorded the first of three consecutive 50-plus goal campaigns. The Pats made it to the league championship that year, losing to Edmonton, and Sobchuk led all scorers in the playoffs. He capped things off by winning Rookie-of-the-Year honours. In his sophomore season he finished second in the scoring race behind Medicine Hat's Tom Lysiak and won the league's Most Valuable Player award. In a game against Brandon he equalled a WHL record by scoring 10 points, 6 goals and 4 assists.

In his third season, 1973–74, Sobchuk played on the Pats top line with Rick Uhrich and Clark Gillies. Once again he finished second in scoring, this time to Ron Chipperfield of the Bran-

Pats scoring star Dennis Sobchuk never played a full season in the NHL.

don Wheat Kings. He led the playoffs in scoring for the second time, then won the Memorial Cup for his team by notching a decisive hat-trick in the final game against the Quebec Remparts.

Sobchuk spent most of his pro career in the WHA, first with Phoenix, then with Cincinnati, and finally in 1978–79 with the Edmonton Oilers, where he shared the centre ice position with Wayne Gretzky. In his first professional season with Phoenix, Sobchuk scored a respectable 77 points in 78 games. Then after scoring 72 points in his second season, he had his best professional season, scoring 44 goals and 96 points and finishing 11th in league scoring. Unfortunately, Sobchuk's career went down the tubes after that 1976–77 season; the next year he only played in 36 games, and after another sub-par WHA season with Edmonton, he moved on to the NHL with Detroit, where he only scored 10 points in 33 games. But he did not last long in the Motor City; he opted to travel to Switzerland where he played for three years. In 1982–83 he was back in the NHL very briefly, playing two games for the Quebec Nordiques before closing out his career.

After leaving the ranks of active players, Sobchuk returned to the WHL and the Regina Pats for two seasons as assistant coach under Doug Sauter. When Sauter left in 1988, Sobchuk took on the dual role of head coach and general manager, but after a disappointing season his contract lapsed and he faded from the hockey scene. He later became involved in the sporting goods business in Calgary.

Doug Wickenheiser

In many ways Doug Wickenheiser's hockey career resembles the career of another Regina Pats star, Dennis Sobchuk. Both were standouts during their junior years, leading their teams to league championships and winning various individual awards. Yet for one reason or another both were unable to attain the NHL stardom expected of them.

Born March 30, 1961, Wickenheiser first played junior hockey with the Regina Pat Blues of the Saskatchewan Junior Hockey League and enjoyed an 88-point season. The Blues were a farm team for the Pats so it was natural that, in 1977, Wickenheiser graduated to the WHL. The young centre played three seasons for the Pats and really came into his own in his final year, 1979–80, when he won the league goals-scoring and points-scoring titles by producing 170 points and 89 goals in 71 games. He also led all scorers in the playoffs, where Regina won the WHL Championship. Not only was Wickenheiser recognized as the Most Valuable Player in the WHL that season, he also was voted the finest major junior player in Canada.

The Montreal Canadiens chose Wickenheiser first overall in the 1980 amateur draft. He had his best professional season in a Canadiens uniform in 1982–83, when he only scored 25 goals and finished with 55 points, but this was not the kind of output Montreal expected and after three and a half seasons he was traded to St. Louis. The change in teams did not bring a change in Wickenheiser's play. He was hampered by nagging rib and knee problems and was the Blues third centre after Bernie Federko and Doug Gilmour. So he was traded again, ending up in Vancouver, then in New York to play with the Rangers, and then in Washington. In 1990 Wickenheiser went to Italy where he played in Asiago for two seasons before returning to North America to play in 1992–93 for St. Louis's farm team, the Peoria Rivermen of the International Hockey League. He managed to lead the Rivermen in points with 78, good enough to place him 18th overall in IHL scoring.

Garth Butcher

Garth Butcher was born on January 8, 1963 in Regina, Saskatchewan. He commenced his junior hockey career in the city of Regina, like many players before him and lots since. It all began for Garth in the 1978–79 season as a midget with the Regina Pat Canadians and before long, in 1979–80, he had advanced to the Regina Pat Blues of the Saskatchewan Junior Hockey League. Later that same season, Garth was given the opportunity to dress in 13 games for the Regina Pats of the Western Hockey League and he has never looked back since.

After two seasons of play with Regina, where he learned his hockey from such coaches as Brian Murray, Jack Sangster and Bill Laforge, Butcher carved out a solid career in the National Hockey League with the Vancouver Canucks and the St. Louis Blues. Schooled in the Bill Laforge mode of tough hockey, Butcher quickly acquired a reputation in the Western Hockey League as a rugged customer, piling up 546 penalty minutes in two seasons as a Pats defenceman. Despite this, and the reputation that Butcher established for himself in the NHL, he was an excellent offensive defenceman. In his first full season with the Pats, he scored 82 points, and in his final junior season, he accumulated 24 goals and 92 points! He was also named to the WHL's first all-star team in 1980–81 and 1981–82 and was a standout on coach Dave King's World Junior Championships gold medal-winning team.

The Canucks made him their first choice, tenth overall in

No. 5 - **Garth Butcher** - Def.

Garth Butcher was a big scorer in Regina.

the 1981 entry draft, and were so impressed that they awarded Butcher a five-game tryout in mid-January 1982. Later in that season, Butcher saw some action in the final game of the Stanley Cup Final on May 16, 1982 against the New York Islanders.

Butcher later returned to the Western Hockey League for a short interval as a member of Bill Laforge's Kamloops Junior Oilers in 1982–83 but, except for a tour of duty with the Fredericton Express of the American Hockey League in 1984–85, he has remained in the National Hockey League ever since. With the Canucks, he joined forces once again with Bill Laforge in 1984–85 as Laforge appeared behind the Canucks bench in a short-lived venture that failed miserably.

"The Strangler" has now played in over 700 NHL games and was awarded the Fred J. Hume award as Unsung Hero and Most Valuable Teammate by his Canuck teammates in 1986–87.

The Canucks had a tremendous opportunity to improve their team

Pats star Jock Callender faces off in a 1981 game with Winnipeg.

on March 5, 1991 and Butcher was traded. Although the deal has turned out to be one-sided in the Canucks' favor they do miss Butcher significantly. In Vancouver, he established himself as one of the league's finest defensive defencemen and a fan favorite. The trade featured Butcher and Dan Quinn going from Vancouver to St. Louis for Geoff Courtnall, Robert Dirk, Cliff Ronning, Sergio Momesso and future considerations.

Butcher continued to play well for the Blues and his highlight of the 1992–93 playoff season was scoring the winning goal on May 7, 1993 in a 4–3 Blues victory in St. Louis during the Norris Division Final against the Toronto Maple Leafs. Unfortunately for Butcher, the Blues were eliminated in seven games by Toronto. That Stanley Cup Final that he played in as an unexperienced 19-year-old could very well be his only one.

Dale Derkatch

One of the most prolific goal scorers in WHL history was also one of the smallest. Standing only 5'5" and weighing between 140 and 150 pounds, Dale Derkatch nevertheless holds a clutch of individual scoring records. Probably the most satisfying is his record of three consecutive 60-goal seasons, a feat unequalled by any other WHL player.

Born in Preeceville, Saskatchewan, October 17, 1964, Derkatch moved to Winnipeg as a youngster and learned his hockey at community clubs in the city. He attended the famous Athol Murray College of Notre Dame at Wilcox, Saskatchewan, where he led the school's midget team to the 1981 national championship. He was named Most Valuable Player of the tournament.

Leaving the midget ranks behind, Derkatch arrived in Regina that fall to play junior hockey with the Pats. In his first season he sniped 62 goals, set a record for most points by a rookie (142) and tied another for most rookie assists (80). He also set a record for most assists in a playoff game. Not surprisingly, this outpouring of points won him WHL Rookie-of-

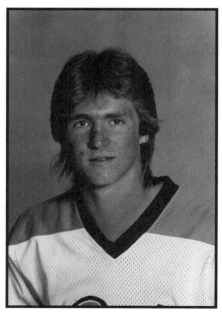

Scoring whiz Dale Derkatch graduated to a pro career in Europe.

the-Year honours. Teammate Dave Michayluk was the finest of the rookie crop the previous year, making Regina the only team in WHL history to have two consecutive winners.

In Derkatch's second junior campaign, he led the WHL in goals (84), assists (95) and points (179). As well, he tied the record for first goals of a game with 13, and established a new record for game-winning assists with 17. Having confidence that he could overcome his size disadvantage in the NHL, the Edmonton Oilers drafted Derkatch as an underage junior late in the 1983 entry draft.

In the 1983–84 season, his last in Regina, Derkatch missed ten games yet still managed to hold onto third place in the scoring parade with 72 goals and 159 points. In post-season play, Derkatch led the Pats to the WHL final where they were eliminated by the Kamloops Junior Oilers in seven games. In the playoffs that spring, he set new records for most assists with 41 and most points with 53. His junior career goal total of 222 ranks him fourth overall.

Derkatch didn't manage to impress the Oilers in training camp, so he went to Europe, where he prefers to play and enjoy his entire professional career with financial security. He has played in Italy, Finland, Germany, and most recently in Zurich, in the Swiss Elite First Division.

SASKATOON

The Saskatoon Blades

When the Western Hockey League began play in 1966 it was called the Canadian Major Junior Hockey League and it had entries from seven cities. With two exceptions, all those original teams are gone. The Edmonton Oil Kings moved to Portland; the Estevan Bruins are now in Kamloops, by way of New Westminster; the Moose Jaw Canucks and the Weyburn Red Wings are both defunct; and the Calgary Buffaloes franchise eventually migrated south to Kennewick, Washington, to become the Tri-City Americans. The Regina Pats are still in the league, but for a couple of seasons back in the late 1960s they dropped out. All of which means that the Saskatoon Blades are the grand old franchise of the WHL. No other team has been in the league, year in and year out, since it began operation.

Stability, in other words, has played a big part in fashioning one of the most successful major junior franchises in all of North America. Over the years the Blades have gone through just two ownership changes and have not experienced nearly as many coaching changes as other clubs in the league.

The original owner of the Blades was Jim Piggott. Back in the early 1960s, Piggott was Mr. Hockey in Saskatoon. He owned the Saskatoon Quakers of the now defunct Western Hockey League, a professional circuit, as well as a team in Los Angeles called the Blades. But he really longed to own a junior team in his home town of Saskatoon.

In 1964 Piggott made good his dream. The Quakers had fallen by the wayside so he purchased a local entry in the Saskatchewan Junior Hockey League, changed its name to the Blades to correspond to his Los

GRADUATES TO THE NHL

Saskatoon Blades
SJHL Franchise

1965: **Keith Magnuson**—Chicago, Vancouver, Boston, Edmonton, Colorado. **Bobby Schmautz**—Chicago Blackhawks

Saskatoon Blades
WCHL Franchise

1967: **Gerry Pinder**—Chicago, California.
1970: **Barry Cummins**—California. **Don Saleski**—Philadelphia, Colorado. **Bill Hogaboam**—Atlanta, Detroit, Minnesota.
1971: **Orest Kindrachuk**—Philadelphia, Pittsburgh, Washington. **Bill Hajt**—Buffalo. **Jerry Engele**—Minnesota.
1972: **Larry Sacharuk**—NY Rangers, St. Louis.
1973: **George Pesut**—St. Louis, California. **Dave Lewis**—NY Islanders, Los Angeles, New Jersey, Detroit. **Russ Walker**—Los Angeles. **Dennis Abgrall**—Los Angeles.
1974: **Bob Bourne**—Kansas City, NY Islanders, Los Angeles.
1975: **Pat Price**—NY Islanders, Edmonton, Pittsburgh, Quebec, NY Rangers, Minnesota. **Bob Hoffmeyer**—Chicago, Philadelphia, New Jersey. **Bill Oleschuk**—Kansas City, Colorado.
1976: **Blair Chapman**—Pittsburgh, St. Louis. **Fred Williams**—Detroit. **Bernie Federko**—St. Louis, Detroit.
1977: **Dave Parro**—Boston, Washington.

Angeles pro team, and hired George Agar as coach and general manager. The new team finished sixth that season in an eight-team league, with a roster that included Bobby Schmautz and Keith Magnuson.

In 1966–67, the first season of operation for the Canadian Major Junior Hockey League, the Blades came fifth out of seven teams, one game above 500. The Pinder brothers, Herb and Gerry, owned the city back in those days. Gerry won the first scoring title with 78 goals and 140 points in 55 games, while Herb finished third and led the league in assists with 75.

In their first years the Blades battled mediocrity, eventually bottoming out in 1969–70 with the worst record in the league. At the end of that season Agar handed over the coaching job to Jackie McLeod, who joined Saskatoon after a lengthy stint with Canada's national hockey program. In his nine years behind the bench (he also served for a while as president and general manager), McLeod turned the franchise around, leading the

1978: **Terry Johnson**—Quebec, St. Louis, Calgary, Toronto. **Neil Hawryliw**—NY Islanders.

1979: **Brent Ashton**—Vancouver, Colorado, New Jersey, Minnesota, Quebec, Detroit, Winnipeg, Boston, Calgary. **Pat Conacher**—NY Rangers, Edmonton, New Jersey, Los Angeles.

1980: **Ron Loustel**—Winnipeg.

1981: **Marc Habscheid**—Edmonton, Minnesota, Detroit, Calgary. **Bruce Eakin**—Calgary, Detroit. **Grant Ledyard**—NY Rangers, Los Angeles, Washington, Buffalo.

1982: **Perry Ganchar**—St. Louis, Montreal, Pittsburgh. **Dave Brown**—Philadelphia, Edmonton. **Daryl Stanley**—Philadelphia, Vancouver.

1983: **Lane Lambert**—Detroit, NY Rangers, Quebec. **Joey Kocur**—Detroit, NY Rangers. **Dale Henry**—NY Islanders. **Brian Skrudland**—Montreal, Calgary, Florida.

1984: **Trent Yawney**—Chicago, Calgary.

1985: **Wendel Clark**—Toronto. **Grant Jennings**—Hartford, Pittsburgh.

1986: **Brian Glynn**—Calgary, Minnesota, Edmonton. **Tim Cheveldae**—Detroit. **Todd McLellan**—NY Islanders. **Larry DePalma**—Minnesota, San Jose. **Randy Smith**—Minnesota.

1987: **Kevin Kaminski**—Minnesota, Quebec. **Shaun Van Allen**—Edmonton, Anaheim.

1988: **Curtis Leschyshyn**—Quebec. **Tony Twist**—St. Louis, Quebec. **Kelly Chase**—St. Louis.

1989: **Ken Sutton**—Buffalo. **Mike Greenlay**—Edmonton.

1990: **Scott Scissons**—NY Islanders.

1991: **Richard Matvichuk**—Minnesota, Dallas.

Blades to three first-place finishes and three visits to the league championship. It was his misfortune, however, to run into some very stiff opposition. In 1972–73, the revitalized Blades held the league's best record, 46–11–11, only to lose in the final to a Medicine Hat Tigers team powered by the high-scoring duo of Tom Lysiak and Lanny McDonald. From 1974–76 Saskatoon twice finished atop the east division and twice met Ernie McLean's New Westminster Bruins in the final, with the same result. The Bruins went on to the Memorial Cup tournament and the Blades went home.

The reputation of Saskatoon as a hockey town took a severe beating in the middle of the 1975–76 season. The Blades were playing at home against the Victoria Cougars, coached by Pat Ginnell. The trouble started when Blades defenceman Bryan Baron was struck in the eye by a high stick belonging to Victoria's Tim Williams. The ensuing brawl resulted in a 50-minute delay in play. Before the game was over the casualty list included not just Baron, who had to be hospitalized, but three other Saskatoon players: Glen Leggott and Bruce Hamilton, both hospitalized with concussions, and Fred Williams who needed 14 stitches to close a gashed lip. The city shut down the arena so that a scheduled rematch between the two teams could not take place and four players—three Cougars and one Blade—received suspensions. Four days after the game, which the Blades won 8–2, Pat Ginnell resigned as coach, saying, "If I am responsible for violence in hockey, I don't want to be in it." However, come playoff time, Ginnell was back behind the bench and he was never fined or suspended for his part in the brawl.

At the end of that turbulent season Jim Piggott sold the franchise to three partners, coach McLeod, contractor Nate Brodsky and Joe Reich. McLeod remained general manager and part-time coach until December 1980, when he resigned and the Brodsky family took sole control of the team.

By this time the Blades were struggling again. In 1980–81 they finished 22–47–3, last in their division. Daryl Lubiniecki arrived on the scene as coach and general manager mid-way through the season, and the change paid immediate dividends. The Blades enjoyed two of their most successful seasons under Lubiniecki before he stepped aside in 1984 to concentrate on the general manager's job. His replacement, Marcel Comeau, remained for five seasons, during which he saw the inauguration of the new Saskatchewan Place arena, on February 9, 1988. Comeau's tenure as coach was capped off in 1989 with Saskatoon's only appearance in the Memorial Cup tournament. The Blades were a respectable team that year—in the playoffs they made it to the East Division Final before losing—but they automatically made it to the tournament because Saskatoon was hosting it. The town went hockey mad. Attendance at the all of the games, which totalled 77,256, broke all previous records. And the Blades surprised everyone by making it to the final game, losing a thriller in overtime to their East Division rivals, the Swift Current Broncos.

When Comeau left to take a shot at coaching in the American Hockey League, he was replaced by Terry Ruskowski, the former Swift Current standout and NHL veteran. Ruskowski lasted a season and a half. He was succeeded on an interim basis by Bob Hoffmeyer, and then in 1991 Lubiniecki hired present coach Lorne Molleken away from the Moose Jaw Warriors.

Molleken led the team to a fourth overall finish at the end of the Western Hockey League's regular season and almost took them to the Memorial Cup in Seattle. In the WHL playoffs the Blades knocked off Lethbridge four games to one, beat Swift Current three games to one and won over Prince Albert, a team that finished 21 points ahead of them in the regular season, four games to two. Saskatoon was clearly the underdog heading to the League Championship series where they were to play the Kamloops Blazers, the Memorial Cup favourites. The Blades didn't capture the WHL Championship, but they surprised WHL fans from Victoria to Brandon by winning three games and taking the Blazers, who had finished first overall in the regular season standings, to the seventh and final game. Saskatoon's top players during the playoffs were goalie Norm Maracle (2.58 goals-against average), captain Richard Matvichuk, leading scorer Jeff Buchanan (24 points in 22 games), over-ager David Struch (23 points), and leading goal-scorer Ryan Fujita (13 goals and 22 points). At the end of the season Richard Matvichuk won the Bill Hunter Trophy as the league's top defenceman and East Division first team all-star honours went to Matvichuk and Trevor Robins, the Blades' goaltender. After losing Matvichuk, Buchanan, Robins and Struch, Molleken's Blades finished fifth in the WHL and made it to the second round of the playoffs in 1992–93.

Over the years some pretty good hockey players have worn the blue and gold: Wendel Clark, and his brother Kerry; Tim Cheveldae, the goaltending pride of Melville, Saskatchewan; the Kocur cousins, Joey and Kory; "Big Bird" Don Saleski; Orest Kindrachuk, Bill Hajt, Pat Price, Curtis Leschyshyn, Bob Bourne, Blair Chapman, Bruce Eakin, Gerry and Herb Pinder, Richard Matvichuk, Bernie and Ken Federko and the Ashtons—Gary, Ron and Brent. For the most part, the Blades have provided an entertaining, quality brand of hockey. In return, the fans have made Saskatoon one of the most reliably successful franchises in the Western Hockey League.

The Pinder Brothers

The first real superstars of Saskatoon hockey were the Pinder brothers, Herb and Gerry. The Pinder family was involved in the drugstore business in Saskatoon for years. In 1964 Herb and his younger brother Gerry began their junior hockey career with the brand new Blades franchise in the Saskatchewan Junior Hockey League. They finished that season as the top two scorers on the team. When the Canadian Major Junior Hockey League began operations in 1966, Saskatoon signed on and the Pinders were still on the roster. The Blades didn't do so well, finishing fifth out of seven teams, but the Pinders gave the fans their money's worth. The brothers combined on a line with Bernie Blanchette to terrorize the league's netminders. Gerry led all scorers with 78 goals and 140 points, winning the scoring title. Herb finished third in the scoring parade and accumulated a league-leading 75 assists. Both brothers appeared in the all-star game that year and Gerry won MVP honours at the end of the season.

Gerry's biggest night came on March 12, 1967, when he scored six

Blades scoring ace Gerry Pinder.

goals and added four assists in a 17–5 shellacking of the woeful Calgary Buffaloes. The Buffaloes only won four games that season, the fewest wins ever posted by a WHL team. Gerry's ten points in a single game has been matched several times but never bettered.

In 1967 the Pinders joined Canada's Olympic team in Winnipeg where they attended classes at the University of Manitoba. The coach at the time was Jackie McLeod, later the part-owner, coach and general manager of the Blades. Herb tore up his knee while he was with the Olympic program and, after a brief spell with the Vancouver Canucks in the old Western Professional Hockey League, he retired from hockey and returned to school. He graduated from Harvard to become a lawyer and player agent back in his native Saskatoon.

After two seasons with the Olympic team, Gerry Pinder turned professional with the Chicago Blackhawks in 1969. He played two seasons with Chicago, and another with the California Golden Seals, before jumping to the World Hockey Association in 1972. He played in the WHA with Cleveland, San Diego and Edmonton before retiring during the 1977–78 season to operate Gerly Holdings, a real estate development company in Calgary.

There is a third Pinder brother, Tom, the youngest of the clan. He played at centre for the Blades 1970–72, then graduated to the International Hockey League for a brief professional career. Like his brother Gerry, he became a businessman in Calgary.

Bernie Federko

Foam Lake, Saskatchewan, may not be much more than a dot on the Yellowhead Highway east of Saskatoon but it has produced some remarkable hockey talent. Former Detroit standout Dennis Polonich was born in Foam Lake. So was Pat Elynuik, the all-star from Prince Albert, now playing in the NHL with the Washington Capitals. And so was the finest player ever to skate in a Saskatoon uniform, Bernie Federko.

Federko began his celebrated three-year career with the Blades in

1973, but he came of age as a scorer in his sophomore season, 1974–75, when he teamed with Blair Chapman on right wing and Danny Arndt on left wing. Saskatoon made the first of two consecutive trips to the league finals that year, losing to New Westminster in seven games. Federko led all scorers with 15 goals in 17 playoff games. The following season, his third and last in the WHL, his wingers were Chapman and Neil Hawryliw. The trio led the Blades back into the playoffs for another losing confrontation with New Westminster. Federko finished the season with 72 goals in as many games and 187 total points to win the scoring race. He was a member of the first all-star team and won the league's Most-Valuable-Player award. In the playoffs he, Chapman and Hawryliw finished one-two-three in scoring. At the time, Federko held league records for most points in a single season, most points in a single playoff season, 45, most assists in a single playoff season, 27, and most goals in one playoff period, three.

Bernie Federko was the finest Saskatoon grad.

The St. Louis Blues drafted Federko seventh overall in the 1976 amateur draft. After a season in the Central Hockey League with the Blues' Kansas City farm team, where he won Rookie-of-the-Year honours, Federko joined the parent club where he remained for the next 13 years. He posted seven 30-goal seasons with the Blues and holds most of the team's all-time individual scoring records, including most career goals (352), most career assists (721) and most career points (1073).

In 1989 Federko was traded to Detroit where he played one more season, then retired. He now lives in Chesterfield, Missouri, where he works for a television station and owns a restaurant. In the summer of 1993, Federko started a coaching career with the St. Louis Vipers of the new Roller Hockey International League.

Wendel Clark

No player in recent seasons has come out of the Saskatoon Blades organization and made a greater impact in the NHL than the Maple Leafs' hard-driving winger, Wendel Clark. A native of Kelvington, Sas-

173

katchewan, Clark played midget hockey at the famous Notre Dame College in Wilcox, Saskatchewan. He joined the Blades in 1983 as a defenceman and played two seasons in Saskatoon. The team finished under .500 during his stay but Clark was a standout. He made the first all-star team during 1984–85 and was named the league's top defenceman. At the Christmas break that season he helped the Canadian Junior National Team win a gold medal at the World Championships in Finland.

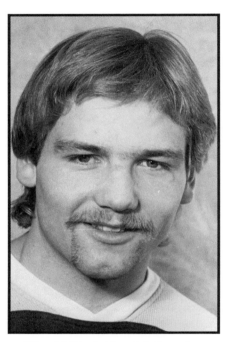

Wendel Clark played defence for the Saskatoon Blades.

Toronto chose Clark first overall in the 1985 NHL draft. He did not take long to prove the Maple Leafs had made a wise choice. Converted from defence to left wing, he established a club record for rookies by scoring a team-high 34 goals and was selected Rookie of the Year by both *The Sporting News* and *The Hockey News*. In his sophomore season Clark played in every game and increased his scoring total to 37 goals.

Clark only knows how to play at one speed, full ahead, and his aggressive style has brought him into contact with a lot of heavy hitters. As a result, injuries have plagued his NHL career since the 1987–88 season. Nonetheless, he was named captain of the Maple Leafs in 1991 and, despite persistent trade rumours, when he is healthy he remains a potent part of Toronto's offense. Despite scoring only 39 points in 66 games in 1992–93, Clark proved with his strong physical presence and apt scoring touch in the '93 playoffs (20 points in 20 games) that he is still one of the few players in the NHL that can totally dominate a game, with or without the puck.

SEATTLE

The Seattle Thunderbirds

Major junior hockey arrived in Seattle in 1977 when Ephraim Steinke, owner of the Kamloops Chiefs, moved his franchise south of the border. The first WHL team in Washington State, the Breakers, as they were known for eight seasons, finished their inaugural campaign with a creditable 32–28–12 record, better than half of the teams in the league yet not good enough to make the playoffs in their own division. Since that time the Seattle franchise has rarely finished above .500 and is still looking for its first divisional pennant. Nonetheless, fan support has grown steadily, especially when the Tacoma Rockets come to town, and Seattle has produced some standout individual performers who have gone on to star in the NHL.

The first top draft pick to play in Seattle was Ryan Walter, the six-foot centre from Burnaby, BC. Walter began in the WHL with Kamloops, then moved with the franchise to Seattle in 1977. After an exceptional 1977–78 season—he was WHL Player of the Year, the Most Valuable Player, and a starting all-star—Walter went second overall in the 1978 amateur draft. The next potential superstar to come out of Seattle was Petr Nedved. No other junior player ever created as much excitement in Seattle as the young Czech defector from Litvinov, and the Vancouver Canucks took him second overall in the 1990 draft, where he and Walter played together for the Canucks, one in the twilight of a long career, the other just beginning to prove how good he can be.

For all the success of Walter and Nedved, some of the most heralded players in Seattle history were largely overlooked in the NHL draft. The fact that neither Glen Goodall nor Craig Endean was a high

GRADUATES TO THE NHL

Seattle Breakers

1978: **Ryan Walter**—Washington, Montreal, Vancouver. **Dwayne Lowdermilk**—NY Islanders, Washington. **Peter Dineen**—Los Angeles, Detroit.

1979: **Errol Rausse**—Washington. **Tim Hunter**—Atlanta, Calgary, Quebec, Vancouver.

1980: **Joe Ward**—Colorado. **Glenn Anderson**—Edmonton, Toronto.

1981: **Wayne Van Dorp**—Edmonton, Pittsburgh, Chicago, Quebec.

1982: **Ken Daneyko**—New Jersey. **Mitch Wilson**—New Jersey, Pittsburgh. **Steve Dykstra**—Buffalo, Edmonton, Pittsburgh, Hartford.

1984: **Brent Severyn**—Winnipeg, Quebec.

1985: **Jamie Huscroft**—New Jersey.

Seattle Thunderbirds

1986: **Craig Endean**—Winnipeg.

1987: **Chris Joseph**—Pittsburgh, Edmonton. **Matt Hervey**—Winnipeg, Boston, Tampa Bay. **Shawn Chambers**—Minnesota, Washington, Tampa Bay.

1988: **Trevor Sim**—Edmonton. **Danny Lorenz**—NY Islanders.

1990: **Petr Nedved**—Vancouver. **Turner Stevenson**—Montreal.

1991: **Dody Wood**—San Jose.

pick has to be attributed to their small size; their skill level was certainly never in question. Goodall was playing major hockey in Seattle at the age of 14 and holds the all-time WHL mark for most games played in the league (399). It is one record that probably will never be broken since players are now restricted from playing in the league until they are at least 16. Goodall, who played for Seattle from 1984 to 1990, also was the WHL all-time career scoring leader with 573 points, until Tri-City forward Brian Sakic eclipsed the record in 1992. Despite these statistics, Goodall was a 10th-round draft pick by the Detroit Red Wings and has yet to make a name for himself in the NHL. Craig Endean put in three seasons in Seattle, turning into one of the league's most prolific goal scorers, before finishing his junior career with the Regina Pats. Like Goodall, Endean was drafted fairly low, in the fifth round by the Winnipeg Jets, and failed to make the transition to the NHL.

Slightly more fortunate was goaltender Danny Lorenz, a third-round pick of the New York Islanders in 1988. Lorenz, a two-time all-star and in 1988–89 the league's top goalie, holds many career records for the Seattle organization, including best goals-against average (3.60). His career 224 games played is the most by any goaltender in WHL history.

As far as first-round NHL draft picks go, six of the seven to come out of Seattle have come since 1987, testimony to the growing on-ice success of the franchise. Three went to Montreal—Lindsay Vallis in 1989, Turner Stevenson in 1990 and Brent Bilodeau in 1991. As well, defenceman Chris Joseph was drafted fifth overall by Pittsburgh in 1987 and tough rearguard Brendan Witt was taken 11th overall by Washington in 1993.

The mid-1980s marked a turning point for the Breakers franchise. In 1985 Earl Hale bought the struggling team and, as part of a new look, he changed the name to the Thunderbirds. Then, in 1988, the new owners brought in the proven winning combination of Russ Farwell as general manager and Barry Melrose as coach. The two had worked together to bring a Memorial Cup to Medicine Hat in 1987–88 and although their stay in Seattle was brief they instilled some of their winning tradition in the franchise.

Seattle's best season came in 1989–90, with Peter Anholt coaching a team that boasted Goodall with 76 goals, rookie sensation Nedved with 65 and 64 from Victor Gervais. They finished second overall in the standings, but dropped the division final to Kamloops. (Not long after the franchise left for Seattle, Kamloops had returned to the league, first as the Junior Oilers and now as the Blazers.) While Portland and Tacoma are their biggest rivals and best fan draws, it is ironic that Kamloops, the town that gave them birth, should be the Thunderbirds' biggest nemesis over the years. In playoff action, Seattle has a record of 2–19 against the Blazers. At the end of the 1991–92 season, the Thunderbirds made it to the Memorial Cup in Seattle as the host team. In that year's playoffs they made it to the West Division final where they were eliminated by Kamloops, who also went on to take them out of the Memorial Cup and win it themselves. The Blazers have been such an adversary to Seattle, that after their local team was eliminated at the 1992 Memorial Cup, Seattle fans jumped on the bandwagon of the Sault Ste. Marie Greyhounds rather than cheer for the western team, Kamloops.

Despite its lack of playoff success to date, the Seattle franchise is showing signs of gaining the continuity of management that helps to build long-term success on the ice.

Ryan Walter

Born in New Westminster, BC, in 1958, Ryan Walter played his minor hockey in the neighbouring municipality of Burnaby. When he was 15 he joined the Langley Lords of the BC Junior Hockey League where he enjoyed two outstanding seasons before graduating to the Kamloops Chiefs of the WHL. Walter spent two full seasons in Kamloops, 1975–76 and 1976–77, posting respectable numbers with the team. During his second season he was captain of a league all-star team which won a Christmas tournament against junior teams from Quebec, Ontario and the Soviet Union.

Before the 1977–78 season the Chiefs franchise moved to Seattle to be re-born as the Breakers, so Ryan Walter completed his junior career in the American city. And what a year it was. As captain of the Breakers, he scored 54 goals and added 71 assists to finish ninth in the scoring race. Seattle finished out of the playoffs, but Walter was chosen Most Valuable Player in the league as well as WHL Player of the Year. He was also captain of the 1978 Canadian junior team at the World Junior Hockey Championships in Montreal.

Washington chose Walter second overall in the 1978 draft, right behind top pick Bobby Smith, who went to Minnesota. In his first season with the Capitals he scored 28 goals and was runner-up to Smith in the voting for NHL Rookie of the Year. The next year he was named the team captain, despite the fact he was only 21 years old. Walter's best season in the NHL was 1981–82 when he scored 38 goals. The Capitals traded him to Montreal that summer along with Rick Green for four players and he spent nine solid seasons with the Canadiens, including the Stanley Cup winning year of 1986.

Montreal released Walter following the 1990–91 season, when he went scoreless in 25 games. He signed on with the Vancouver Canucks as a free agent and although he stopped showing the scoring punch of his younger days, he gave the team valuable leadership. In May 1992, Walter was named NHL Man of the Year for his sportsmanship and extensive community service work.

Seattle MVP Ryan Walter, second from left.

Craig Endean

From the beginning of his hockey career as a young player in Prince George, BC, Craig Endean has been a gifted natural scorer. As a 14-year-old bantam player, he accumulated an incredible 278 scoring points for the Prince George Chieftains and led the team to the Western Canadian bantam championship in Winnipeg in April 1983. In the tournament's final round, Craig was chosen the first star in three games and in the sudden-death game, he scored three times as the Prince George side defeated the Red Deer Moose Chiefs.

In 1983–84 Endean became the first 15-year-old to crack the starting lineup for the Seattle Breakers. "His moves are incredible and his hockey sense is unbelievable," marvelled Jake Goertzen, Seattle's director of player personnel. Still young enough to be playing bantam, Endean got into 67 games with the Breakers and even contributed a couple of goals in the team's first-round playoff loss to Kamloops.

The next season, 1984–85, Endean became more comfortable in Seattle and his point total blossomed to 97, tied for the team lead with right-winger Scott Robinson. As his draft year approached, there was much talk that Endean would become Seattle's first-ever number one draft pick. He did not go quite that high, but after he scored 58 goals and 70 assists during the 1985–86 campaign the Winnipeg Jets picked him 92nd overall in the draft.

Craig Endean was one of the WHL's great scorers.

Endean was still young enough to spend two more seasons in the WHL. At the conclusion of his draft year, Seattle traded him to Regina where he really came into his own as a scorer. In 1986–87 he notched 136 points and won the East Division scoring title. He also won the league's most sportsmanlike player award and a place on the second all-star team. The Jets brought him up to the NHL for two games and he managed to collect an assist, little realizing at the time that these would be the only two NHL games he would ever play.

After one more season with Regina, during which he made the divisional all-star team and finished seventh in league scoring, Endean went to the Jets training camp but failed to make the team. He divided the 1988–89 season between the Moncton Hawks and the Fort Wayne Komets of the International Hockey League. During the next season the Jets released him and he signed on as a free agent to play briefly with Adirondack in the American Hockey League. The Philadelphia Flyers gave him an opportunity to make the team at their 1990 training camp, but before long he found himself back in Prince George without an organization to play for. The Minnesota North Stars gave Endean one more chance at the NHL during their training camp preceding the 1991–92 season, but once again, he was an early cut from the roster. From 1991–1993, Craig played in the East Coast Hockey League for Doug Sauter's Winston-Salem Thunderbirds and the Roanoke Valley Rampage. He returned to the league in 1993–94 as a member of the new Charlotte Checkers franchise.

Glen Goodall

Glen Goodall played for Seattle from 1984 to 1990, six seasons in which he established Western Hockey League records for most games played (399), most goals scored (262) and most points (573). Brian Sakic broke his career points record in 1992, but it is doubtful whether the games and goals marks will ever be surpassed, not because there will never be another player as good as Goodall but because it is unlikely another player will ever spend as long in the junior ranks.

A native of Fort Nelson, BC, Goodall skated into the WHL with Seattle in the fall of 1984 when he was just 14 years old. Not only was he young—boys that age are no longer permitted to play in the league—but he was also skinny and only grew to be 5'8". Nonetheless, he turned out to be a dazzling goal scorer, the most prolific the Seattle franchise has ever seen. Four times in his WHL career Goodall scored more than 50 goals in a season. His best year was 1989–90 when the Thunderbirds finished second overall in regular season play, and Goodall scored 76 times to come second in the scoring race behind Len Barrie of Kamloops. He started at centre ice for the West Division all-star team that year, and was named the league's Most Valuable Player.

The Seattle Thunderbirds retired Goodall's uniform when his WHL career finally ended, yet none of his junior heroics translated into a job in the NHL. The Detroit Red Wings chose him in the tenth round of the 1988 draft but sent him to their American Hockey League affiliate. In 1991 he signed as a free agent with the New York Rangers but so far he has remained in the minor pro leagues, with teams like the Adirondack Red Wings, Binghamton Rangers, San Diego Gulls and Erie Panthers, waiting for his chance in the big show.

Russ Farwell

Russ Farwell's career in hockey began in the 1970s in Terrace, BC, when he showed up for tryouts for a team Scotty Munro was operating as an affiliate of his Calgary WHL franchise. During the 1974–75 season Farwell ended up playing one game with another Calgary affiliate, the Pass Red Devils of the Alberta Junior Hockey League, but Munro recognized early on that the young man did not possess the on-ice skills to succeed as a player.

There was something about Farwell, though—his enthusiasm perhaps, and his willingness to do just about anything to stay in hockey—that made Munro think that he might have a future in some team's front office.

By the late 1970s Farwell was a coach of the Calgary Canucks in the Alberta Junior circuit. The 1981–82 season found him in Billings, Montana, as a member of the Bighorns executive. Pressed into service behind the bench, he coached the team to a first-round loss in the playoffs.

At the end of that season the Billings franchise closed its doors and Russ Farwell was on his way to Medicine Hat as general manager. In his six years with the Tigers he hired four different coaches, but despite the revolving door behind the bench Farwell had tremendous success with the franchise. His teams reached the East Division finals five times, won back-to-back Memorial Cup titles in 1987 and 1988, and compiled a 281–135–16 record for a .699 winning percentage.

After the second Memorial Cup, Farwell received an offer to join the Seattle Thunderbirds organization as general manager. During his two years in Seattle the team went 85–52–7; following the 1989–90 season Farwell received the Lloyd Saunders Trophy as the WHL's top executive.

On June 6, 1990, Farwell was named general manager of the Philadelphia Flyers. It was the first time an NHL general manager had jumped directly from the junior ranks since Wren Blair went from the Oshawa Generals to Minnesota back in 1967.

Farwell will always be remembered as the general manager who landed Eric Lindros. Selected first overall in the 1991 NHL entry draft, Lindros refused to report to Quebec City. After prolonged negotiations, Farwell acquired the budding superstar in exchange for five players, a future draft pick, future considerations and $15 million US.

Time will tell whether the Lindros trade and other moves work the same magic for the Flyers as Farwell managed during his championship years in Medicine Hat.

Petr Nedved

It was Christmas, 1988, and Petr Nedved was in Calgary playing in a midget hockey tournament with his team from Litvinov, Czechoslovakia.

Almost no one else knew that while the tournament was taking place, young Nedved was hatching a plan to defect to the West. On January 2, while the other players travelled back to Czechoslovakia, Nedved walked away from his team and his native country and asked for refugee status in Canada. Before the winter was over he was playing hockey for the Calgary franchise in the Alberta Junior Hockey League and in June, 1989, the Canadian government granted him landed immigrant status.

Born in 1971 in the small town of Liberec, Czechoslovakia, Nedved learned his hockey from his father Jaroslav, who was a local coach. (Nedved has a brother playing defence in the Czech first division.) When he defected, his rights belonged to the Moose Jaw Warriors of the WHL but it was felt that Nedved would be able to adjust more easily to North American life in a larger city and so the Warriors traded him to Seattle where he started for the Thunderbirds as the 1989–90 season began.

Nedved became a WHL superstar almost overnight. He finished his only season in the league with 145 points, a rookie record. His 80 assists tied another rookie mark. He finished sixth in the league in scoring and played for the West Division in the WHL all-star game, where he notched a goal and an assist. Not surprisingly he was named Rookie of the Year in both the WHL and the Canadian Hockey League.

Vancouver chose Nedved second overall in the 1990 amateur draft, right behind Owen Nolan from the Cornwall Royals. Much has been made of how he has emulated Wayne Gretzky in his style of play. The Canucks brought him along slowly and he disappointed many fans with his weak upper-body strength, inconsistency and immaturity in his first two seasons. In the 1992–93 season he silenced his critics, scoring 38 times and establishing himself as the team's second-best goal-scorer after Pavel Bure.

SPOKANE

The Spokane Chiefs

Junior hockey got off to a shaky start in Spokane in 1980. The previous season the Great Falls Americans had tried to make a go of it as a WHL expansion franchise in the Montana city, and had failed after 28 games. Reorganized as the Spokane Flyers, the franchise struggled to a 17–54–1 record in its first year. The Flyers name was a throwback to the glory days of the Western International Hockey League in the city when the senior Flyers won four Allan Cup senior hockey titles. But the junior Flyers were a different story indeed, and after winning just three of 26 games in the early going of the 1981–82 season, the franchise folded.

By this time, however, the success of WHL teams in Portland and Seattle was proving that the future for league expansion lay south of the border and in 1985 Spokane got a second chance. This time it was the Kelowna Wings franchise that was in trouble. After three seasons in the league the Wings were icing a competitive team, but the Kelowna arena was proving too small for a successful franchise. At the beginning of the 1985–86 season the Wings were reborn as the Spokane Chiefs.

From 1985 to 1990 the Chiefs enjoyed modest success, recording two winning seasons and once, in 1987–88, advancing as far as the West Division finals. But nothing prepared Spokane fans for the season of 1990–91. It was a year of spectacular success in which the Chiefs broke nearly every team and individual record and steam-rolled all opposition in one of the most awesome runs to the Memorial Cup ever seen.

The season began with new ownership. George Brett, the future hall-of-fame baseball player, and his brother Bob purchased the franchise in 1990 and brought an enthusiastic spirit to a team already blessed with

GRADUATES TO THE NHL

Spokane Chiefs

1987: **Mick Vukota**—NY Islanders.
1988: **Link Gaetz**—Minnesota, San Jose. **Darcy Loewen**—Buffalo, Ottawa.
1989: **Travis Green**—NY Islanders.
1991: **Pat Falloon**—San Jose. **Ray Whitney**—San Jose. **Steve Junker**—NY Islanders. **Jon Klemm**—Quebec.
1992: **Valeri Bure**—Montreal.

head coach Bryan Maxwell, a veteran skipper who had led Medicine Hat to the Memorial Cup in 1987. Maxwell had some exceptional talent to work with. Pat Falloon, in his third season, established the franchise record for goals in a career (146) and won the Brad Hornung Trophy for most sportsmanlike player. Ray Whitney led all scorers in the league, with 67 goals and 118 assists, setting team records for career assists (207) and total points (348) and finishing the season as WHL Most Valuable Player and Player of the Year. On defence, Kerry Toporowski set a team single-season mark for penalty minutes (505) and in goal, Scott Bailey registered four shutouts. To ensure a successful post-season, the Chiefs traded some young prospects to Brandon for Trevor Kidd, arguably the best junior netminder in Canada.

After finishing the regular 1990–91 season in second place behind the Kamloops Blazers, the Chiefs embarked on one of the most impressive playoff runs in major junior hockey history. In the opening round the team dropped one game to the Seattle Thunderbirds, then did not lose another game in post-season play. They blanked Kamloops in the West Division final, captured the WHL pennant with a 4–0 sweep of Lethbridge, then posted four straight victories at the Memorial Cup tournament. The Chiefs not only went unbeaten at the Memorial Cup, they were invincible. Out-scoring their opponents 27–9, their closest game was the 5–1 championship victory over Drummondville.

Falloon and Whitney were outstanding. Falloon was the tournament MVP and won the scoring title, just ahead of linemate Whitney who was voted the tournament's most sportsmanlike player. Falloon at right wing, Whitney at centre and Brent Thurston on left wing formed the starting forward line on the Memorial Cup first all-star team. So impressed were the NHL expansion San Jose Sharks that they snapped up three Spokane players in the June draft—Falloon, Whitney and Toporowski. Steve Junker and Brent Thurston escaped the Sharks; taken by the New York Islanders and the Vancouver Canucks respectively. Highlights for the Chiefs after 1991 included finishing second in the West Division in 1991--92, producing seven NHL draft picks in 1992, Valeri Bure finishing second in league scoring in 1992–93, upsetting the Tacoma Rockets in the 1993 WHL playoffs, and having Bure, Maxim Bets and Bryan McCabe being picked in the first two rounds of the draft.

Junior hockey took root firmly in Spokane. Attendance in 1991–92 jumped by 30%, solidifying plans for a new 12,000-seat arena in 1995.

Ray Whitney

Ray Whitney began playing bantam hockey in his hometown of Fort Saskatchewan, Alberta, during the winter of 1987–88. In a 71-game schedule, young Ray scored 80 goals and added 155 assists. Playing as a centre, he even found time to spend 119 minutes in the penalty box. At 5'8", 150 pounds, he was not a big player, but that did not discourage the scouts of the Spokane Chiefs who spotted Ray as a "can't miss" prospect.

As a WHL rookie in 1988–89 Whitney scored 17 times and registered 50 points. That same winter Pat Falloon joined the Chiefs and the two rookies met instant success, playing together on the same line. In 1989–90 Whitney netted 57 goals, and then in the magical 1990–91 season he exploded for 67, finishing at the top of the league scoring race. The scoring championship was just one of several honours he took home that season. He was the league's Most Valuable Player, starting centre on the West Division all-star team, leading scorer in the playoffs, Most Sportsmanlike Player in the Memorial Cup tournament and, finally, WHL Molson/Cooper Player of the Year.

In June 1991, Whitney was the first player selected in the second round of the NHL amateur draft, by the expansion San Jose Sharks. It was something of a Chiefs reunion in San Jose, as the Sharks also selected Pat Falloon and Kerry Toporowski and added Murray Garbutt in the 1991 dispersal draft. Whitney balked at signing a contract with the Sharks and headed over to Europe to play professionally in Cologne, Germany. It was a disappointing experience and he returned to North America before the end of November, signing as a free agent with Don Waddell's San Diego Gulls of the International Hockey League. The Gulls were an independent team with a reputation for free spending. In San Diego, Whitney scored 90 points in 63 games, impressing the Sharks enough to sign him to a multi-year contract in April 1992. Whitney had a disappointing rookie season with the Sharks, amassing only 10 points in 26 games and being sent to San Jose's farm team in Kansas City, where he scored 53 points in 45 games.

Pat Falloon

Born on September 22, 1972, in Birtle, Manitoba, Pat Falloon was raised on a farm near Foxwarren. He learned his skating skills on the frozen sloughs of southwestern Manitoba and in 1987–88 was playing midget hockey with the Yellowhead Chiefs of the Manitoba Triple A League. In just 52 games as a 15-year-old he scored 74 goals and added 69 assists. Yet somehow the hometown Brandon Wheat Kings failed to spot him and the Spokane Chiefs snapped up his rights in a trade with Regina.

The Chiefs were not sure that Falloon, at age 16, was quite ready to make the jump to junior hockey, leaving home, as he was, for the first time and moving across the border to the United States. But he adjusted with relative ease and won Rookie-of-the-Year honours that first season, finishing with 22 goals and 78 points. Falloon's scoring touch really showed itself in 1989–90, when he played right wing on a line with Ray Whitney and piled up 124 points.

Falloon's last year in a Spokane uniform was the dream year of 1990–91, when the Chiefs won the national championship. He finished fourth in league scoring that season, was named to the West Division all-star team and was chosen the most sportsmanlike player in all of Canada. In the Memorial Cup tournament he tied a record by scoring eight goals and was named the tournament MVP. As well, he was a member of the gold-medal-winning national team which won the World Junior Hockey Championship in Saskatoon.

The San Jose Sharks picked Falloon second overall behind Eric

Pat Falloon accepts silverware from league president Chynoweth.

Lindros of the Oshawa Generals at the 1991 entry draft. He went on to enjoy an excellent 1991–92 rookie campaign in the NHL with the Sharks, leading them in scoring with 25 goals and 34 assists. Mainly due to a shoulder injury, his numbers went way down in the 1992–93 season, but the Sharks were still counting on Falloon to be a major contributor in the years ahead.

Bryan Maxwell

Bryan Maxwell, coach of the Spokane Chiefs, has had two careers in the WHL. First of all, in the early 1970s, he was a hard-nosed defenceman for the Medicine Hat Tigers. Then, after a professional career that spanned eight NHL seasons and four teams, he returned to the junior league as a coach, becoming one of the few coaches in junior hockey to lead two different franchises to Memorial Cup wins.

Born in North Bay, Ontario, Maxwell grew up in Lethbridge, Alberta, and joined the Medicine Hat Tigers in the middle of the 1972–73 season when coach Jack Shupe spotted him playing in the Alberta Junior Hockey League. During two and a half years in Medicine Hat, the muscular Maxwell amassed a sizeable number of penalty minutes and was never known to back away from a fight. On one famous occasion in Winnipeg, with Medicine Hat losing 5–0 to the Clubs, Tiger centre Ryan Wecker took a spear to the cheek from Winnipeg's Paul Baxter. Thinking the attack was instigated by Clubs coach Gerry Brisson, Maxwell fired the puck at the Winnipeg bench, hitting a player and narrowly missing the coach. Then he advanced on the bench, stick swinging. The inevitable bench-clearing brawl ensued and both teams were banished to the dressing room to cool down. Eight players were gone from the game when play resumed.

When he left Medicine Hat in 1975, Maxwell joined the Cleveland Crusaders of the World Hockey Association. Over

3. BRYAN MAXWELL

Spokane coach Bryan Maxwell played for four NHL teams.

the next ten years he made enough stops with enough teams to publish his own road map. In the WHA he played for Cleveland and Cincinnati. In the NHL he played for Minnesota, St. Louis, Winnipeg and Pittsburgh. And his minor-league itinerary included Springfield, Binghamton, Oklahoma City, Salt Lake City and Baltimore.

Released by the Pittsburgh Penguins in 1985, Maxwell launched his coaching career back in Medicine Hat as an assistant to Doug Sauter. Within a year he was the head coach and in his inaugural season behind the bench, 1986–87, took the Tigers to the league championship and then to the Memorial Cup. The Tigers repeated as national champions in 1988, but by that time Maxwell was in Los Angeles working as an assistant coach with the Kings. He remained in the City of Angels for two seasons, including the beginning of the Wayne Gretzky era, then returned to junior ranks, this time with Spokane.

In his first year in Spokane, 1989–90, the Chiefs finished well back in the standings but since then Maxwell has enjoyed tremendous success with the team. In 1991 he led Spokane to his second Memorial Cup championship, then in 1992 won WHL Coach-of-the-Year honours with a team that finished second in its division.

Valeri Bure

The first Russian-born junior to play in the WHL, Valeri Bure played with the famous Red Army team before coming to North America and joining the Spokane roster for the 1991–92 season. Valeri is the brother of Vancouver Canucks scoring sensation Pavel Bure, the "Russian Rocket," and hockey observers think that the younger Bure is very similar in style. "If he's anything like his brother," says Vancouver coach and general manager Pat Quinn, "there's not too much to worry about."

In the meantime Valeri has been developing quickly on right wing for Spokane. He finished his rookie season with 27 goals and a total of 49 points in 53 games, but really proved himself in the playoffs, leading the team with 11 goals and 17 points in 10 games. Afterwards, the Montreal Canadiens drafted him 33rd overall. Pat Quinn was criticized by some Vancouver fans for not taking Pavel's brother with the Canucks' first-round pick (21st overall) and after Valeri's improved 1992–93 campaign, he probably wishes that he did. In his sophomore year in the WHL, 1992–93, Bure scored 147 points to become the league's second-highest scorer for a Spokane team which finished well below .500. His 68 goals broke Ray Whitney's record for the most goals by a Chief in one season.

Valeri's stats seemed to indicate hockey fans were going to be treated to another "Pocket Rocket" in the NHL.

SWIFT CURRENT

The Swift Current Broncos

The history of the Swift Current Broncos neatly divides into two parts. Part one saw the Broncos join the WHL in 1967 and play in the league for the next seven seasons. Swift Current was the smallest city in the world to have a major junior hockey franchise and, given the population base, it became harder and harder to support the team. In 1974 the club was forced to leave the city. But a few dedicated hockey people refused to let the dream die and after persistent negotiating the Broncos returned to Swift Current in 1986 to begin part two of their story. After scrambling to get the team back, the city was stunned by a tragic accident which claimed four young lives, then marvelled as the team bounced back to win a national championship. Tragedy and triumph—it could have been scripted in Hollywood.

The original Broncos were a pretty mediocre team. Only once between 1967 and 1974 did they win more games than they lost, and that was in their last season, 1973–74, when they made it to the second round of the playoffs. Still, some fine young players with dreams of playing professionally passed through Swift Current. Gene Peacosh scored 52 goals and 100 points during the franchise's first season, good enough for sixth spot in the league scoring race. And that was for a team, under coach Harvey Roy, that only scored 242 goals and only won 16 games. The next big-time scorer to come along was Don Kozak, who later played seven NHL seasons with Los Angeles and Vancouver. His 74 points, including 40 goals, ranked him tenth in the league in 1969–70. The following year Ken Tarnow, a left-winger, struck for 52 goals. Defenceman Joe Zanussi played three seasons in the NHL but is famous among

GRADUATES TO THE NHL

Swift Current Broncos

1968: **Joe Zanussi**—NY Rangers, Boston, St. Louis.
1969: **Dave Schultz**—Philadelphia, Los Angeles, Pittsburgh, Buffalo.
Brian Spinner"Spencer—Toronto, NY Islanders, Buffalo, Pittsburgh.
1971: **Larry Giroux**—St. Louis, Kansas City, Detroit, Hartford.
1973: **Kelly Pratt**—Pittsburgh.
1974: **Bryan Trottier**—NY Islanders, Pittsburgh. **Dave "Tiger" Williams**—Toronto, Vancouver, Detroit, Los Angeles, Hartford. **Terry Ruskowski**—Chicago, Los Angeles, Pittsburgh, Minnesota.
1987: **Joe Sakic**—Quebec. **Ryan McGill**—Chicago, Philadelphia. **Bob Wilkie**—Detroit.
1988: **Sheldon Kennedy**—Detroit.
1989: **Dan Lambert**—Quebec.
1990: **Geoff Sanderson**—Hartford. **Kimbi Daniels**—Philadelphia.
1991: **Tyler Wright**—Edmonton.

trivia buffs for being the third man offered by the New York Rangers, along with Brad Park and Jean Ratelle in 1975, to acquire Phil Esposito and Carol Vadnais from Boston. The Broncos had some standout goaltenders in their time as well. Probably the finest was Roger Kosar, who played there from 1968 to 1971, though Bill Oleschuk and Henry Durkin also come to mind.

Curiously, the best Broncos team was also the last, at least for the early years. The 1973–74 club was led by Terry Ruskowski, who finished fifth in the scoring race that season, Tiger Williams, a 52-goal scorer, rookie Bryan Trottier, who added 41 goals, and big right-winger and future NHLer Ron Delorme. Stan Dunn won Coach-of-the-Year honours for guiding the Broncos to a third-place finish in their division. In the first round of the playoffs they edged past Flin Flon four games to three, bringing them face to face with the powerful Regina Pats and their scoring ace, Dennis Sobchuk. Swift Current lost four games to two but they didn't go quietly. In the fifth game of the series, Regina leading 6–2, Tiger Williams was serving a penalty when he charged out of the box into the stands after an obnoxious fan. The bench followed and it took 50 police officers half an hour to get the teams into their dressing rooms. Play finally resumed with the Broncos bench surrounded by badges and blue uniforms. After the game Williams, Terry Ruskowski and Ron Delorme were slapped with assault charges and eventually fined.

Regina went on to win the Memorial Cup that spring while the Broncos returned home to a state of uncertainty. Rumours that the team was going to move away from Swift Current recurred after every season. It was no secret that the franchise, controlled by majority owner Bill Burton, was in financial trouble, always had been. The arena only sat 2500 fans and the city only had 15,000 people. Lethbridge, on the other hand, a community without a major junior franchise, was building a two-million-dollar sports centre for the 1975 Canada Winter Games. Burton asked for, and received, league permission to move and on May 6, 1974, it was official: the Broncos would be playing in Lethbridge in 1974–75.

For the next decade, hockey fans in Swift Current had to be content with watching Tier II Saskatchewan Junior Hockey League play. The SJHL Broncos, with Dunn coaching and Willie Desjardins sniping goals, won the league title in 1974–75. In 1984 that franchise, too, disappeared, replaced by the Swift Current Indians under head coach Pat Ginnell.

Through it all, local hockey enthusiast John Rittinger was working hard behind the scenes to bring a major junior franchise back to the city. Along with a few others, Rittinger organized a sale of shares and collected $250,000 to begin the hunt for a team. Kelowna, Calgary, Seattle, Kamloops, Winnipeg, New Westminster, Victoria, Regina and Brandon; all at one time were targeted for a move to Swift Current and all, for one reason or another, fell through. Rittinger and his group came very close with Seattle but at the last minute the league decided it did not want to lose a team from the West Division and bought the Seattle franchise itself. Another close call involved the Winnipeg Warriors, who were planning to transfer to Moose Jaw. Backers in Moose Jaw were having difficulty coming up with the money, however, so Rittinger stepped in. Two days short of the deadline, Moose Jaw found the money and Swift Current lost the Warriors.

Perhaps the most interesting might-have-been was in 1985 when Rittinger came close to landing the Regina Pats, the oldest junior hockey franchise in the world. Herb Pinder Jr., the owner of the Pats, was having trouble with the Regina Exhibition Association, which controlled the arena, and wanted to sell. It was all arranged to move the team to Swift Current over Christmas and play out the rest of the season there. Once again the league stepped in at the last minute, buying the Pats and reselling them to a group of Regina businessmen.

It began to look as if the Swift Current group was fated to be frustrated in its search for a team when suddenly the wheel came full circle and Rittinger began hearing rumours of problems in Lethbridge. At first the Lethbridge Broncos' owner, Dennis Kjeldgaard, offered to sell half the franchise, dividing up the team so that there would be teams in both Lethbridge and Swift Current. Pat Ginnell jumped at this offer, but Rittinger wanted the whole loaf. After long negotiations the price was set at $375,000 and on April 11, 1986, the Broncos moved back to Swift Current.

Almost immediately the new owners signed 33-year-old Graham James as head coach and general manager of the revitalized Broncos. Despite his youth, James was a junior hockey veteran. He had scouted for Saskatoon, Flin Flon and Winnipeg and had coached at the Tier II level in Manitoba. He was a promoter of the finesse game, preferring speed and skill to the rough stuff. Let the other team take the penalties, then apply the knock-out blow with your power play; that was his philosophy. And it worked. In 1986–87, his first season in Swift Current, the Broncos were the least-penalized team in the WHL. The following season they repeated; the closest team to them averaged 17.7 penalty minutes more per game. And in 1988–89 the Broncos' power play struck for a record 180 goals in 526 chances for a 34.2% success rate. In one game the power play unit scored ten times, still a league record.

The new franchise was hardly back in business when it was struck by a tragedy that is still echoing through the Western Hockey League. On December 30, 1986, the Broncos boarded a bus to travel to Regina for a game against the Pats. A wet snow was falling and the trip was just beginning when the bus blundered off the highway into a ditch. Four players—Scott Kruger, Trent Kresse, Brent Ruff and Chris Mantyka—lost their lives. The city, the WHL, the entire hockey world, was stunned at the news. Donations in memory of the players poured into the team

The 1971–72 Swift Current Broncos:
Back row: Larry English (trainer), Ed Lang, Vern McCormick, Graeme
Bennett, Glen Toner, Lyal Knudson, Virgil Gates, Kelly Pratt, Terry
Ruzkowski, Brian Back, Stan Dunn (coach).
Front row: Alec Kogler, Dave Williams, Terry McDougall, Dan
McCarthy, Henry Durkin, Bret Nakrayko, Brent Leavins, Gord Engele,
Wayne Inglis, Kevin Joll.

office and were used to set up an education fund, administered by the city. Another fund raised money to replace the damaged bus. Even if it was fixed, James said, his team would never ride in it again.

In the aftermath of the tragedy, John Rittinger threw down a challenge. "It's up to the players and the fans now," he said. "We aren't ready to throw in the towel." The fans did what they could to show their commitment. At the end of the 1986–87 season a group of local supporters known as the Hockey Hounds raised enough money that Rittinger was able to pay off the bank and declare the franchise debt-free. "I think after the bus accident . . . that galvanized the spirit of the community," James said later. "I think that was a catalyst. Since then we've had to provide a product that's been worthy of fans coming, but I think that incident certainly rallied the community."

The payoff came with the 1988–89 season. It began with 12 straight victories. By the time the Christmas break rolled around the Broncos had a record of 28–5–0 and were riding a ten-game winning streak. They ended the season with the best record in the league, and their home

The 1992–93 Swift Current Broncos::
Back row: Todd Holt, Regan Mueller, Rich Girard, Tyler Wright,
Jason Horvath, Russ Hewson, Chris Low, Paul Nichols, Dean
McAmmond, Andy Schneider.
Middle row: Doug Mosher (head scout), Paddy Maclore, Craig Miller,
Keith McCambridge, Darren McLean, Heath Weenk, Ryan Brown, Ashley
Buckberger, Darren Perkins, Bill Hooson, John Foster (PR director)
Front row: Milan Hnilicka, John Rittinger (president), Graham James
(coach & GM), Brent Bilodeau, Trent McCleary, Jason Krywaluk, Rob
Daum (assistant Coach & GM), Ian Gordon, Carol Beyer (office manager).

record of 33–2–1 established a new league mark for most wins by a team at home. Five players scored 100 points or more: Tim Tisdale (139), Peter Kasowski (131), Sheldon Kennedy (106), Dan Lambert (102), and Brian Sakic (100). Darren Kruger finished with 97 points and set a WHL record with 63 power-play assists. His twin brother, Trevor, was the team's goalie. Their brother Scott was one of the players who died in the bus crash.

The Broncos cruised through the playoffs without losing a game, another league first, sweeping Moose Jaw, Saskatoon, then Portland in the final. Next it was off to the Memorial Cup tournament, held in Saskatoon that year. After the round robin was over, it came down to a showdown between Swift Current and the host team, the upstart Blades. The final was a thriller, undecided until the 3:25 mark of sudden-death overtime when Tim Tisdale tipped in a centring pass from Darren Kruger and the Cup belonged to the Broncos. Combining regular season and playoff records the team finished at 71–17–1, one of the finest records ever compiled by a WHL club. All this from a team just a season and a half away from the tragic deaths of four of its members. James said that the accident "is something we downplay, but it meant something to the players who were there and the people involved with the franchise . . . I think it's a great tribute to the guys (Kresse, Kruger, Mantyka and Ruff) and we can let them rest in peace." It really was a story made for Hollywood.

The Swift Current Broncos rebounded from an average 1991–92 campaign to record the franchise's second best season in history after 1988–89. The team finished the regular season with a league-leading 100 points, won the league championship in the playoffs, and made it to the Memorial Cup tournament in Sault Ste. Marie, Ontario. Compared to the three other CHL teams that were in the tournament, the Broncos clearly had the strongest lineup on paper, but they only managed to win one game. The game they did win was against the eventual champions, the Sault Ste. Marie Greyhounds, but after losing two round-robin games and then a tiebreaker match against the Laval Titan, they were the first team eliminated. That strong lineup featured one player who was the top goals- and points-scorer in the WHL and the CHL, and the Western League's Most Valuable Player. Jason Krywulak, a 21-year-old centre, scored an even 81 goals and 81 assists for 162 points to lead the WHL in regular season goals, assists and points scoring. Included in those totals were 47 power play goals, enough to break both the Western Hockey League and Canadian Hockey League single season records. His goals and points totals broke the Broncos' individual single season records set by Joe Sakic in 1987–88. Rick Girard, Todd Holt, Andy Schneider, Brent Bilodeau, Tyler Wright, Dean McAmmond, Ashley Buckberger and goalie Milan Hnilicka also made great contributions to the team's success.

Terry Ruskowski

Born and raised in Prince Albert, Saskatchewan, Terry Ruskowski came to the Broncos from Humboldt, where he spent 1970–71 playing in the Saskatchewan Junior Hockey League. A left-shooting centreman, he made up for what he lacked in size with hard work and an upbeat, take-charge attitude. In three seasons with Swift Current, 1971–74, two of them on a line with "Tiger" Williams and Bryan Trottier, he produced 78 goals and 273 total points. In his last year he finished fifth in the league scoring race and led all scorers in the playoffs with 23 assists in 13 games.

In 1974 Ruskowski joined his first professional team, the Houston Aeros of the WHA. He played with the legendary Gordie Howe and in 1975 was part of the Houston team which won the WHA championship. After four seasons, the Aeros merged with the Winnipeg Jets to produce another championship team under coach Tom McVie. In 1979 four WHA teams joined the NHL and Ruskowski found himself with the Chicago Blackhawks, who had drafted him back in 1974. He was stunned when, after just 12 games, coach Ed Johnston named him team captain. After three seasons in Chicago, it was on to Los Angeles, then Pittsburgh and Minnesota before finally wrapping up his pro career, after 999 games, in 1989.

Ruskowski had always wanted to get into coaching and the opportunity came in 1989 when he learned that the Saskatoon Blades needed to replace Marcel Comeau. The transition from player to coach was more difficult than he expected—"I found out that sitting there and standing there are two different things"—but his first season was a pretty successful one. The Blades finished third in their division and made it to the second round of the playoffs before losing to Lethbridge in seven games.

Ruskowski was replaced as coach midway through his second season in Saskatoon, so he moved on to the East Coast Hockey League, where he coached the Columbus Chill in 1992–93.

Terry Ruskowski centred Tiger Williams and Bryan Trottier.

Dave "Tiger" Williams came to Swift Current as a defenceman but found his niche as a fighting forward.

Dave "Tiger" Williams

A native of Weyburn, Saskatchewan, south of Regina, Dave "Tiger" Williams gained his nickname when he was a kid. "My brother Leonard was refereeing a game once and he called a penalty on me. I warned him not to do it—who calls a penalty on his own brother? But he did and I knocked him over and then people started calling me Tiger." Williams played his bantam and midget hockey in his home town, then jumped to the Broncos as a 17-year-old for the 1971–72 season. When he arrived in Swift Current, Williams played defence but he was a slow, awkward skater who had trouble moving backwards so coach Stan Dunn put him on the forward line. From then on everything fell into place.

Williams played a rough-and-ready brand of hockey—"I like to hit guys and I don't feel I'm in the game unless I am hitting," he once said—but he began to cut down on bad penalties in his second year. He was a very durable player, never missing a game in three seasons of WHL play. Playing on a line with Bryan Trottier and Terry Ruskowski, he improved his game to such a degree that the Toronto Maple Leafs took him in the second round of the 1974 NHL entry draft.

Williams spent 14 seasons in the NHL, seasons notable for his boisterous style of play. Seven times he led the league in penalty minutes, in either the regular season or the playoffs, and he holds the record for career penalty minutes, 3966 in 962 regular season games. Most of these minutes were a result of fighting. "Fights are a way of letting off steam so that things don't get worse," Williams once insisted in his own defence. "It's when the sticks start swinging that you get bad scenes. I throw my fists, not my stick—I'm not a dirty player." Of course, Williams talents were not confined to his fists. During his NHL career he posted 241 goals and 272 assists and had one 30-plus goal season.

After six seasons with the Leafs, "Punch" Imlach traded the Tiger to Vancouver, where he played a key role in the 1982 playoffs, helping the Canucks go all the way to the Stanley Cup Finals. He also played briefly for Detroit, Los Angeles, and Hartford before dropping his gloves for good following the 1987–88 season. He stayed in Vancouver, where he enjoyed life as a sports celebrity, an accomplished after-dinner speaker and a tireless worker for various charities. In 1993, Williams was named as the head coach of the Vancouver Voodoo, a new roller hockey team playing out of Vancouver's PNE Agrodome.

Bryan Trottier

Beside the highway on the outskirts of Val Marie, a tiny community in the southwest corner of Saskatchewan just north of the Montana border, a large sign proudly declares: "Val Marie—Home of Bryan Trottier." Like

Future superstar Bryan Trottier wasn't drafted until the second round.

so many NHL stars, Trottier honed his hockey skills as a young boy on the frozen rivers and ponds of the western prairie. Dreaming of a future as a professional hockey player, he would linger on the ice long into the evening to practise shooting the puck at the border collie he had taught to play goal.

Progressing through the minor leagues in Val Marie and nearby Climax, Trottier began making the 75-mile commute down the road to Swift Current where, in 1972, he led his midget team, the Swift Current Legionnaires, to the Saskatchewan championship. That fall he graduated to the WHL and the Swift Current Broncos. "Tiger" Williams, who played for the Broncos at that time, recalled noticing Trottier at training camp and marking him out for future success. "The little son-of-gun always had the puck," marvelled Williams, whose assessment turned out to be prophetic. By his second year in the league Trottier had broken into the ranks of the top-ten scorers, and in 1974–75, playing with the transplanted Broncos franchise in Lethbridge, he finished second in scoring with a league-leading 98 assists and won the WHL Most Valuable Player award.

As his career advanced, Trottier just kept getting better. He was not chosen until the second round of the NHL draft, but he skated straight into the lineup of the New York Islanders and quickly proved himself an indispensable part of the dynasty that coach Al Arbour and general manager Bill Torrey were building on Long Island. In 1975–76 Trottier debuted in the NHL with the first of nine consecutive 30-plus goal seasons, setting a team record for most assists (63) and points by a rookie (95) and winning the Calder Trophy as Rookie of the Year. He also held NHL records for the most assists and points in a season by a rookie, before they were broken by Peter Stastny in 1980–81. He was a first-team all-star in 1978 and 1979, and a member of the second team in 1982 and again in 1984. In 1978–79 he led the league in scoring and also won the Hart Trophy for Most Valuable Player. Trottier can also claim the unique distinction of having played for two different countries in the Canada

Cup. In 1981 he suited up for Canada; in 1984 he became a US citizen and played for the Americans. And, of course, there were the four straight Stanley Cups, 1980–83. Trottier contributed 107 points in 75 playoff games during the streak, winning the Conn Smythe Trophy as the Most Valuable Player in the 1980 playoffs. The line of Trottier at centre, Mike Bossy on right wing and Clark Gillies on the left, is one of the most fearsome ever to have played in the NHL.

Every dynasty has its day, however, and one by one the heroes departed—Stefan Persson, Dave Langevin, Gillies, John Tonelli, Bob Nystrom, Denis Potvin, Bossy—some of them to be reunited in the Hall of Fame. By 1990 Trottier was the last member of the Cup teams still with the Islanders and it looked as if retirement was inevitable. Instead, he gave himself a second life by signing as a free agent with Pittsburgh and winning two more Stanley Cups in a Penguins uniform. He retired in the summer of 1992 to work in the Islanders' front office, but after one season out of hockey he decided to make a comeback as a playing assistant coach for the 1993–94 Pittsburgh Penguins. The little son-of-a gun who always had the puck became the 15th-highest goal-scorer (520), the fifth-highest assist-scorer (890) and the sixth-highest point-scorer (1410) in NHL history .

Graham James

Graham James, one of the most colourful coaches to patrol the bench in the Western Hockey League, was born and raised in Winnipeg and played his minor hockey in the suburb of St. James. While he attended the University of Manitoba he maintained his interest in hockey and had quite a bit to do with Anders Hedberg, Ulf Nilsson and Lars-Eric Sjoberg, helping the three Scandinavian imports to the Winnipeg Jets get accustomed to their new home. James has always maintained that the three Europeans taught him another way of looking at the game and helped to shape his coaching philosophy, with its emphasis on speed and finesse.

Coach Graham James, who stripped "down to his pants."

James began his coaching career at the midget level, taking the St. James Canadians to the final of the Air Canada Cup in

1978–79. He was also doing some scouting for the Flin Flon Bombers and the Saskatoon Blades. In 1979 James stepped up to the Manitoba Junior A Hockey League as assistant coach, then head coach, of the Fort Garry Blues. He remained with the Blues through the 1982–83 season, after which he took on the jobs of assistant coach and director of player personnel for the troubled Winnipeg Warriors franchise in the WHL.

During his one year with the Warriors the franchise suffered a brutal season on the ice and at the box office. The only solution seemed to be to relocate to a city which really longed to support a junior hockey team. That city turned out to be Moose Jaw. Moose Jaw had had a team in the Canadian Major Junior Hockey League in 1966–67 and 1967–68, the Canucks, and the city was eager to welcome a new franchise.

Moose Jaw retained the Warriors name and wasted no time in hiring Graham to be the first coach on May 23, 1984. As things turned out he only stayed one season. After the 1984–85 campaign the owners brought in Barry Trapp, from Regina, as general manager. James and Trapp did not see eye to eye and it wasn't long before Trapp was the Warriors' coach as well and James was back in the Manitoba Junior Hockey League coaching the Winnipeg South Blues. James had good success that year, 1985–86, coaching the Blues to the Abbott Cup final game, but he still wanted to coach in the WHL. The opportunity came in the spring of 1986 when the Lethbridge Broncos franchise moved back to Swift Current and the owners hired James as coach and general manager, a position he still holds.

James has had a lot of success in Swift Current, highlighted by the Broncos' Memorial Cup victory in 1989. But he is perhaps best known for his famous "striptease" of October 30, 1990. The Medicine Hat Tigers were visiting Swift Current. The Broncos led 7–3 in the second period when the roof caved in. The Tigers scored six third-period goals, the last one, the game winner, coming with just 13 seconds remaining in the game. James blew his top. He charged onto the ice, screaming at referee Kevin Muench until he was restrained by the linesmen and some of his players. Returning to the bench, the irate coach threw sticks and water bottles onto the ice and then began removing his clothes. Off came the jacket and tie, off came the shirt. He was down to his pants and one shoe when the players escorted him back to the dressing room. The crowd went wild. A television camera got all the action on tape and the performance was seen on the *Tonight Show* with Johnny Carson, *Late Night with David Letterman* and *Hockey Night in Canada*. Two days later James was slapped with a six-game suspension and a $2000 fine.

James, one of the senior coaches in the WHL, was only 40 years old as the 1992–93 season wound down, a lot of coaching years still ahead of him.

Joe Sakic

Joe Sakic, now a high-scoring centre with the Quebec Nordiques in the NHL, was born in Burnaby, BC, where his working-class parents settled after emigrating from Croatia. Young Joe played bantam and midget hockey in Burnaby, leading his teams at both levels to the Western Canada regional championships.

Future NHL star Joe Sakic of Burnaby BC, skating in Swift Current Broncos colours.

As a 17-year-old junior rookie, Sakic arrived in Swift Current in the fall of 1986 at the same time the Bronco franchise moved back to the small city in southwestern Saskatchewan. The Broncos finished a lowly sixth in their division that season, and suffered the tragic loss of four members of the team in a highway accident. But Sakic's play provided one of the bright spots in an otherwise dismal year. His 60 goals and 73 assists earned him fourth place in the WHL scoring race and Rookie-of-the-Year honours, the first time a Swift Current rookie had won the award. He was also named Most Valuable Player in the East Division.

That summer, 1987, he was drafted as an underage pick by the Nordiques, 15th overall in the first round. After attending the Quebec training camp, he returned for another season with Swift Current and proceeded to win another case-full of trophies. He led the league with 78 goals and shared the overall scoring championship with Moose Jaw sniper, Theoren Fleury. He was the Most Valuable Player in the league, made the all-star team, and in January helped Team Canada win the World Junior Hockey Championship in Moscow. Sakic topped off a fantastic year when he was selected the Canadian Junior Player of the Year.

By his sixth season with the Nordiques, Sakic had become Quebec's captain and one of the league's leading offensive threats, regularly scoring over 100 points a year and doing his best to turn the youngest, most promising team in the league into the NHL's next dynasty.

TACOMA

The Tacoma Rockets

The Tacoma Rockets joined the ranks of the Western Hockey League's West Division in time for the 1991–92 season. Tacoma's hockey history dates back to the 1930–31 season in the Pacific Coast Hockey League. More recently the name Tacoma Rockets saw action as memebers of the Pacific Coast Hockey League from the 1946–47 season right thgouth the 1952–53 season. The league became professional in 1948–49 and changed its name in the 1952–53 season to the Western Hockey League.

The Rockets have been guided in their infancy as a hockey franchise by a "Saskatoon Connection" which included Bruce Hamilton, the Rockets' governor/general manager and president. Lorne Frey, a former Saskatoon Blades coach, serves the Rockets as an assistant general manager, alternate governor and a director of player personnel. Rounding out this connection is Marcel Comeau, who coached the Saskatoon Blades and Calgary Wranglers previously. Donn Clark, a former Saskatoon Blade who served the Rockets as an assistant coach, left the organization to become the Prince Albert Raiders' new coach in 1993–94. Jamie Reeve, a former Regina Pats netminder and Moose Jaw Warriors assistant coach, joined the Rockets to replace Clark as assistant coach. The team had a dismal first season on the ice with a 24–43–5 regular-season record in the West Division and suffered a quick elimination from the playoff scene at the hands of the Kamloops Blazers four games to zero, being outscored 31 to 7 by the Blazers.

The tremendous affection shown by the rabid Tacoma fans to their new Rocket heroes was amazing. On opening night, October 11, 1991, a huge crowd of 14,975 showed up at the 17,000-seat Tacoma Dome for a game against arch-rival Seattle Thunderbirds. Later in the season, crowds of 14,975 and 15,240 on January 25, 1992, also against Seattle, established an all-time attendance record for a single WHL game. Three Tacoma players were selected in the 1992 NHL entry draft—Tuomas Gronman by the Quebec Nordiques, John Varga by the Washington Capitals and Michal Sykora by the San Jose Sharks.

The 1992–93 season was simply incredible for the sophomore team. A 45-game victory, 90-point regular season were highlighted by a WHL and Canadian Hockey League record 24-game home winning streak from October 28, 1992 to February 18, 1993. The Rockets held first place in the West Division for much of the season, finally being overtaken in the last week of the schedule by the Portland Winter Hawks, who finished at 93 points. Marcel Comeau was awarded the Dunc McCallum Memorial Trophy emplematic of the WHL Coach-of-the-Year honours for his fine coaching efforts. Bruce Hamilton was also the winnter of the Lloyd Saunders Trophy as the WHL's Executive of the Year.

At the conclusion of the regular season the Rockets slumped, winning only three of their last ten games. The dismal ending continued on into the post-season when the Rockets blew a three-games-to-two advantage over the Spokane Chiefs to lose the opening-round series in seven games. It was a tough playoff defeat as two games, including the final one, were decided in overtime. The Rockets also managed to outscore the Chiefs 31 to 30 in the series.

Five Tacoma skaters made the West Division all-star voting lists—goaltender Jeff Calvert, defenceman Jason Kwiatkowski, Michal Sykora and centres Jamie Black and Allan Egeland. Egeland was one of two Rockets selected in the 1993 NHL draft. He was chosen by the Tampa Bay Lightning in the third round and will spend the 1993–94 season in Petersburgh, Florida. Goaltender Todd MacDonald was selected in the fifth round by the Florida Panthers.

There is little doubt that the Rockets have a bright future, with many good seasons in store for their excited fans in this Washington city.

AMERICANS

TRI-CITY

The Tri-City Americans

Franchises come and franchises go but the Western Hockey League Tri-City Americans is a franchise that seemed to take root. After just four years in the league, the fans of the three cities of Kennewick, Pasco and Richland have shown great support for their team.

"We have around 3800 season ticket sales and draw fans from all three communities, as well as from places like Walla Walla and Northeast Oregon," says Tom Lathen, who helps with marketing and public relations for the team.

It may have been the first time in the history of major junior hockey that an owner gambled on moving a franchise into a market area where the sport literally had no roots. But in the first four seasons, all the growing pains that are so much a part of this fast paced and, at times, turbulent game have been seen by Tri-City fans.

While the team still waits its first playoff series win or first championship trophy, it has been competitive from the outset, usually emphasizing the kind of high-powered offence that today's fans want to see.

The club has also weathered it's share of turmoil. On March 24, 1990, the intense feelings between Tri-City and state arch-rival Seattle Thunderbirds erupted into an ugly stick-swinging scene involving the Americans, their coach Rick Kozuback, and Thunderbirds fans at the Seattle Coliseum. Fines and suspensions against the Tri-City organization followed.

On December 17, 1990, when the controversial Bill Laforge was hired by Americans owner Ron Dixon to help well-liked Rick Kozuback with the team's coaching, more contention followed. Laforge's reputa-

GRADUATES TO THE NHL

Tri-City Americans

1989: **Stu Barnes**—Winnipeg. **Olaf Kolzig**—Washington.
1990: **Scott Levins**—Winnipeg, Florida.
1991: **Vladimir Vujtek**—Montreal, Edmonton. **Bill
Lindsay**—Quebec, Florida. **Jason Marshall**—St. Louis.
1992: **Jason Bowen**—Philadelphia.

tion as an intimidating coach who preached a physical, goon-style type of game made his hiring unpopular with Tri-City fans and players. After his first "pep talk" at a practice, 20 players walked out and refused to play hockey for him. Without much of a choice, team owner Ron Dixon announced that after only a couple of weeks as a coach, Laforge had been reassigned to be in charge of team scouting and that Kozuback would resume full head-coaching reins. Laforge eventually left the Tri-City organization.

Ron Dixon, in turn, sold the franchise to Ron Toigo, son of the late Vancouver businessman and owner of the White Spot restaurant chain Peter Toigo. Toigo, through his Vancouver connections, in turn hired the former Vancouver Canucks coach Bob McCammon to eventually become the president, general manager and coach of the Americans. "In a city this size to have a personage like Bob McCammon here coaching is perceived as if we were to have Tom Lasorda here coaching the baseball team," says Lathen of the response of the community to McCammon as coach.

Except for the 1992–93 season, the Tri-City Americans have always been a solidly competitive team. In the team's first five seasons it played solidly over or around .500, although being eliminated from the playoffs every one of those seasons and never finishing higher than third in the division standings. The Americans slumped in 1992–93, finishing the season 28 and 41, 13 games under .500.

In back-to-back games in 1990–91, Tri-City was a 19–3 winner in Seattle and returned home to bounce Victoria 16–3. The 35 goals in two consecutive games may never be challenged and, as well, the 20 power-play goals that the Americans amassed in the same two games will require a long-long time to be topped.

The team has scored goals, lots of them, and with intense state rivalries with Seattle and Spokane, as well as with perennially powerful Kamloops and surprisingly, even with the Victoria Cougars, the fans have fully supported the cause.

As a team, Tri-City has had a reputation as a run-and-gun style club that emphasized offence and suffered defensively. With the exception of the inaugural season, when goaltender Olaf Kolzig was a first-round draft pick of the Washington Capitals, stopping goals has been a problem for the Americans. The offence, led by players like Stu Barnes, Brian Sakic, Kyle Reeves, Scott Levins, Bill Lindsay, Vladimir Vujtek and defenceman Todd Klassen, has been magnificent. These players, and some of the forwards that the Americans have owned the rights to—Paul Kariya, Peter and Chris Ferraro, Libor Polasek and Robert Petrovicky—proved that the Americans could attract good young talent. With fans in the stands and talent on the ice, it only remained for Tri-City to achieve a high position in the standings for the franchise to be declared a total success.

Kyle Reeves was ranked second in scoring in the WHL behind Brian Sakic.

Stu Barnes

Raised in the Edmonton suburb of St. Albert, Stu Barnes' introduction to junior hockey action came with the St. Albert Saints of the Alberta Junior Hockey League. The young centre was barely 16 years old during the 1986–87 season when he scored 41 goals, had 34 assists and earned 75 points. Barnes' play caught the attention of Roy Henderson, director of player personnel for the New Westminster Bruins, who arranged for Stu to try-out with the Bruins in autumn of 1987. Barnes not only cracked the Bruins lineup, he became an impact player immediately, scoring 37 times and adding 64 assists for 101 points. He was named WHL Rookie of the Year and was the centre for the West Division second all-star team.

In 1988 the owner of the Bruins, Ron Dixon, decided to move the franchise to Kennewick, Washington, where the team became the Tri-City Americans. Barnes made the move as well, and expanded on his scoring feats during the 1988–89 season, finishing second in the league scoring race with 141 points. Impressed by such a sensational campaign, the Winnipeg Jets chose Barnes fourth overall in the entry draft of June 1989.

After attending the Jets training camp, Barnes returned to Kennewick for the 1989–90 season to sharpen his defensive skills. During his third year of WHL play he finished a very respectable seventh in league scoring with 144 points, including 52 goals.

Still concerned about Barnes' defensive play, the Jets sent him to Calgary to play for the Canadian Olympic Team under the watchful eye of coach Dave King. He joined the Jets for the 1991–92 season and has divided his time between the parent club and the Moncton Hawks of the American Hockey League. In 1992–93, Barnes only played 38 NHL games, but impressed the Jets by showing bright spots and scoring 22 points in limited ice time.

Brian Sakic

Lightning-fast hands and a proven scoring touch were the hallmarks of Brian Sakic's play during his five junior seasons in the WHL. A native of Burnaby, BC, Brian is the younger brother of Joe Sakic, the high-scoring captain of the Quebec Nordiques. Both Sakic boys got their hockey training in the Burnaby minor system. As a bantam in 1986–87, Brian scored 89 goals and added 117 assists to earn a phenomenal 206 points in just 56 games.

Brian followed his brother Joe to the Swift Current Broncos. At the age of 16 in his first season, 1987–88, he produced a modest 49 points, playing in the shadow of Joe, who won the league scoring title that year

Brian Sakic—between Sakic and Kyle Reeves they had 104 points in 19 games.

and was chosen the country's best junior player. The next season, with Joe graduated to the NHL, Brian came into his own, posting the first of four consecutive 100-point seasons. It was a glorious campaign for the Swift Current team, as they not only won the WHL championship but went on to defeat Saskatoon in overtime to win the 1989 Memorial Cup.

During the 1989–90 season Swift Current traded Sakic to the Tri-City Americans where he continued to pile up the points. He ended the year fourth in scoring with an assist total one shy of the leader, signalling even better things to come. At the 1990 NHL Draft at Vancouver, he was chosen 114th overall, in the sixth round, by the Washington Capitals. Sakic was probably chosen so late because of his size—5'10", 156 pounds—and the perception that he was weak defensively. In 1990–91 Sakic earned himself a position on the West Division all-star team by finishing second in scoring and leading the league in assists with 122. In a game against Seattle on October 3rd, 1990 he earned eight assists and ten points to set a record for most assists in one game and tie another for the most points scored in one game. A dangerous performer on the powerplay, Sakic also tied a league record that season for most assists on the powerplay, 63.

After another season as one of the league's most prolific scorers, Sakic ended his junior career as the WHL's all-time leader in assists, 405, and points, 591. On August 13, 1992, the New York Rangers showed confidence in Sakic by signing him as a free agent. During the 1992–93 season he skated with the Erie Panthers of the East Coast Hockey League.

VICTORIA

The Victoria Cougars

Long before the Victoria Cougars junior franchise played its first game in the WHL in 1971, the Cougars name was well known to hockey fans. The original Cougars were owned by Lester Patrick who, with his brother Frank, organized their own professional league, the Pacific Coast Hockey Association, in 1911. The Patricks built Canada's first artificial ice rink in Victoria, and in 1925 the Cougars defeated Montreal to win the Stanley Cup, the last time a non-NHL team did so. The next year Patrick sold his club to a new NHL franchise in Detroit and the Cougar name disappeared for a while. But following World War Two, Patrick, his glory days with the New York Rangers behind him, returned to Victoria and re-established the club as a member of the Pacific Coast Hockey League. Until the early sixties, this team too was known as the Cougars.

In 1967, Victoria's entry in the Western Professional Hockey League packed its bags and relocated down south in sunny Phoenix. The departure of the pros created an opportunity for promoters of junior hockey to catch the attention of fans on Vancouver Island. A group of Victoria businessmen, headed by Robert Reid, organized the public sale of shares and a community-owned team was born. And what better name to adopt than the Cougars? Under coach Doug Anderson the new franchise played in the BC Junior Hockey League and, in only the second year of operation, captured the league championship in 1969.

The Cougars were hugely successful at putting fans in the seats. It was not unusual for the rafters of Memorial Arena to be ringing with the noise of three or four thousand fans. In the 1971 playoffs against the

Vernon Essos, the Cougars attracted a crowd of 5219. These numbers made the supporters of major junior hockey sit up and take notice. A Calgary group, headed by sportscaster Eric "The Earache" Bishop, purchased the franchise and immediately upgraded the Cougars to the Western Canada Hockey League for the 1971–72 season.

As the newest member of the league, the Cougars struggled for the first three seasons, going through three coaches—Fred Hucul, Mitch Pechet and Ollie Dowhoy—before Bishop and his group gave up in despair and sold the franchise to Pat Ginnell at the end of 1973. Three times the WCHL Coach of the Year with the Flin Flon Bombers, Ginnell immediately lifted the Cougars to respectability, guiding them to first place overall in his first full year behind the bench, 1974–75. Ginnell was blessed with the scoring punch of Mel Bridgman, the top scorer in the league, ably assisted by Peter Morris (43 goals, 72 assists), Danny Lucas (57 goals, 56 assists) and WHL Defenceman of the Year Rick Lapointe. However, the Cougars under Ginnell were better known for their brawling style than their scoring finesse. His three years in Victoria were marked by some wild melees. On one occasion, the mayor of the city, Peter Pollen, even left his seat at a game to berate the coach during a donnybrook on the ice. In 1976–77 the subsequent mayor, Mike Young, wanted Ginnell to include a non-violence clause in the Memorial Arena rental contract!

By 1977 the Cougars had tumbled to the bottom of their division and it was time for Ginnell to go. He was replaced by Jack Shupe, over from Medicine Hat, where he had helped to mould the Tigers into a contender. In 1977–78 Shupe took the club to the division finals and shared Coach-of-the-Year honours with Dave King, but he had his greatest on-ice success in 1980–81. The Cougars that season were loaded with talent—Grant Fuhr in goal, Bob McGill on defence and Tony Feltrin, Paul Cyr, Barry Pederson, Torrie Robertson, Stu Kulak, John Mokosak, Rich Chernomaz and Geoff Courtnall up front. They finished the regular season with a record of 60–11–1, then defeated Calgary to win the league championship for the only time in their history. The season ended with a whimper, however, when the team only managed to win one game at the Memorial Cup tournament in Windsor. In both of the next two seasons, Victoria finished second in the West Division but never made it past the first round of the playoffs.

Trying to operate a major junior hockey franchise on an island has its disadvantages. Travel costs are higher and inclement weather can wreak havoc on the ferry schedules. Still, an island location has its benefits as well, the main one being that the audience is a captive one. It is a costly, time-consuming jaunt across to the mainland to watch the Canucks, so for most fans on the lower island the Cougars are the only game in town.

From the middle of the 1980s to the early 1990s, the Victoria franchise sank into the lower regions of the league standings, actually

GRADUATES TO THE NHL

Victoria Cougars
BCJHL Franchise

1970: **Ron Grahame**——Boston, Los Angeles, Quebec.
1971: **Bruce Cowick**——Philadelphia, Washington, St. Louis.

Victoria Cougars
WCHL Franchise

1972: **Gary Donaldson**——Chicago.
1975: **Mel Bridgman**——Philadelphia, Calgary, New Jersey, Detroit, Vancouver. **Rick Lapointe**——Detroit, Philadelphia, St. Louis, Quebec, Los Angeles. **Don Cairns**——Kansas City, Colorado. **Kim Clackson**——Pittsburgh, Quebec. **Gordie Roberts**——Montreal (drafted in 1977 from New England of the World Hockey Association), Hartford, Minnesota, Philadelphia, St. Louis, Pittsburgh, Boston.
1976: **Jeff McDill**——Chicago. **Lorry Gloeckner**——Boston, Detroit. **Danny Lucas**——Philadelphia. **Al Hill**——Philadelphia.
1977: **Archie Henderson**——Washington, Minnesota, Hartford.
1978: **Curt Fraser**——Vancouver, Chicago, Minnesota. **Glen Cochrane**——Philadelphia, Vancouver, Chicago, Edmonton.
1979: **Gary Lupul**——Vancouver. **Geordie Robertson**——Buffalo.

setting a record for ineptitude in 1989–90 by winning only five games while losing 65. Even while they struggled, however, the Cougars featured some standout performers, among them Simon Wheeldon, who counted 96 assists and 157 points during 1985–86 to finish second in the scoring race; Ken Priestlay, a 73-goal-scorer in the same season; league all-stars Randy Hansch, Brent Hughes, Andrew Wolf and Jackson Penney; as well as Adam Morrison, Clayton Young, Gerry St. Cyr, Steve Passmore and Scott Fukami. During the 1980s the Cougars produced four first-round NHL draft picks: Grant Fuhr, the all-star goaltender with Edmonton (1981), Paul Cyr, a left-winger with Buffalo for several seasons (1982), Russ Courtnall, most recently with the Minnesota North Stars (1983), and Joel Savage, picked by Buffalo in 1988.

Pat Ginnell

Born in Dauphin, Manitoba, on March 3, 1937, Pat Ginnell was one of the most controversial personalities ever associated with the Western Hockey League. His junior playing career began in 1954 with the Port

1980: **Brad Palmer**—Minnesota, Boston. **Barry Pederson**—Boston, Vancouver, Pittsburgh, Hartford, Boston. **Bob McGill**—Toronto, Chicago, San Jose, Detroit. **Torrie Robertson**—Washington, Hartford, Detroit. **Tony Feltrin**—Pittsburgh, NY Rangers. **Greg C. Adams**—Philadelphia, Hartford, Washington, Edmonton, Vancouver, Quebec, Detroit.

1981: **Grant Fuhr**—Edmonton, Toronto, Buffalo. **Rich Chernomaz**—Colorado, New Jersey, Calgary. **Mark Morrison**—NY Rangers. **Stu Kulak**—Vancouver, Edmonton, NY Rangers, Quebec, Winnipeg. **John Mokosak**—Hartford, Detroit.

1982: **Paul Cyr**—Buffalo, NY Rangers, Hartford.

1983: **Russ Courtnall**—Toronto, Montreal, Minnesota, Dallas. **Geoff Courtnall**—Boston, Edmonton, Washington, St. Louis, Vancouver.

1984: **Dave Mackey**—Chicago, Minnesota, St. Louis. **Tom Martin**—Winnipeg (drafted from Kelowna of the BCJHL in 1982), Hartford, Minnesota. **Simon Wheeldon**—Edmonton, NY Rangers, Winnipeg.

1985: **Ken Priestlay**—Buffalo, Pittsburgh.

1986: **Kevin Evans**—Minnesota, San Jose.

1987: **Brent Hughes**—Winnipeg, Boston.

1988: **Joel Savage**—Buffalo. **Len Barrie**—Edmonton, Philadelphia. **Wade Flaherty**—Buffalo, San Jose.

1989: **Jim McKenzie**—Hartford.

Arthur North Stars, part of the Detroit Red Wings organization. After two seasons with Port Arthur he returned to Manitoba to play for Flin Flon, then in the Saskatchewan Junior Hockey League. Coached by Bobby Kirk, the Bombers were the best of the West that season and went on to win the 1957 Memorial Cup.

Ginnell played for a succession of teams during eight years in the professional minor leagues, including Edmonton, Portland, Seattle and Vancouver in the Western League and Troy, NY, Omaha and Des Moines in the International Hockey League. During the 1963–64 season in Des Moines he was almost killed when a fan threw a folding chair out of the stands and struck him on the head. Knocked unconscious, Ginnell was rushed to hospital and he was even listed in the next morning paper's obituary column. He recovered, however, and his next season was probably the finest of his career as he was named the IHL's all-star right-winger.

When Ginnell retired from active play he knew that he wanted to remain in hockey in some capacity. Coaching seemed the best bet and in 1966 he returned to Manitoba and the Flin Flon Bombers. His first season behind the bench was a splendid success. Spearheaded by Bobby Clarke and Reg Leach, the Bombers breezed to the championship of the Manitoba Junior Hockey League and on to the Abbott Cup final, which they lost to Port Arthur. After that season, the Bombers made the jump to the Western Canada Junior Hockey League where they immediately established themselves as a top contender, reaching the championship series four years in a row and winning it twice. Three times Ginnell won WHL Coach-of-the-Year honours.

Midway through the 1973–74 season, Ginnell left Flin Flon. He purchased 49% of the ailing Victoria Cougars franchise from Eric "The Earache" Bishop, and took over as coach and general manager of the team. During his three and a half years in Victoria he promoted a tough, brawling style of hockey which earned him a host of detractors. At one point he even had the mayor of the city at the players' bench hollering his opinion of Ginnell's tactics.

Ginnell's toughest, meanest, best Victoria team was in 1974–75. It featured league scoring champion Mel Bridgman, and included Peter Morris and Danny Lucas, both of whom finished in the top ten in scoring, Don Cairns, Jim Gustafson and future NHLers Gordie Roberts, Kim Clackson, Rick Lapointe and Curt Fraser. The team finished the season with the best record in the league, but not without some wild scenes of mayhem. Particularly memorable was a mid-January road trip that took the Cougars to Manitoba. Playing against the Winnipeg Clubs, Bridgman was belted to the ice by Jerry Rollins, who immediately was jumped by five Cougars. Rollins, who led the league with 473 penalty minutes that year, took on all five of them, levelling Curt Fraser into the boards and leaving two others collapsed on the ice, before triumphantly exiting the scene without a scratch on his face. By the time tempers cooled the referee, Joe "Butch" Cassidy, had handed out 13 minor penalties, 19 majors and a ten-minute misconduct, and eight players were tossed out of the game. Celebrating a 10–3 victory, Ginnell laughed, "That's my kind of hockey." Moving on to Brandon the following evening, the Cougars were pummelled 9–2 in another fight-filled game. Ginnell threw all his sticks onto the

Pat Ginnell—a hot temper and a tough style of hockey.

ice in the direction of referee Murray Harding, and in the end had to be restrained from going after Harding. League president Ed Chynoweth had seen enough. In two games the Cougars had piled up 425 minutes in penalties. He slapped Ginnell with a five-game suspension. None of which stopped Ginnell from winning his fourth Coach-of-the-Year award, or the Cougars from advancing to the second round of the playoffs, where they lost to a powerful New Westminster squad.

During 1975–76 Ginnell and his Cougars continued to earn their reputation as the bad boys of the league. On October 4, in a home game with the struggling Calgary Centennials which Victoria won 9–2, a 20-minute brawl resulted in more than 100 minutes of penalties. Victoria's mayor, Peter Pollen, left his seat in back of the penalty benches, circled Memorial Arena, clambered up into the Cougars' player bench and engaged Ginnell in a heated discussion. "I asked him if he was going to get his animals under control or the other animals under control," Pollen later explained. "Is this the example we set for our young people? This is a complete disgrace. If I have my way, they won't play here anymore and this isn't sport—it's barbarism." Later in the season, in Saskatoon, the game was interrupted for 50 minutes while the Cougars and the Blades pounded each other with their fists. At one stage fans, coaches, trainers and the police all joined in to put a stop to the melee. When it was finally over the referee assessed a total of 223 penalty minutes.

In neither of these incidents was Ginnell disciplined by the league. He stepped down as coach temporarily four days after the Saskatoon game but returned in time for the playoffs. The next season, however, the Cougars fell to the bottom of their division and by the summer of 1977 Ginnell was gone as coach.

Ginnell's career in the WHL was far from over. He coached at Lethbridge for one season and Medicine Hat for three before ending up with New Westminster in 1985. On October 14, 1981, when Ginnell was coaching the Medicine Hat Tigers, he made the most controversial move of his career. While the Tigers and the Lethbridge Broncos were in the middle of a bench-clearing brawl, Ginnell stepped into the middle of it and exchanged blows with linesman Gary Patzer. Ginnell was charged with assault by the Medicine Hat RCMP, given a 36-game suspension, the longest in WHL history, and removed from his position of Medicine Hat's head coach and general manager at the completion of the season.

It took three years before Ginnell was rehired in the WHL, and when he was, with the New Westminster Bruins, it sure didn't take him long to get into even more controversy. In his very first outing as coach of the Bruins, during an exhibition game with Seattle, one of his defencemen steamrolled over the Seattle goalie. When one of the Thunderbirds retaliated, Ginnell emptied his bench. Attitudes in the

WHL had changed. This kind of tactic was tolerated in the 1970s. In 1985 it earned Ginnell a five-game suspension and a $500 fine. Ignoring orders to stay away from the rink during the suspension, the irrepressible coach showed up at a game wearing a fake moustache and dark glasses. His disguise didn't work and another game and $250 was added to his sentence.

The Bruins are no longer in New Westminster, moving to Kennewick, Washington in 1988, and neither is Pat Ginnell. The WHL lost one of its most colourful characters when he retired from junior coaching to become a scout in the St. Louis Blues organization.

Mel Bridgman

Mel Bridgman is the only player from the Victoria Cougars ever selected first in the NHL entry draft. Born in Ontario but raised in Victoria, Bridgman played his minor hockey for the Victoria Cubs, the provincial Junior B champions in 1969–70, and the Nanaimo Clippers of the BC Junior Hockey League. By 1973 he was ready to graduate to the WHL and to the Victoria Cougars.

The Cougars were a mediocre team when Bridgman arrived. It was only their third year in the league and they finished well back of the front runners, out of the playoffs. As a rookie centre, young Bridgman contributed a respectable 65 points, but in his second season, 1974–75, he

Mel Bridgman was a scoring machine in Victoria.

developed into a scoring machine. The Cougars topped the regular-season standings that year and Bridgman led all scorers with 66 goals and a total of 157 points, a franchise record that he shares with Simon Wheeldon. It was Victoria's first appearance in the playoffs and the team made it to the second round before losing to New Westminster, the eventual league champions. Pat Ginnell won Coach-of-the-Year honours, Rick Lapointe was the league's top defenceman and Bridgman tied Bryan Trottier in the voting for all-star centre.

In 1975 Bridgman joined a powerful Philadelphia team which had just finished winning two consecutive Stanley Cups. As a professional he was unable to match his junior goal-scoring heroics, though he played six solid seasons with the Flyers, serving as team captain for two years and twice reaching the Stanley Cup finals. Not long into the 1981–82 season, Philadelphia began restructuring the team and traded Bridgman to Calgary for Brad Marsh. Two years later he was on the move again, this time to New Jersey. After a stint with the Detroit Red Wings, he decided to give European hockey a try in 1988–89, but returned to the NHL to play out the last games of his career with Vancouver in the spring of 1989.

After hanging up his skates, Bridgman enrolled in the University of Pennsylvania's prestigious Wharton School of Business. Equipped with an MBA, he was hired in 1991 as general manager of the brand new Ottawa Senators franchise which began play in the NHL in 1992–93. Unfortunately, the 1992–93 Senators established themselves as one of the worst teams in NHL history (10 wins, 70 losses, and 4 ties), and Bridgman was replaced at the end of the season.

Curt Fraser

Curt Fraser was born in Cincinnati, Ohio on January 12, 1958. At an early age he moved with his family to Winnipeg and then to North Vancouver. There he honed his hockey skills at the North Shore Winter Club. Then it was on to Don Culley's Kelowna Buckaroos of the British Columbia Junior Hockey League for the 1973–74 season, where he experienced playing on a championship side.

The Buckaroos, after getting by Brian Sutter's Red Deer team in five games, lost in the western Abbott Cup final to the Selkirk Steelers of Manitoba in a tremendous seven-game series. The Steelers eventually became the Centennial Cup champions. During this time, the Victoria Cougars had been taking notice and they placed the 16-year old Fraser on their roster. Fraser completed a solid four-year junior career with the Victoria Cougars under the coaching eyes of Pat Ginnell and Jack Shupe. Statistically, Fraser's best junior season was in 1975–76 when he scored 43 goals and 107 points, but he really developed himself into an NHL-quality player in his final junior season, 1977–78, when he picked up 48 goals and 92 points and showed that he could handle himself with 256 penalty minutes. The Vancouver Canucks made the solid left-winger, 6' and 195 pounds, their second-round choice, 22nd overall in the 1978 amateur draft.

After his junior career in which he scored 142 goals, 181 assists for the total of 323 points, he stepped directly into the lineup of the 1978–79 Vancouver Canucks. The Canucks were not disappointed with their catch and he was recognized as one of the NHL's better fighters, which developed as a result of years of weight-lifting. He never looked to start many of the altercations that he became involved in but the big, strong left-winger was generally around to finish the scenes. With the Canucks he improved his annual point production for four seasons (1978–79 until 1981–82) until being traded to the Chicago Blackhawks after a disappointing 1982–83 season for the up-and-coming right-winger Tony Tanti. Probably his biggest hockey thrill came with the Canucks in 1982, when he played a role in their amazing run to the Stanley Cup Finals.

Fraser went on to enjoy five seasons with the Blackhawks and was on the move once again in 1988 when the Chicago Blackhawks, in a steal of a trade, shipped Fraser to the Minnesota North Stars for Dirk Graham. Graham became the Hawks' captain and played with them well into the nineties.

Curt played two and a half seasons for the North Stars before ending his playing days. He has become the coach of the Milwaukee Admirals, an unaffiliated team in the International Hockey League. His final statistics over a 12-year National Hockey League career were 193 goals and 240 assists for a total of 433 points in 704 games played. During his career he piled up 1306 minutes in penalties.

Barry Pederson

When you ask NHL centreman Barry Pederson to recall his three seasons in the WHL with the Victoria Cougars he will tell you about the ferries. They didn't run after midnight, so when the Cougars were on the mainland for an away game, as often as not they spent the night curled up in the bus at the terminal waiting for the dawn run. "We *always* had a problem with the ferry," laughs Pederson. "To this day I don't ever want to take that ferry again. Whenever my wife and I go over to the island, we fly."

However, bus rides aside, Barry Pederson has some great memories of his years in Victoria, beginning in 1978 and culminating in 1980–81 with a WHL championship and a trip to the Memorial Cup. These were the glory days of the franchise, with Grant Fuhr in net, Jack Shupe behind the bench, and the arena jammed with fans every night. And one big reason for the success was the play of Pederson. A native of Big River, Saskatchewan, he grew up in Nanaimo, so Victoria was almost a home team. In his second year he had 88 assists to go along with 52 goals and finished third in the scoring race, propelling the Cougars past Seattle and Portland into the championship final. Following the season he was drafted by the Boston Bruins and he began 1980–81 in the NHL, returning to Victoria for most of the regular season, and all of the playoff run that saw the Cougars advance all the way to the Memorial Cup. Once again Pederson finished third in league scoring (65 goals and 82 assists in only 55 games) and almost certainly would have won the scoring title had he played the full season. In any event, he was named the outstanding player in the WHL.

Pederson graduated to the NHL for good in 1981–82 and enjoyed a marvelous rookie season with Boston, finishing runner-up to Dale Hawerchuk in balloting for the Calder Trophy. Playing every game of the regular season he scored 44 goals and his 92 total points lasted 11 years as a team record for a rookie. He followed that with 107 points in 1982–83 when he became, at 22 years old, the youngest player to lead the Bruins in scoring. After a 116-point season in 1983–84, Pederson seemed well on his way to establishing himself as one of the leading centres in the league when disaster struck. Late in 1984 doctors discovered a non-malignant tumour in his upper right arm and a major operation was needed to remove the growth, along with surrounding muscle, tissue and some bone.

Pederson bounced back in 1985–86 to tally 29 goals for the Bruins, but after the surgery, he never fully regained his scoring touch. When Boston would not offer him a long-term contract, he was happy to accept a trade to Vancouver for Cam Neely and a first-round draft pick. He spent three full seasons with the Canucks but his point production had clearly fallen off and part way into the 1989–90 season Vancouver traded him to Pittsburgh. The Penguins did not use him regularly and he was released. The Hartford Whalers and Boston Bruins each gave him free agent trials in 1991–92 but his skills had eroded. After finishing off the season with Boston's farm team in Maine, he retired from hockey to start a new life in Marblehead, Massachusetts.

Grant Fuhr

Few players have made such an immediate impact on the NHL as Grant Fuhr did in the 1981–82 season, his first in the league. Playing in goal for the Edmonton Oilers, Fuhr lost his professional debut 4–2 to Winnipeg, then did not taste defeat again for 23 games. In fact, he appeared in 48 games that season and only lost five times, finishing with a goals-against average of 3.31 and a berth on the second all-star team. His accomplishment is even more startling considering that it was discovered late in the season that he had been playing with a chronic shoulder injury that needed off-season corrective surgery.

Fuhr began his career in the WHL in 1979 after one season with the Sherwood Park Crusaders of the Alberta Junior Hockey League. His two years with the Victoria Cougars were marked by splendid success, both for himself and the team. In his rookie season he compiled a 3.14 goals-against average, was named to the first all-star team and won Rookie-of-the-Year honours as the Cougars went all the way to the league championship before losing to the Regina Pats. Fuhr returned for an

Grant Fuhr, in action between his Victoria Cougars and the Winnipeg Warriors in 1980–81, butterflies to stop a shot from Bobby Hull Jr.

even better sophomore year. His 2.78 goals-against average and 4 shutouts led the league in both departments and are still franchise records. Behind Fuhr's steady netminding, the Cougars returned to the league championship, only this time they won it, defeating the Calgary Wranglers in the seventh game of the final series. Victoria's visit to the Memorial Cup tournament was disappointing, but Fuhr capped off the season by being named the outstanding goaltender in the WHL.

Drafted eighth overall in 1981, Fuhr performed brilliantly for Edmonton for nine seasons and was the number one goaltender on the Oilers teams which won four Stanley Cups between 1984 and 1988. Aside from the Stanley Cup glory, he won the Vezina Trophy for his performance during the 1987–88 season and was named to the first all-star team. The following season, however, things started to go wrong for Fuhr. Struggling in the nets, he was outplayed at times by Bill Ranford, acquired by the Oilers from Boston, and in 1989–90, when Edmonton once again won the Stanley Cup, it was Ranford who won the Conn Smythe Trophy as the Most Valuable Player in the playoffs.

In 1990 the NHL suspended Fuhr for admitted substance abuse, and he sat out the first half of the 1990–91 season. He marked his return to the ice on February 18 with a shutout against New Jersey (Edmonton's only shutout of the season), and in the playoffs he was once again the team's number one goalie, but before the next season began the Oilers traded him to Toronto. Then, midway through the 1992–93 campaign, the Maple Leafs dealt him to Buffalo for a package that included Dave Andreychuk. In pressure situations with a game on the line there were not many goaltenders a team would prefer to have minding the nets, even in the twilight of his career.

The Courtnall Brothers

Three years separate Geoff and Russ Courtnall in age, but for one season the brothers combined to give fans of the Victoria Cougars a lot to cheer about. Geoff, the elder of the two, was an overage player in 1982–83 when younger brother Russ arrived from Notre Dame College in Wilcox, Saskatchewan, where he played his midget hockey. The boys had been encouraged to take up hockey by their father, Archie, a former minor league professional player himself. Indeed, when their dad died in 1978 the Courtnalls almost abandoned the game. They persevered, however, and went on to have solid careers in the NHL. Together the brothers have played for eight NHL teams, but only once have they played together and that was in the WHL for Victoria in 1982–83.

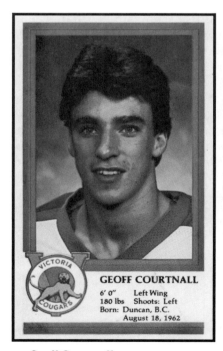

GEOFF COURTNALL

6' 0"   Left Wing
180 lbs Shoots: Left
Born: Duncan, B.C.
August 18, 1962

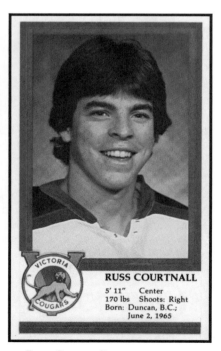

RUSS COURTNALL

5' 11"   Center
170 lbs Shoots: Right
Born: Duncan, B.C.;
June 2, 1965

Geoff Courtnall   *Russ Courtnall*

The top point-getter for the Cougars that season was Mark Morrison, who was winding up a junior career that left him the leading scorer in franchise history. But the Courtnalls made their presence felt as well. Geoff scored 41 goals and added 73 assists for 114 points. Russ, in his freshman season, accumulated 97 points, then potted 11 goals in 12 playoff games as the Cougars made it to the West Division Final round.

Despite his solid performance in his final year with the Cougars, Geoff Courtnall remained undrafted by an NHL team. In 1983 he signed as a free agent with Boston and spent three seasons bouncing back and forth between the American Hockey League and Boston Gardens. By 1986–87 he had earned a regular spot with the Bruins but the following season he was on the move again, traded to Edmonton along with Bill Ranford for Andy Moog. He arrived in Edmonton in time to win a Stanley Cup ring with the Oilers that spring and soon after was traded to Washington. Courtnall enjoyed his most productive NHL seasons with the Capitals, registering 42 goals in 1988–89 and 35 goals the next year. But stability was not a part of his career path. The Capitals traded him to St. Louis for the 1990–91 campaign and before it was over he found himself back in British Columbia in a Vancouver Canucks uniform. By 1992–93 he was the Canucks' third-leading scorer and seemed to have found a permanent home.

Brother Russ took a similarly indirect route into the NHL. Unlike Geoff, Russ went high up in the entry draft, chosen seventh overall by the Toronto Maple Leafs in 1983. He still had a year of junior eligibility remaining and began the 1983–84 season back with Victoria. After 32 games he signed on with Dave King's Olympic program, then landed a starting spot on the Canadian Junior team and was Canada's premier player at the 1983–84 World Junior Championships in Stockholm. Courtnall completed a rather dizzying season by playing in 14 games with the Toronto Maple Leafs. As a regular with the Leafs for four seasons, Russ was a member of the Hound Line, along with Wendel Clark and Gary Leeman. All three had played in Wilcox for the famed Notre Dame College Hounds. A consistent 20-goal-scorer, Courtnall was traded to Montreal early in the 1988–89 season, then traded again in 1992 to Minnesota where he completed his first season in a North Stars uniform as the team's second-leading scorer.

WINNIPEG

The Winnipeg Jets, Clubs, Monarchs and Warriors

The person most responsible for bringing major junior hockey to Winnipeg was millionaire entrepreneur Ben Hatskin. In 1967 Hatskin purchased three Junior A teams—the Winnipeg Rangers, the Winnipeg Braves and the Winnipeg Warriors—then resold them to different local owners. (The Braves have since become the St. James Canadians, the Rangers are the St. Boniface Saints and the Warriors, formerly the St. Boniface Canadians, formed the nucleus of the West Kildonan North Stars.) All three of these teams entered the Manitoba Junior Hockey League for the 1967–68 seasons. Meanwhile, Hatskin used these clubs as the source of players to stock his own expansion franchise in the Canadian Major Junior Hockey League, the forerunner to the WHL, which had formed a year earlier. The Winnipeg Jets, coached by Eddie Dorohoy, did exceptionally well for a first-year team, finishing above .500 and advancing to the first round of the playoffs where they were bombed by an Estevan team on its way to the league championship.

For four seasons the Jets were a great success, both on and off the ice. Attendance boomed, and the team provided an exciting brand of hockey. The highlight of these early years was the semi-final series against Flin Flon in the 1970 playoffs. Led by Chris Oddleifson, the third-leading scorer in the league that season, the Jets took the Bombers to a ninth and deciding game before bowing out. The team began to falter, however, finishing in last place in 1971–72, then winning just 14 games the next season. Hatskin was involved with the professional Jets of the World

GRADUATES TO THE NHL

Winnipeg Jets

1968: **Ron Low**—Toronto (drafted in 1970 from Jacksonville of the East Coast League), Washington, Detroit, Quebec, Edmonton, New Jersey.

1969: **Butch Goring**—Los Angeles, NY Islanders, Boston.

1970: **Jim Hargreaves**—Vancouver. **Chris Oddleifson**—California, Boston, Vancouver. **Bill Mikkelson**—Los Angeles, NY Islanders, Washington.

1971: **Al Simmons**—California, Boston. **Dave Hrechkosy**—NY Rangers, California, St. Louis. **Henry Boucha**—Detroit, Minnesota, Kansas City, Colorado. **Neil Komadoski**—Los Angeles, Colorado.

1972: **Larry Bolonchuk**—Vancouver, Washington. **John Bednarski**—NY Rangers, Edmonton. **Rick St. Croix**—Philadelphia, Toronto.

1973: **Mike Korney**—Detroit, NY Rangers. **Blair Stewart**—Detroit, Washington, Quebec.

Winnipeg Clubs

1974: **Barry Legge**—Montreal, Quebec, Winnipeg. **Paul Bunyan"Baxter**—Quebec, Pittsburgh, Calgary. **Doug Wilson**—Chicago (drafted in 1977 from Ottawa of the Ontario Hockey Association), San Jose.

1975: **Larry Skinner**—Colorado (drafted in 1976 from Ottawa of the Ontario Hockey Association).

Winnipeg Monarchs

1977: **Kevin McCarthy**—Philadelphia, Vancouver, Pittsburgh. **Tom Roulston**—St. Louis, Edmonton, Pittsburgh.

Winnipeg Warriors

1982: **Randy Gilhen**—Hartford, Winnipeg, Pittsburgh, Los Angeles, NY Rangers, Tampa Bay, Florida.

1983: **Darren Boyko**—Winnipeg.

Hockey Association and had little time left for the junior team. In 1973 he sold the junior Jets to coach Gerry Brisson.

The Brisson era, lasting from 1973 to 1977, was a dismal time for the franchise. With a new name, the Clubs, and an unstable coaching situation, the team never managed to get its record above .500. The Clubs made two appearances in the playoffs, both times losing in the first round. One bright spot was the play of Kevin McCarthy. In 1975–76 McCarthy was named the league's top defenceman and he returned the next season to finish fourth in the scoring race with a phenomenal 105 assists in 72 games, a performance that won him WHL Player-of-the-Year honours.

Some 1980–81 Warriors––––clockwise from the bottom, Geoff Wilson, Bobby Hull Jr., Bryan Shettler, Doug Hall, Butch Barkwell.

Meanwhile, the Clubs floundered. Brisson was finding it increasingly difficult to compete for fans with the WHA Jets. In 1976 he attempted to shift the franchise to Spokane, but at the last minute the Spokane Flyers senior team blocked the move and Brisson was forced to remain for another season in Winnipeg. Hoping to breath some life into the team, he renamed it the Monarchs, a famous name from the 1930s and 1940s, when the Winnipeg Monarchs won three Memorial Cups. Along with Kevin McCarthy, the reborn Monarchs featured forwards Tom Roulston, Guy Lash, Jim Malazdrewicz, and Eugene O'Sullivan and defenceman Ray Mawhinney. It was the best Winnipeg team yet, finishing in second place in its division, but still failed to get past the first round in the playoffs.

In the off-season, Brisson finally got the permission he was looking for to move the franchise. In Calgary the Centennials had decided to head south to Billings, Montana, opening an opportunity for another franchise in the city. Before the 1977–78 season began, Brisson had transferred the Monarchs from Winnipeg to Calgary where they were renamed the Wranglers.

Three years passed before the WHL returned to Winnipeg. In 1980, a consortium including Marsden Fenwick, Fran Huck, Bob Cunningham, Tim Ryan, Albert De Fehr and Harry Bueckert tried to buy the ailing New Westminster Bruins franchise for the Manitoba capital. This deal fell through and instead Winnipeg was awarded an expansion franchise

Oil Kings netminder Tim Thomlinson attempts to stop Guy Lash of the Winnipeg Clubs at the Winnipeg Arena in 1975–76.

for the 1980–81 season. The new team was named the Warriors, after a club which had played in the Western Professional Hockey League in the 1950s. Fran Huck and Bruce Southern divided the coaching duties, while Tom Thompson came on board as a scout and later, general manager.

In their four seasons in the league, the Warriors managed to build a contender just once, in 1982–83. Featuring Randy Gilhen, the future NHLer with Winnipeg, Pittsburgh, Los Angeles, New York, Tampa Bay and Florida, and Darren Boyko, who went on to play professionally in Europe, Winnipeg finished in fourth place in their division, 12 games over .500. Unfortunately, the Warriors ran into a red-hot Lethbridge team in the first round of the playoffs and bowed out early.

The 1983–84 season turned out to be a complete disaster for the franchise. The Warriors finished with the worst record in the league, recording only 9 victories against 63 defeats. In the process they established several WHL records for ineptitude, including longest home-ice losing streak (19 games) and most goals allowed in a season (580, or an average of eight per game). The Warriors also suffered one of the worst defeats in WHL history when Medicine Hat crushed them 19–2.

After such a season it was perhaps merciful that a group of Moose Jaw business people purchased the franchise and moved it west to Saskatchewan in time for the 1984–85 season. Once again major junior hockey was dead in Winnipeg.

Butch Goring

Butch Goring, a 16-year veteran of the NHL and a coach in a number of different leagues, played a lot of his minor hockey in and around

Butch Goring made a pair of homemade helmets when he was 11 and continued to wear them for 25 years.

After just half a season in the WHL, Butch Goring went on to a distinguished 16-year career in the NHL.

Winnipeg, though he played in the WHL for just half a season. A native of St. Boniface and the son of a welder, Goring made a special helmet when he was a lad of 11, fell in love with it, and proceeded to wear it for 25 years until his career was over. "I lost track how many times I had it in the paint shop or body shop," he recalled. Goring began his junior career in 1966 as a centre with the Winnipeg Rangers of the Manitoba Junior Hockey League. The next year he headed east to Ottawa to join the national B team, then finished the season back home at the senior level with the St. Boniface Mohawks.

In 1968–69, Goring was still young enough to play junior hockey and after a brief stint with the national team, he began the season with the Winnipeg Jets, then in their second season in the fledgling Western Canada Hockey League. At the midway point coach Eddie Dorohoy was replaced by Frank Boucher behind the Jets bench. Goring did not like the change and left the team, preferring to finish the year with the Dauphin Kings of the MJHL. At that time the winner of the MJHL qualified for Memorial Cup play, and when Regina defeated Dauphin in the finals they invited Goring to join their roster for the national championships, won that year by the Montreal Junior Canadiens.

In the 1969 amateur draft the Los Angeles Kings selected Goring. He played two seasons with the Springfield Kings of the American Hockey League, helping the Kings win a league championship in 1970–71, before graduating to the NHL for good in 1971. During nine solid seasons in Los Angeles, he won the Lady Byng trophy for most sportsmanlike player and the Bill Masterton trophy for "perseverance, sportsmanship and dedication to hockey." Near the end of the 1979–80 season Goring was traded to the New York Islanders for Billy Harris and Dave Lewis, just in time to take part in the first of the Islanders' four consecutive Stanley Cup championships. In 1981 he won the Conn Smythe trophy as the Most Valuable Player in the playoffs.

When his playing days were over, Goring made the transition to the coaching ranks. He has coached in the NHL with the Boston Bruins, in the WHL with the Spokane Chiefs, in the AHL with the Capital District Islanders, and in the IHL with the Las Vegas Thunder. Goring, a member of the Manitoba Sports Hall of Fame, never stopped spending his summers back in his home province.

Kevin McCarthy

Without a doubt, the finest junior hockey player to play in the Western Hockey League in Winnipeg was Kevin McCarthy. McCarthy was born in Winnipeg on July 14, 1957 and was a graduate of midget hockey in the St. James suburb of Silver Heights.

Loudly praised by coach Gerry Brisson as "the franchise," Kevin

Kevin McCarthy, seen here in the road uniform of the Winnipeg Clubs, often amazed WHL fans with his incredible end-to-end rushes.

was part of a trio of sensational 16 year-olds who made the roster of the Winnipeg Clubs during the fall of 1973. He was joined by future NHL star defenceman Doug Wilson, and future NHL netminder Murray Bannerman.

It all began for Kevin as a rookie with the Winnipeg Clubs in 1973–74. From the outset, he looked like something special with his rink-length dashes and puck-handling skills. The NHL took notice soon, and it was not unusual to see the Winnipeg Arena with plenty of scouts peering down on to the ice surface.

In his first season he scored 5 goals and 22 assists. But during the next three years in Winnipeg his natural skills began to produce results as he lived up to his nickname the "Wizard of Winnipeg." After accumulating 81 points in 1974–75, 121 in 1975–76 and 127 in 1976–77, it is not hard to see how he won two individual awards. From top defenceman in 1975–76 to Molson/Cooper Player of the Year in 1976–77, his true talent showed. In one game in 1976 against Calgary, he had five assists in only the second period!

The Philadelphia Flyers wasted little time in selecting McCarthy in the first round of the 1977 draft, 17th overall. But after only one season with the Flyers, McCarthy was traded on December 29, 1978 to the Vancouver Canucks along with Drew Callander for Dennis Ververgaert. After a hip injury kept him in the press box for most of the 1978–79 season, McCarthy wasted little time in proving himself to Canucks fans. He missed only one game in 1979–80 and scored 15 goals and 30 assists. The next season, his high-calibre play caught the eye of hockey scribes around the NHL and they voted him to the Campbell Conference All-Star team. He was also voted the Canucks' Most Valuable Defenceman in 1980–81 and that same season, McCarthy's leadership talents were rewarded with his appointment as team captain.

The popular defenceman of the Vancouver Canucks was having a tremendous season in 1981–82 when he suffered an unfortunate mishap. He broke an ankle two days prior to the start of the Stanley Cup playoffs. During a routine practice, McCarthy fell, in a collision with left-winger Curt Fraser, and could not get up off the ice. It was the second serious injury of the season for the Canuck defenceman, previously having missed eight games in the middle of the season with a partially separated shoulder. Despite these setbacks, McCarthy still led all the Canuck defencemen in scoring with 6 goals and 39 assists for 45 points. While his goal scoring was down from the previous two seasons, McCarthy's outstanding defensive play was a major factor in helping the team to the fifth best defensive record in the NHL. Unfortunately, the Canucks fine defenceman had to miss Vancouver's sensational march to the Stanley Cup final against the New York Islanders in the spring of 1982.

But with the short career of hockey players, McCarthy was to enjoy only one more decent season in the NHL, with the Canucks in 1982–83. He was traded the following season to the Pittsburgh Penguins for a third-round 1985 draft pick. After just a season and a half as a Penguin, McCarthy was on the move again, this time back to the Philadelphia Flyers. By this time, McCarthy's career was pretty much at the end and he dressed in only six games for the Flyers and spent most of his time in the minor leagues with the Hershey Bears of the American Hockey League.

Since leaving the active player ranks, he spent time in the Flyers system as a pro scout and Player Development Coordinator. Most recently, he has assumed the position of assistant bench coach of the Hartford Whalers under longtime Philadelphia Flyers teammate Paul Holmgren.

Index